MathFlare

Name: _____________________

Class: __________

Teacher: _____________________

Introduction

As parents and educators, we recognize the pivotal role mathematics plays in shaping a child's academic journey and future success. Yet, the path to mathematical proficiency can often seem daunting, fraught with challenges and complexities. That's where the transformative power of MathFlare Workbooks shine through, illuminating the way forward with clarity, precision, and purpose.

Introducing MathFlare Workbooks – a beacon of guidance, a testament to excellence, and a catalyst for achievement. Crafted with meticulous care and expertise, MathFlare Workbooks stand as paragons of educational excellence, designed to nurture young minds, ignite a passion for learning, and develop a deep-rooted understanding of mathematical concepts.

Picture this: your child eagerly delves into the pages of Mathflare Workbook, greeted by a step-by-step guide illuminated with vivid examples that demystify complex mathematical concepts. With each turn of the page, they embark on a journey of discovery, encountering thoughtfully curated practice questions that reinforce learning and hone problem-solving skills. And when they unveil the answers to those very questions, a sense of accomplishment blossoms within them – a tangible reward for their hard work and dedication.

But MathFlare Workbooks are more than just tools for learning; they are pathways to comprehension, fostering a deep-seated understanding of mathematical concepts through a sequential, logical flow. From fundamental principles to advanced problem-solving strategies, every chapter builds upon the last, ensuring a robust foundation upon which future knowledge can be constructed.

As parents, we yearn for nothing more than to see our children thrive, to witness the spark of inspiration ignited within them as they conquer academic challenges with confidence and poise. MathFlare Workbooks serve as partners in this noble endeavor, offering not just practice questions, but the keys to unlocking a world of opportunity.

And for teachers, MathFlare Workbooks stand as invaluable allies in the quest to cultivate mathematical proficiency in the classroom. With answers readily available, instructors can focus on guiding and nurturing their students, confident in the knowledge that MathFlare Workbooks provide a solid framework upon which to build.

In the pages of MathFlare Workbooks, we find not just the promise of academic excellence, but the seeds of a brighter tomorrow. So let us embrace the power of mathematics, let us champion the journey of learning, and let us pave the way for a generation of young minds poised to shape the world. With MathFlare Workbooks as our guide, the possibilities are infinite, and the future, bright.

Table of Contents

MathFlare
Grade 2
MATH WORKBOOK
Step by Step Guide
and Essential Practice
with Answers
Addition
Subtraction
Multiplication
Place Value and
Expanded Notations
Geometry
MathFlare Publishing

MathFlare
Grade 2-3
MATH WORKBOOK
Step by Step Guide
and Essential Practice
with Answers
Addition
Subtraction
Multiplication
and Division
Place Value and
Expanded Notations
Geometry
MathFlare Publishing

MathFlare
Grade 3
MATH WORKBOOK
Step by Step Guide
and Essential Practice
with Answers
Multiplication
and Division
Decimals
Place Value and
Expanded Notations
Fractions
and Geometry
MathFlare Publishing

MathFlare
Grade 1
MATH WORKBOOK
Step by Step Guide
and Essential Practice
with Answers
Counting and
Numbers
Addition and
Subtraction
Place Value and
Expanded Notations
Understanding
Time
MathFlare Publishing

MathFlare
Grade 1-2
MATH WORKBOOK
Step by Step Guide
and Essential Practice
with Answers
Counting and
Numbers
Addition and
Subtraction
Place Value and
Expanded Notations
Understanding
Time
MathFlare Publishing

MathFlare
Grade 3-4
MATH WORKBOOK
Step by Step Guide
and Essential Practice
with Answers
Addition
Subtraction
Multiplication
Division
Place Value and
Expanded Notations
Fractions
and Geometry
MathFlare Publishing

MathFlare
Grade 4
MATH WORKBOOK
Step by Step Guide
and Essential Practice
with Answers
Addition
Subtraction
Multiplication
Division
Place Value and
Expanded Notations
Fractions
and Geometry
MathFlare Publishing

MathFlare
Grade 4-5
MATH WORKBOOK
Step by Step Guide
and Essential Practice
with Answers
Multiplication
Division
Place Value and
Expanded Notations
Fractions
and Geometry
Unit
Conversion
MathFlare Publishing

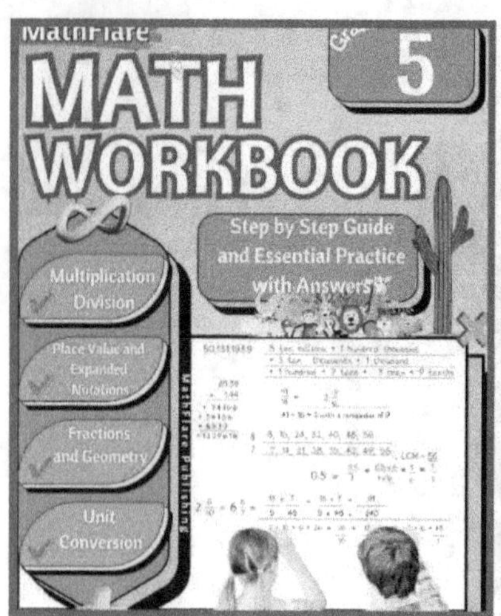
MathFlare
Grade 5
MATH WORKBOOK
Step by Step Guide and Essential Practice with Answers
Multiplication Division
Place Value and Expanded Notations
Fractions and Geometry
Unit Conversion
MathFlare Publishing

MathFlare
Grade 5-6
MATH WORKBOOK
Step by Step Guide and Essential Practice with Answers
Multiplication Division
Place Value and Expanded Notations
Fractions and Geometry
Units and Statistics
MathFlare Publishing

MathFlare
Grade 6
MATH WORKBOOK
Step by Step Guide and Essential Practice with Answers
Integers and Statistics
Arithmetic and Pre-Algebra
Fractions and Geometry
Ratio and Percentage
MathFlare Publishing

MathFlare
Grade 6-7
MATH WORKBOOK
Step by Step Guide and Essential Practice with Answers
Arithmetic and Pre-Algebra
Ratio, Percent Proportion
Geometry
Statistics
MathFlare Publishing

MathFlare
Grade 7
MATH WORKBOOK
Step by Step Guide and Essential Practice with Answers
Pre-Algebra
Ratio, Percent Proportion
Geometry
Statistics
MathFlare Publishing

MathFlare
Grade 7-8
MATH WORKBOOK
Step by Step Guide and Essential Practice with Answers
Pre-Algebra
Ratio, Percent Proportion
Geometry and Cartesian Plane
Statistics
MathFlare Publishing

MathFlare
Grade 8-9
MATH WORKBOOK
Step by Step Guide and Essential Practice with Answers
Pre-Algebra
Ratio, Proportion and Percentage
Linear Equations
Geometry and Cartesian Plane
MathFlare Publishing

MathFlare
Grade 8
MATH WORKBOOK
Step by Step Guide and Essential Practice with Answers
Pre-Algebra
Percentage
Linear Equations
Geometry
MathFlare Publishing

Chapter 1

Counting and Numbers

Counting Up:

Counting the numbers in ascending order or adding numbers in a sequence.

168	169	170	171	172	173	174	175	176	177

Counting Down:

Counting the numbers in descending order or subtracting numbers in a sequence.

249	248	247	246	245	244	243	242	241	240

Counting Patterns:

It refers to sequences of numbers that follow a specific rule or pattern: such as counting by 2s and 3s, adding 2s and 3s in sequence.

Count by 2s

Count by 2 from 312 to 330

312	314	316	318	320	322	324	326	328	330

Compare the Numbers:

We use signs to compare the numbers. Such as, > = greater than, < = less than, and = equal to.

For Instance: if we compare, 754 and 51, we can write:

$$754 > 51$$

This means that 754 is greater than 51. In other words, 754 is a larger number than 51.

Circle the Numbers:

In this lesson, we try to understand and recognize the numbers. The task is to identify the numbers that are smallest, largest, odd or even. For instance, we have circled the smallest and largest numbers in the following numbers.

948, 69, 529, 523, 82

948 is the largest number and 69 is the smallest number.

Missing Numbers:

In this exercise, one or two numbers are given, and the task is to find the numbers that come before, between and after those numbers. For example:

296 _297_ 298 , _472_ 473

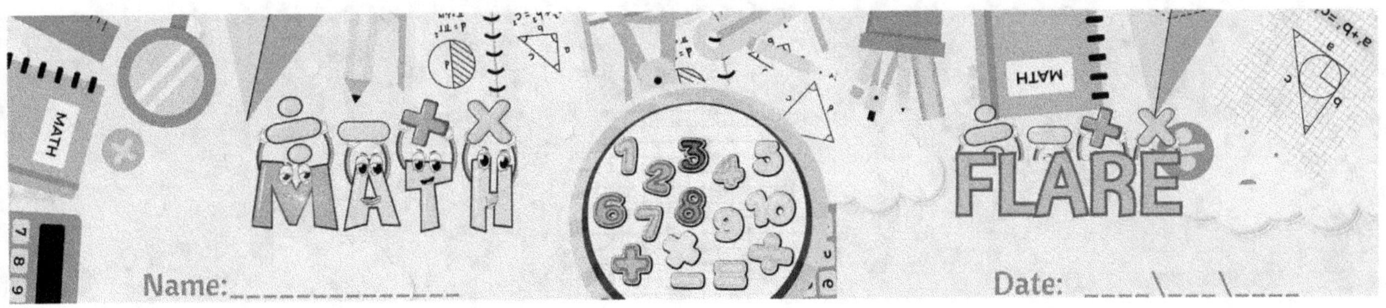

Counting Up

Fill in the missing numbers by counting up.

1)

				323				318

2)

602	601							

3)

		819		817				

4)

275						268		

5)

			111			108		

6)

929							921	

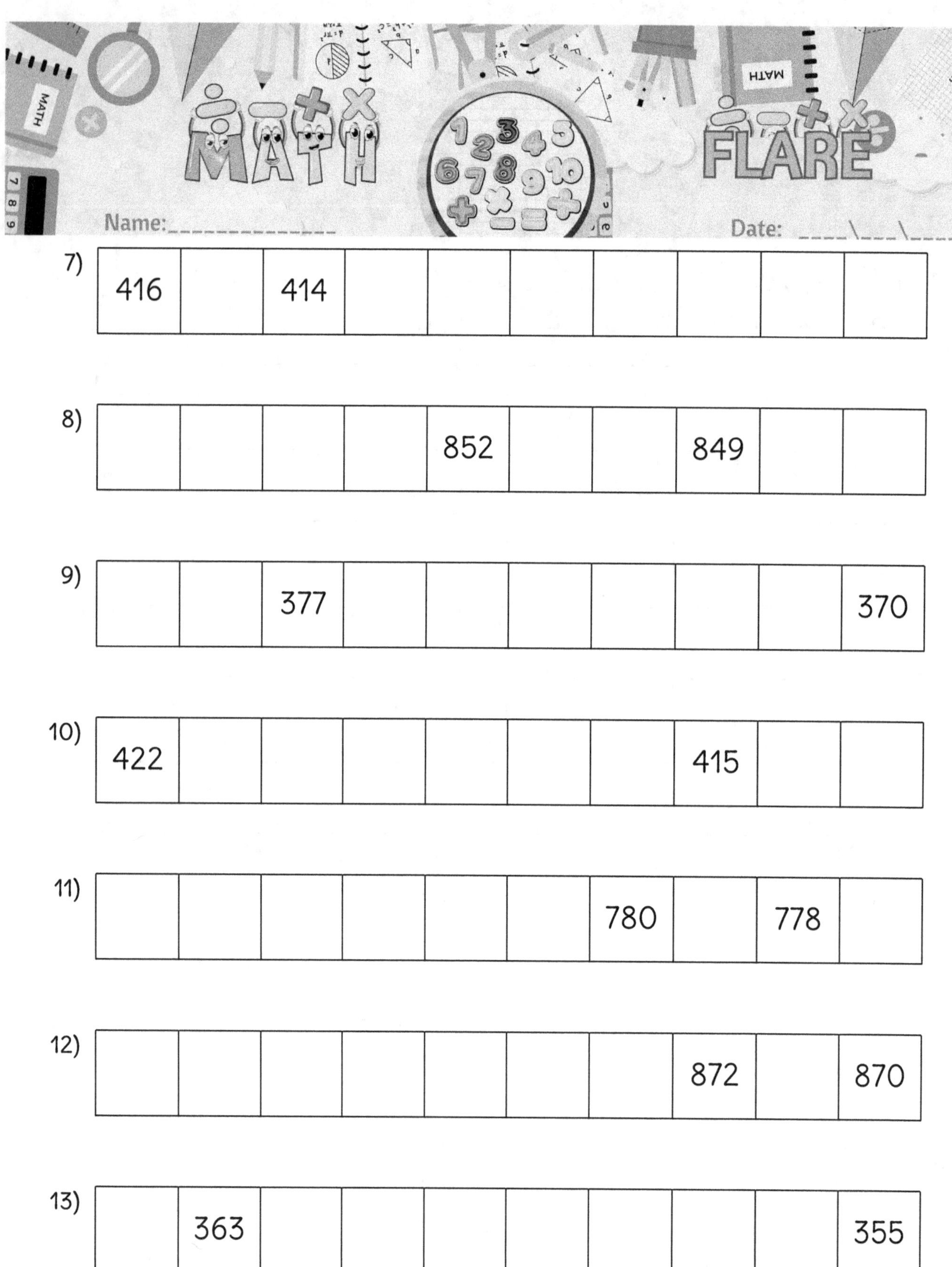

7)

416		414							

8)

				852		849		

9)

		377						370

10)

422						415		

11)

						780		778	

12)

							872		870

13)

	363							355

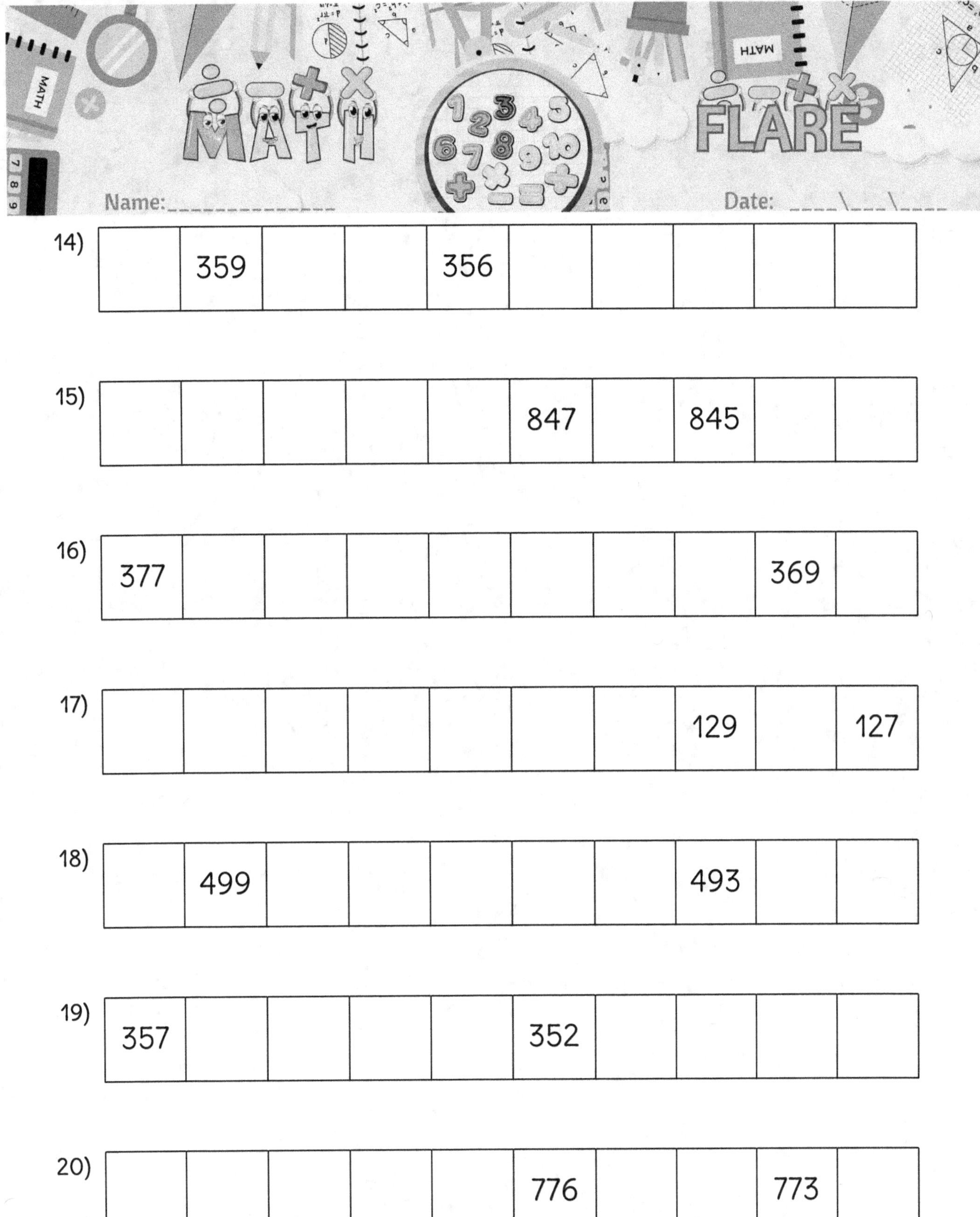

14)

	359			356					

15)

					847		845		

16)

377								369	

17)

								129		127

18)

	499						493		

19)

357					352				

20)

					776			773	

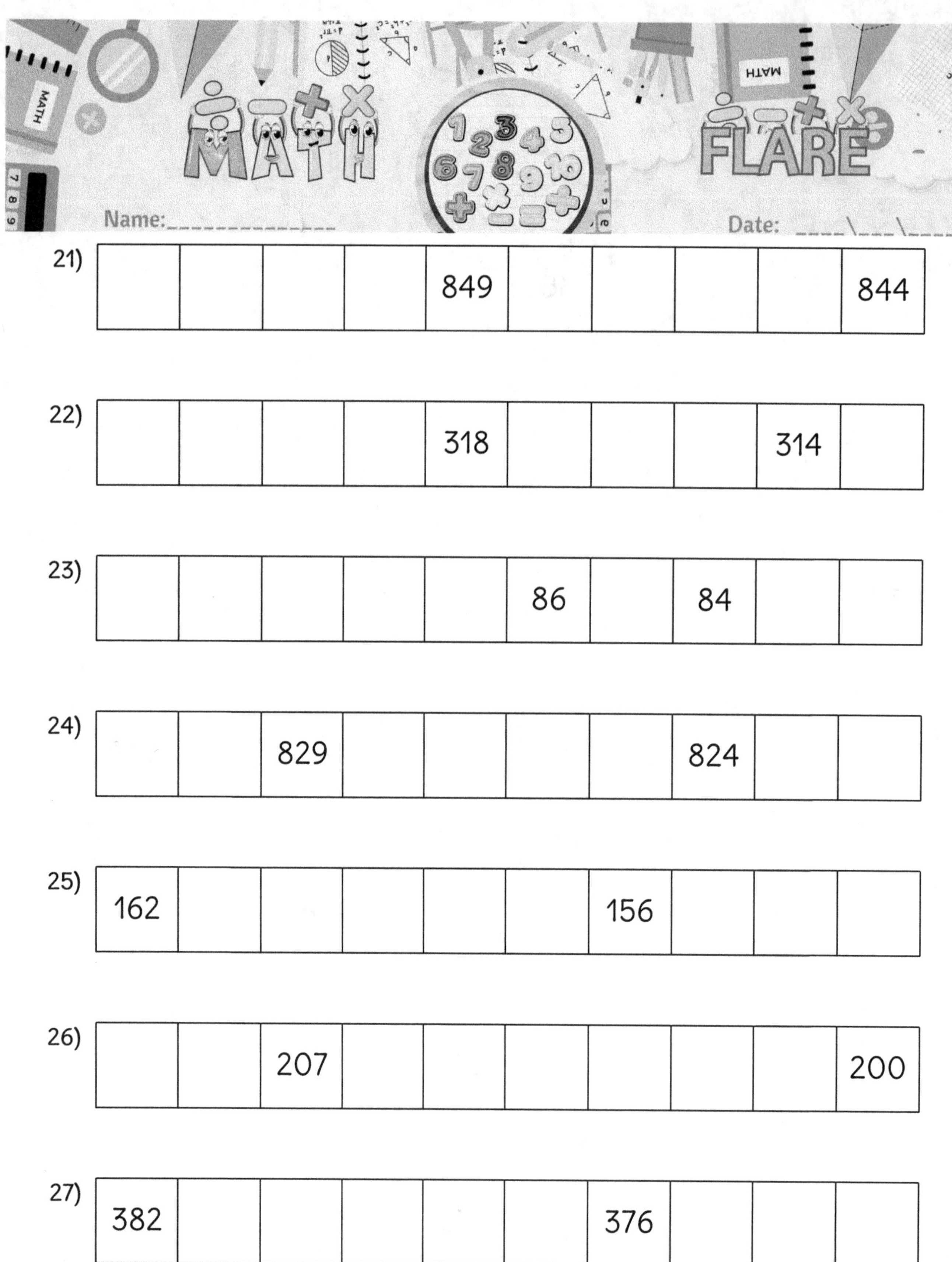

21)

				849				844

22)

				318			314	

23)

					86		84	

24)

		829				824		

25)

162						156		

26)

		207						200

27)

382					376			

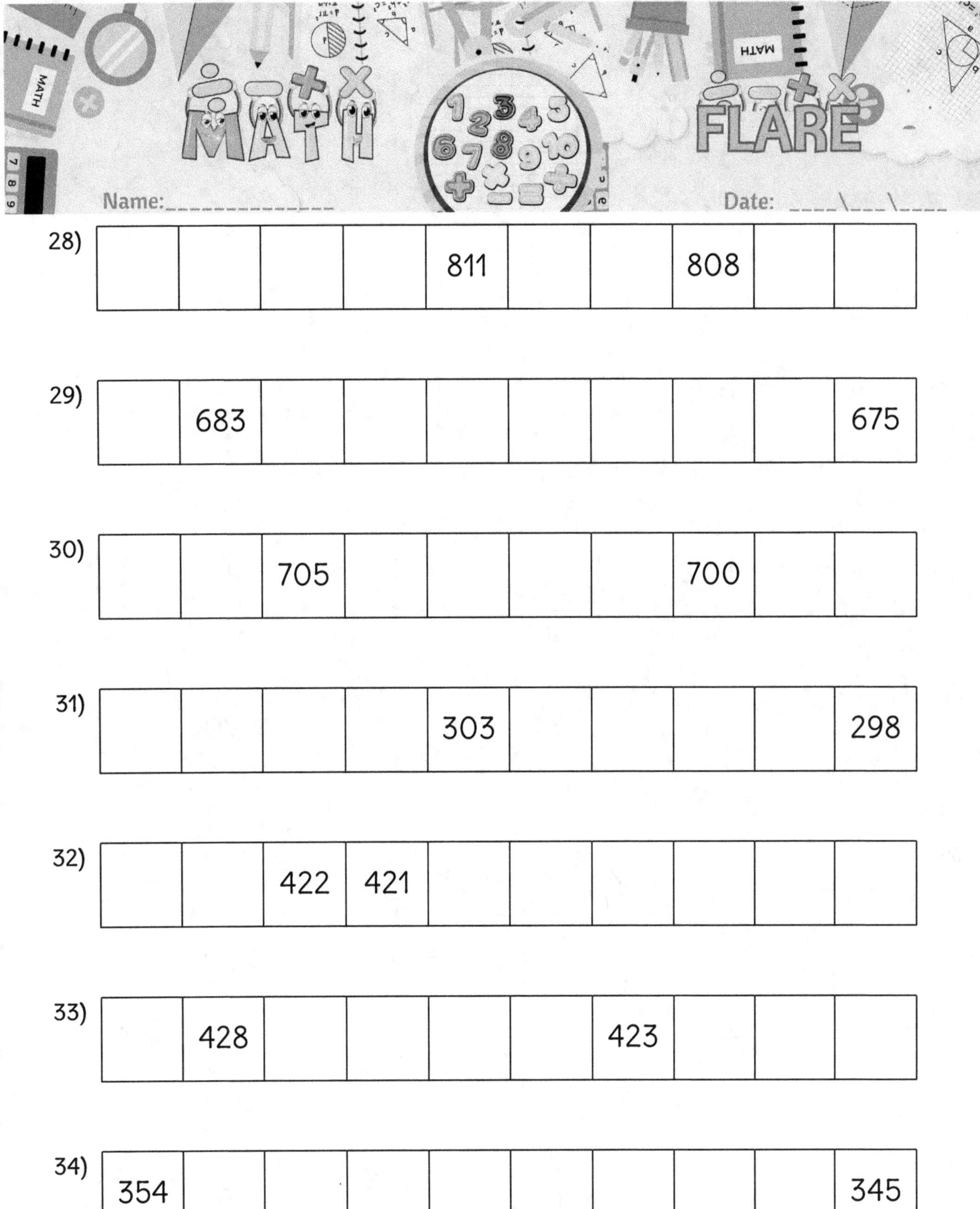

28)

				811			808		

29)

	683								675

30)

		705				700			

31)

				303					298

32)

		422	421						

33)

	428					423			

34)

354									345

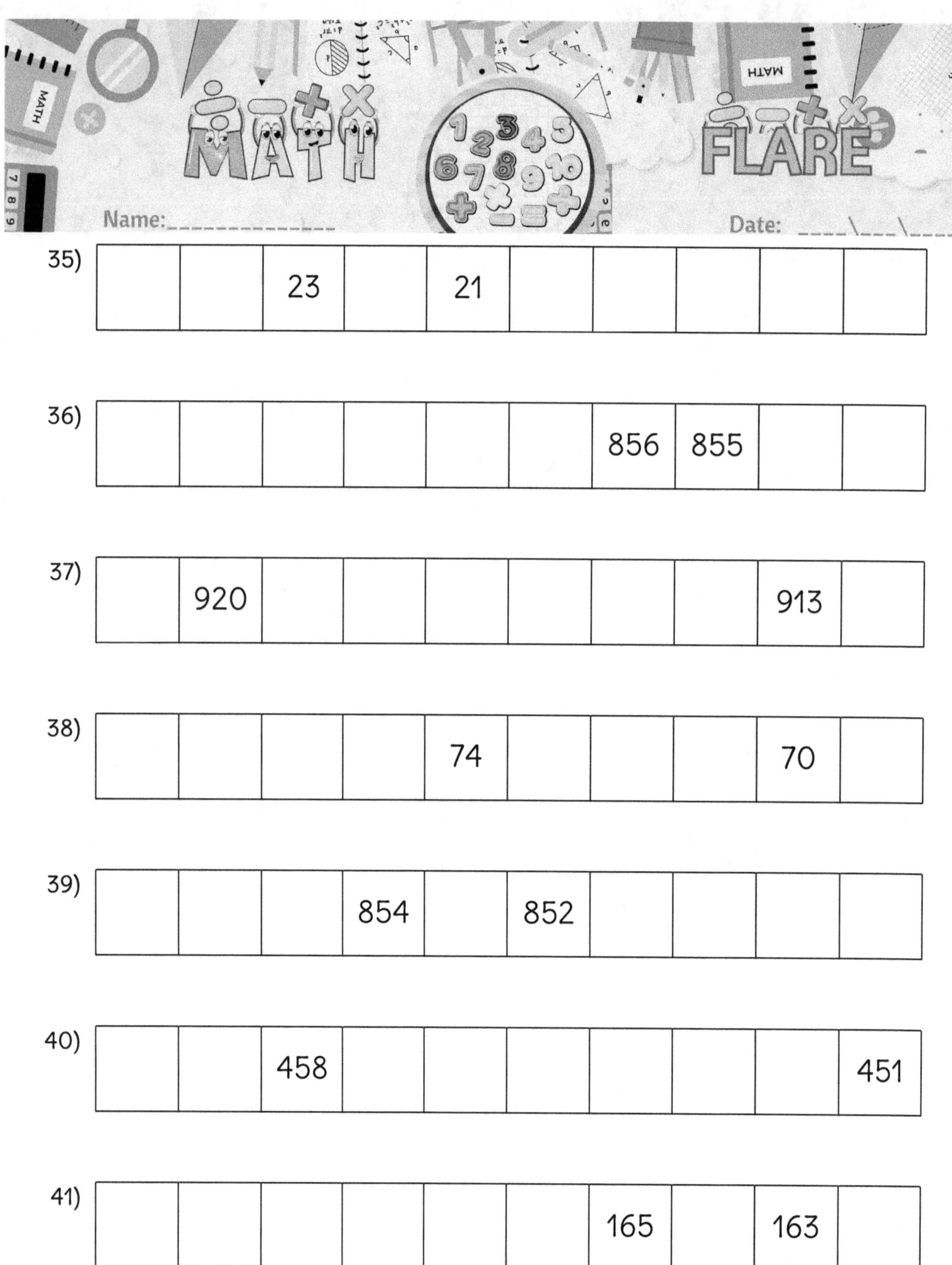

35)

		23		21					

36)

						856	855		

37)

	920							913	

38)

				74				70	

39)

			854		852				

40)

		458							451

41)

						165		163	

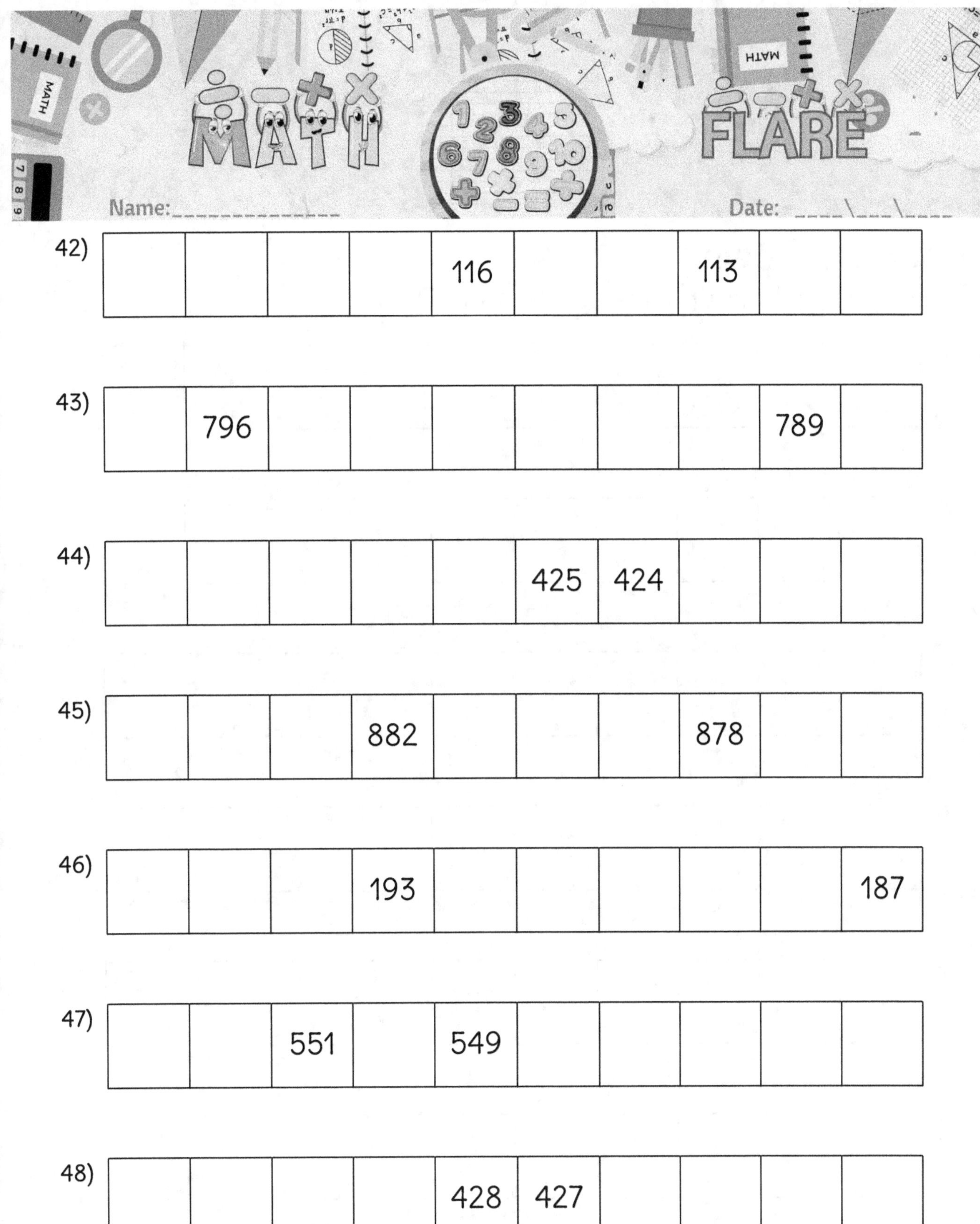

42)

				116			113		

43)

	796							789	

44)

					425	424			

45)

			882				878		

46)

			193						187

47)

		551		549					

48)

				428	427				

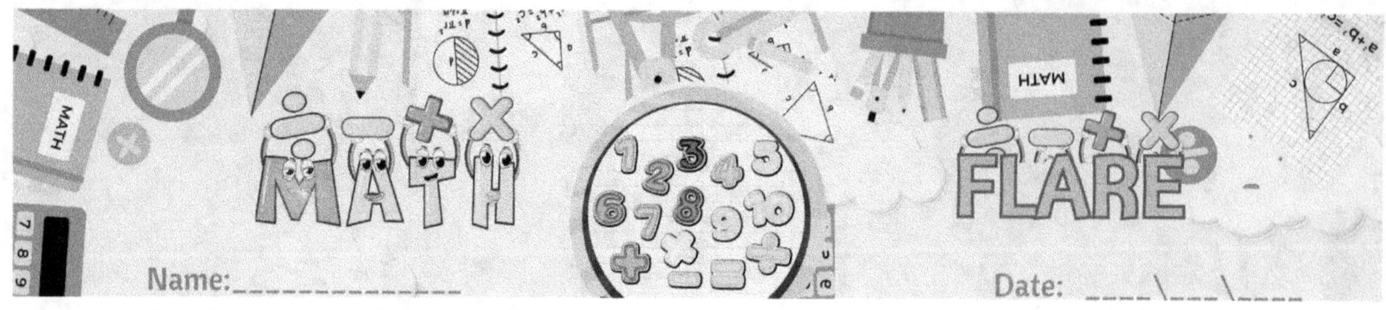

Counting Down

Fill in the missing numbers by counting Down.

1) | | | 247 | 246 | | | | | | |

2) | | | | | | 59 | 58 | | | |

3) | | | 841 | 840 | | | | | |

4) | | | | 375 | 374 | | | | |

5) | | | | 722 | 721 | | | | |

6) | | | | | 611 | 610 | | | |

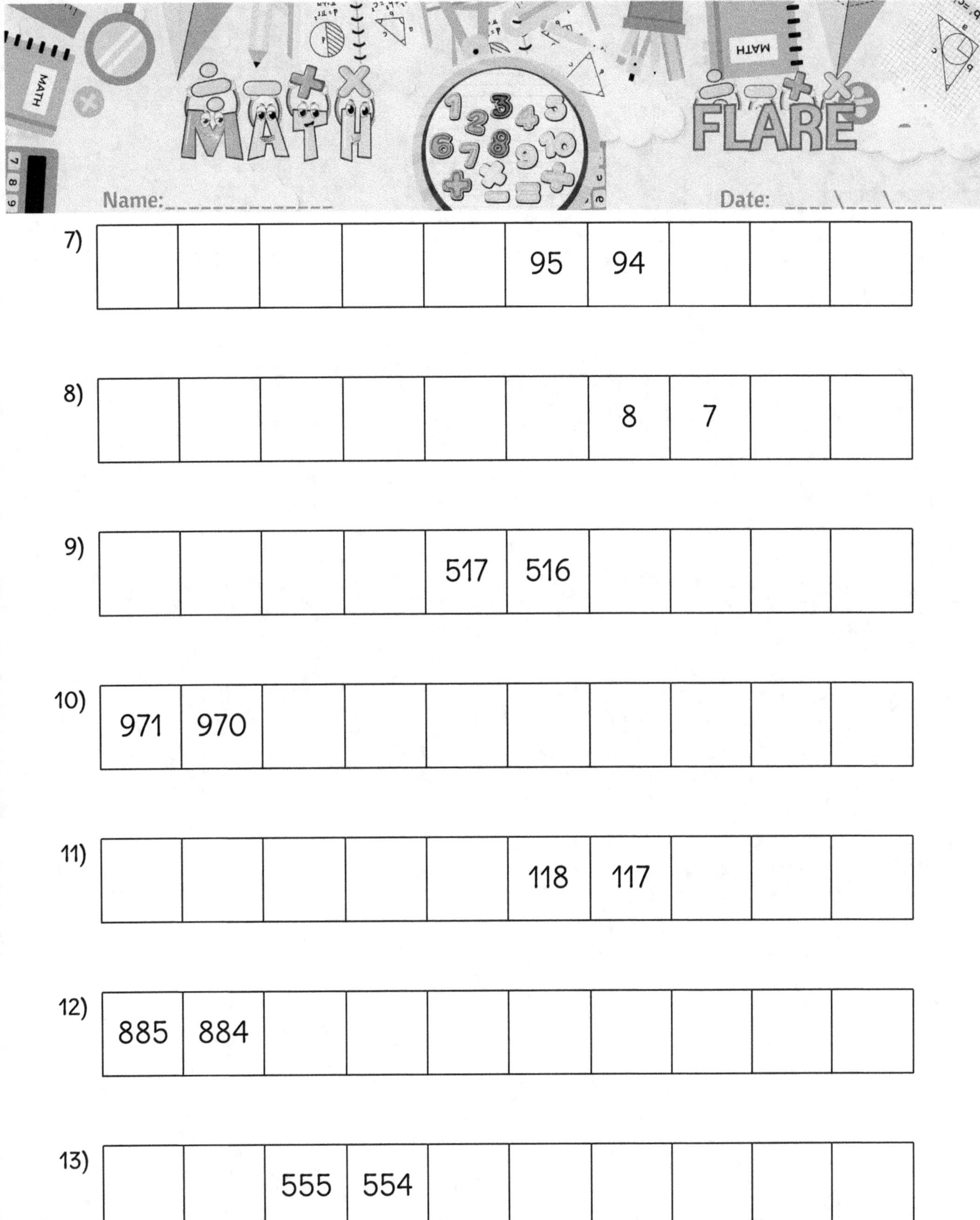

7)

					95	94			

8)

					8	7			

9)

			517	516					

10)

971	970								

11)

					118	117			

12)

885	884								

13)

		555	554						

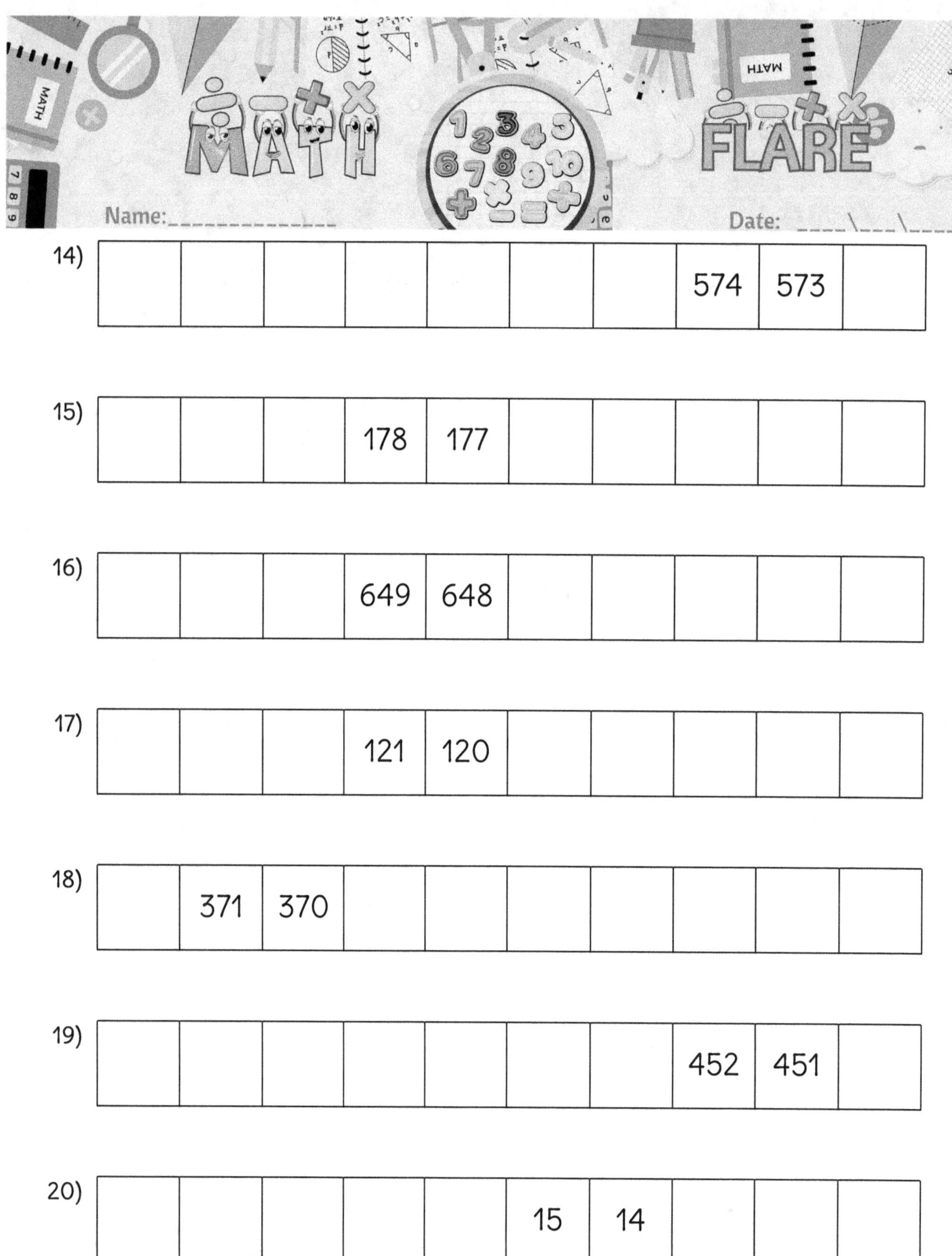

Name: _______________________   Date: _______________

14)

						574	573	

15)

		178	177					

16)

		649	648					

17)

		121	120					

18)

371	370							

19)

						452	451	

20)

				15	14			

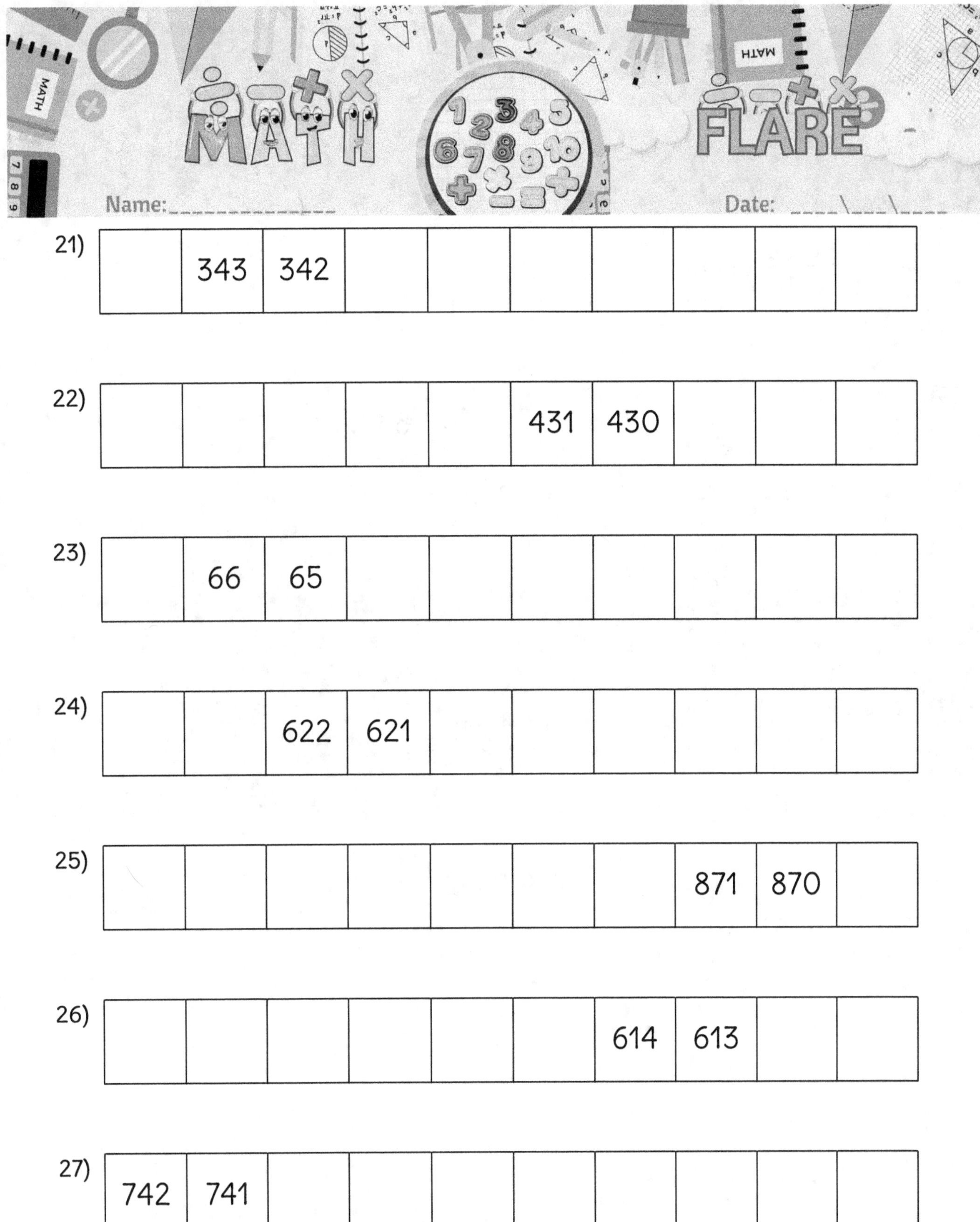

21)

	343	342						

22)

					431	430		

23)

	66	65						

24)

		622	621					

25)

						871	870	

26)

					614	613	

27)

742	741							

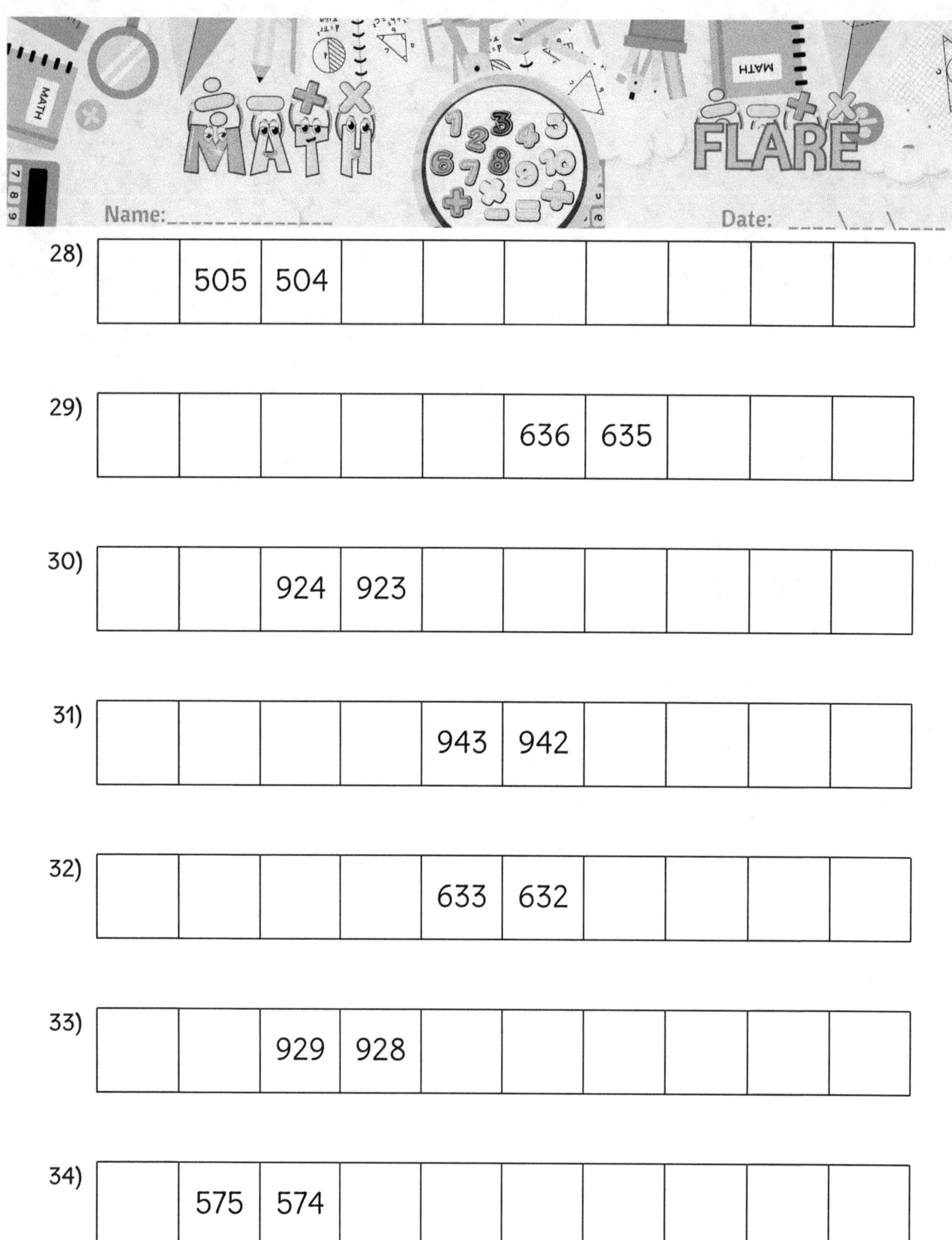

28)

	505	504						

29)

					636	635		

30)

		924	923					

31)

				943	942			

32)

				633	632			

33)

		929	928					

34)

	575	574						

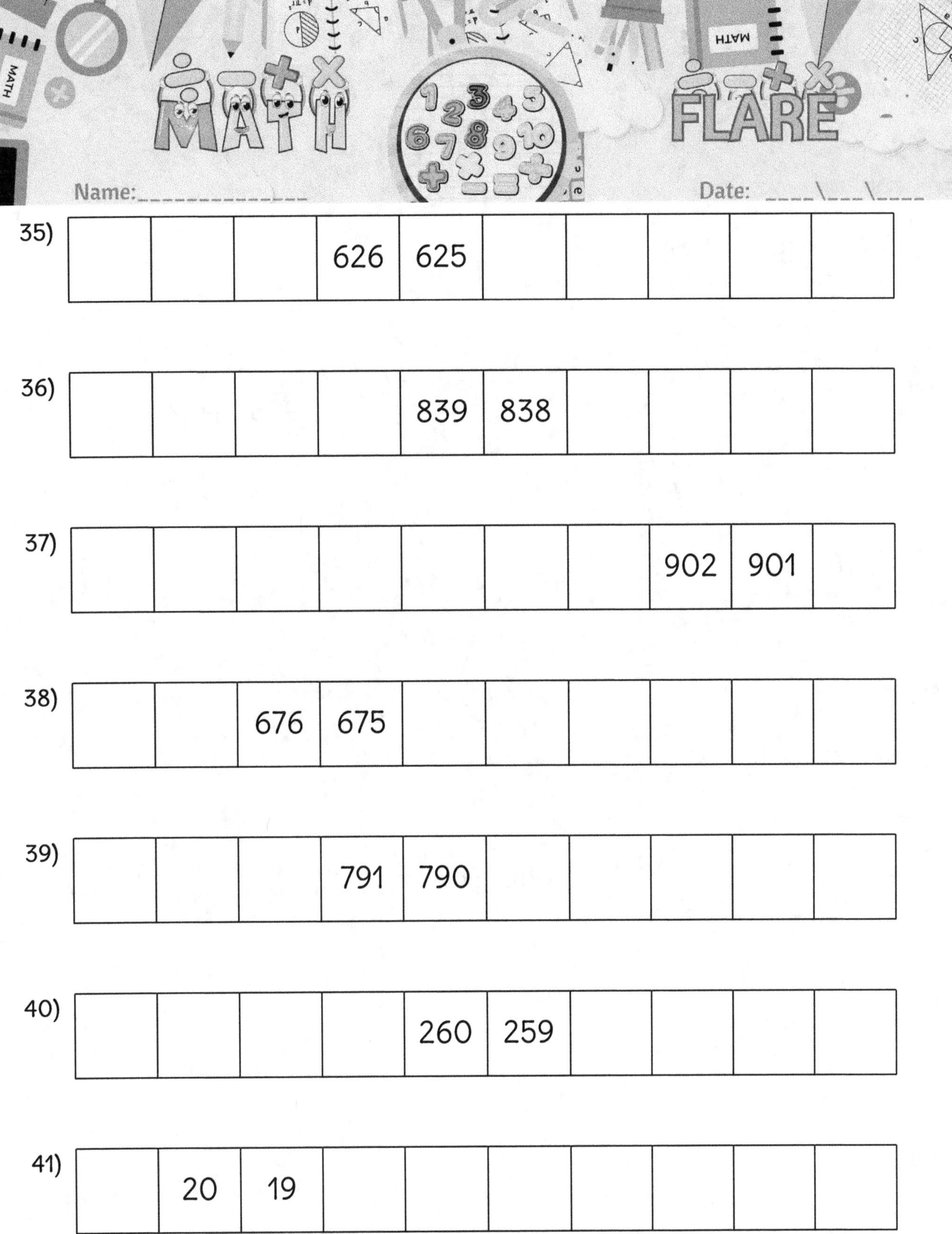

35) | | | | 626 | 625 | | | | |

36) | | | | 839 | 838 | | | | |

37) | | | | | | | 902 | 901 | |

38) | | 676 | 675 | | | | | | |

39) | | | 791 | 790 | | | | | |

40) | | | | 260 | 259 | | | | |

41) | 20 | 19 | | | | | | | |

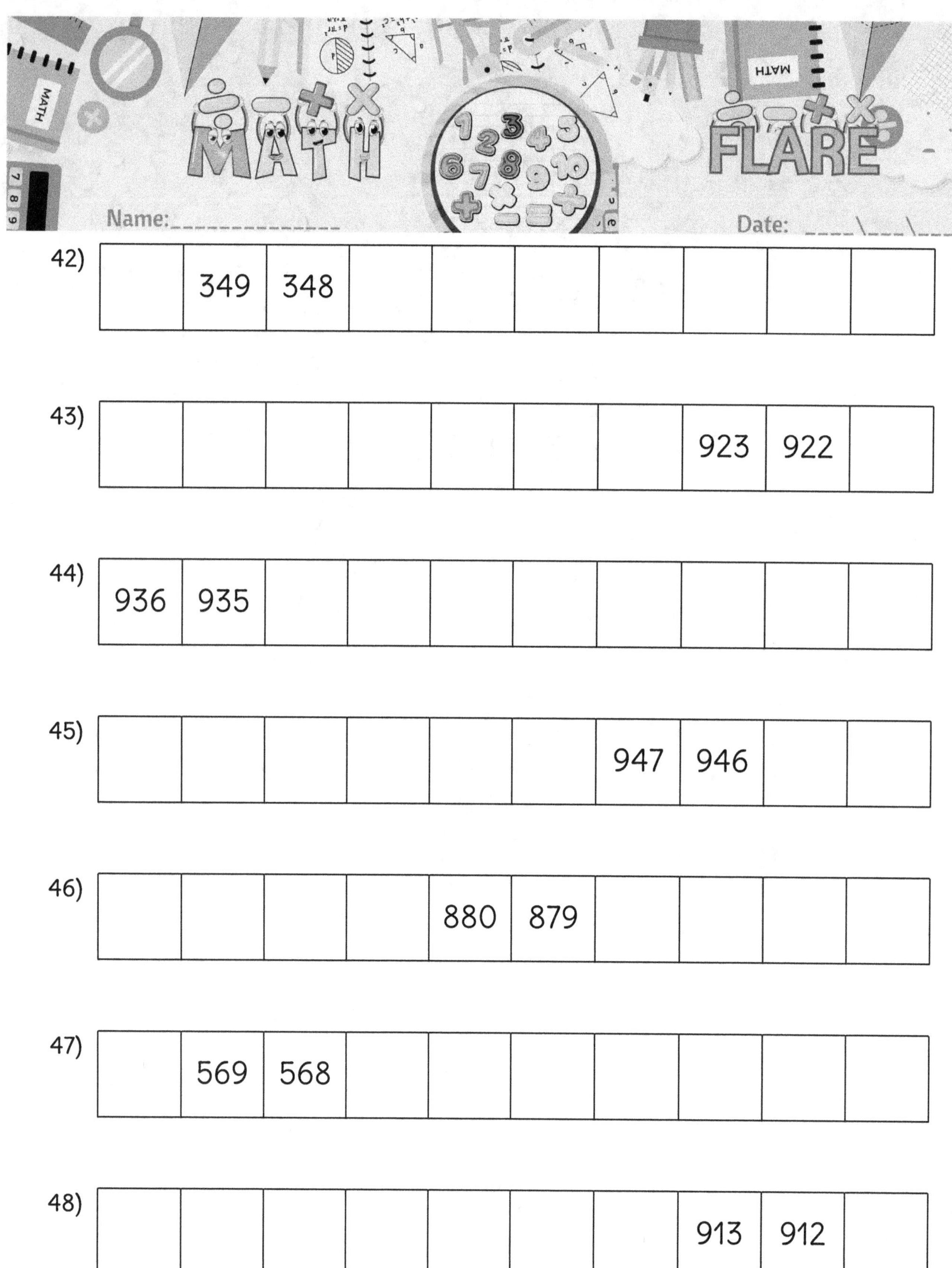

42)

| | 349 | 348 | | | | | | | |

43)

| | | | | | | | 923 | 922 | |

44)

| 936 | 935 | | | | | | | | |

45)

| | | | | | | 947 | 946 | | |

46)

| | | | 880 | 879 | | | | | |

47)

| | 569 | 568 | | | | | | | |

48)

| | | | | | | | 913 | 912 | |

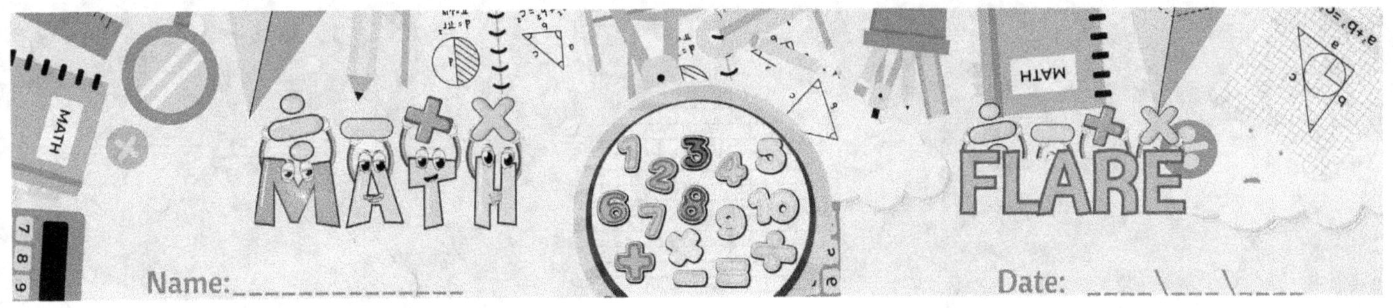

Counting Patterns

Complete the counting tables.

1) Count by 2 from 312 to 330

312	314	316	318	320	322	324	326	328	330

2) Count by 4 from 722 to 758

						746			

3) Count by 4 from 90 to 126

				106					

4) Count by 3 from 611 to 638

					626				

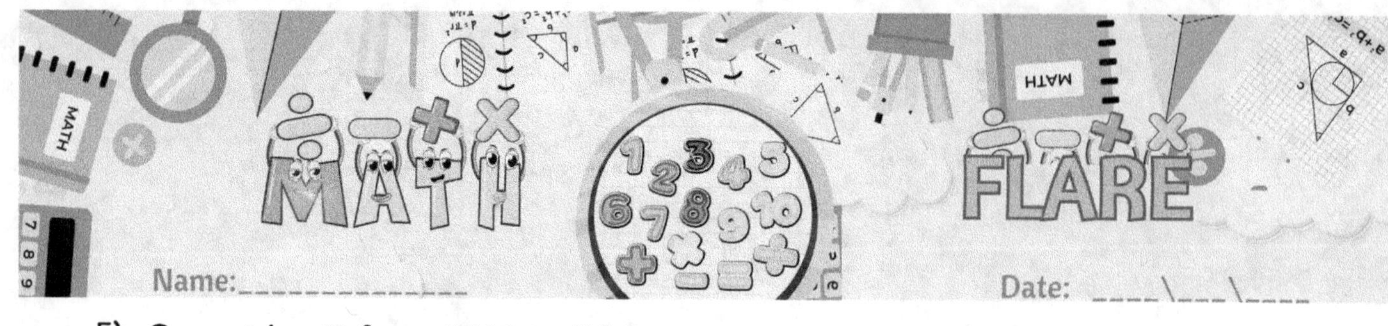

5) Count by 5 from 741 to 786

					766				

6) Count by 5 from 986 to 1031

					1,011				

7) Count by 3 from 489 to 516

			498						

8) Count by 5 from 47 to 92

			62						

9) Count by 2 from 254 to 272

			260						

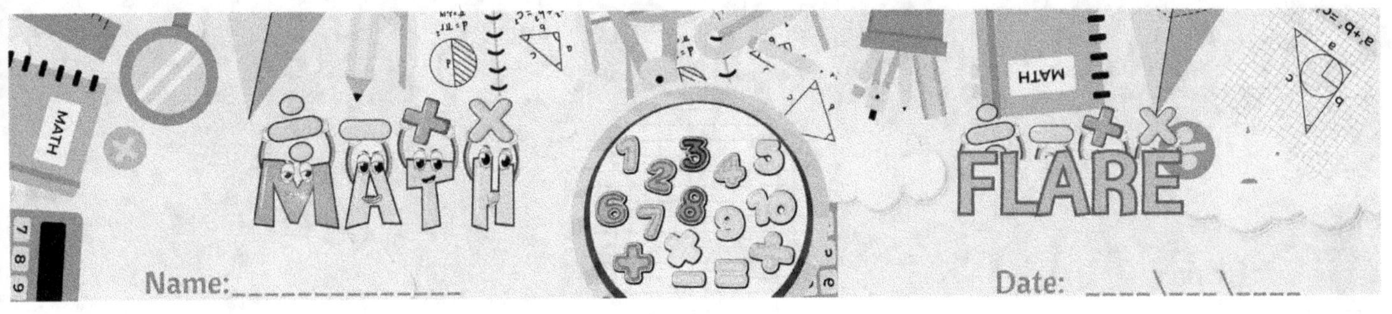

10) Count by 4 from 6 to 42

				22					

11) Count by 4 from 796 to 832

					816				

12) Count by 2 from 678 to 696

									694	

13) Count by 4 from 741 to 777

							769		

14) Count by 3 from 633 to 660

			645					

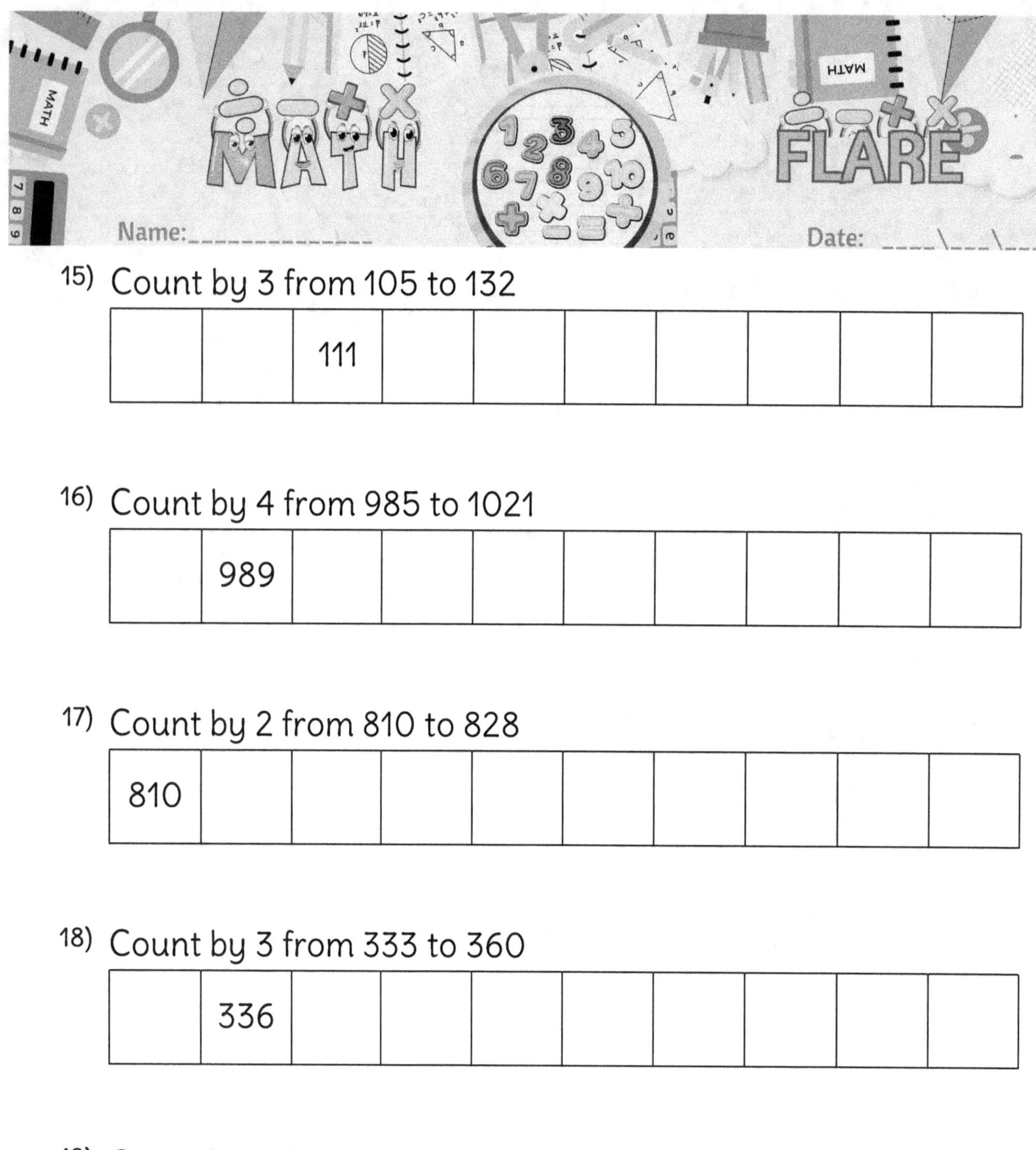

15) Count by 3 from 105 to 132

| | | 111 | | | | | | | |

16) Count by 4 from 985 to 1021

| | 989 | | | | | | | | |

17) Count by 2 from 810 to 828

| 810 | | | | | | | | | |

18) Count by 3 from 333 to 360

| | 336 | | | | | | | | |

19) Count by 3 from 234 to 261

| | | | | | | 252 | | |

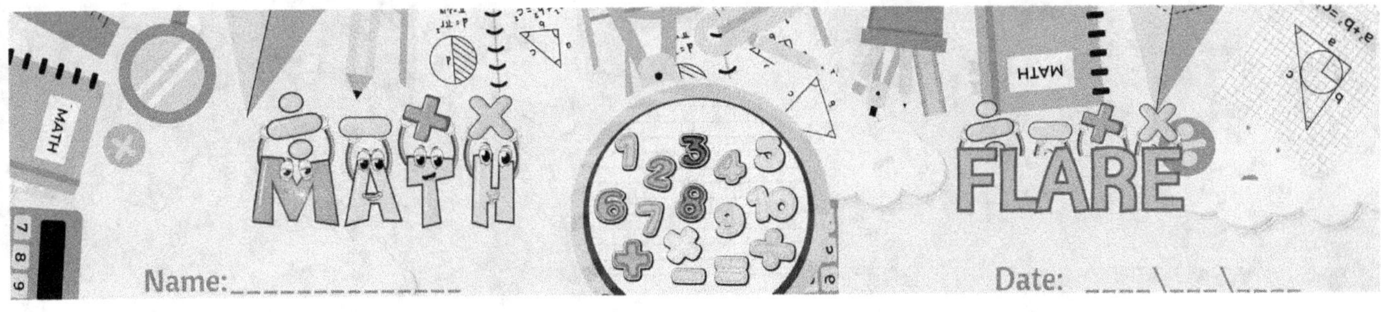

20) Count by 2 from 850 to 868

850									

21) Count by 3 from 21 to 48

	24								

22) Count by 2 from 177 to 195

						189			

23) Count by 5 from 805 to 850

						835			

24) Count by 5 from 514 to 559

								554	

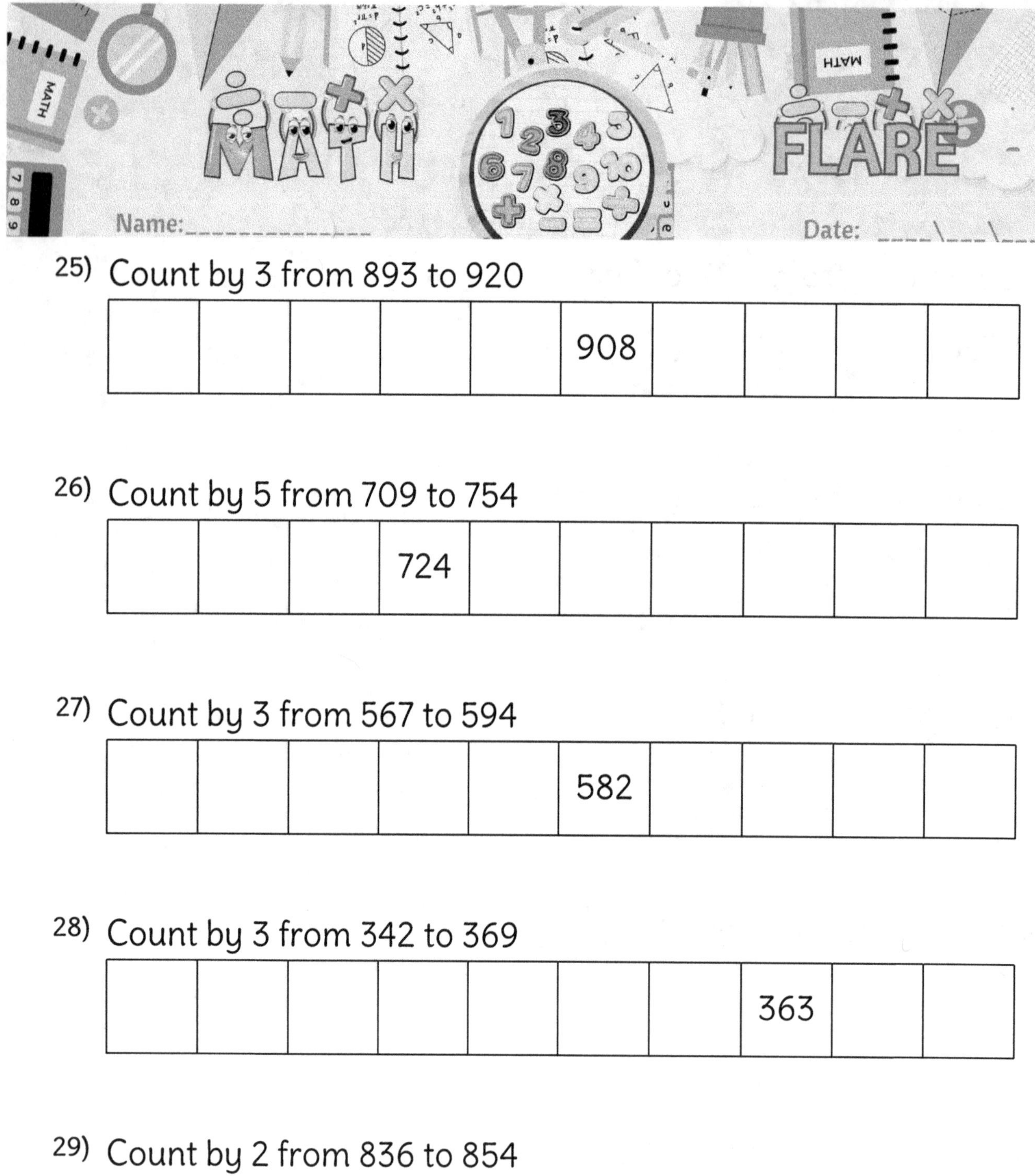

Name:_________________   Date: ____________

25) Count by 3 from 893 to 920

					908				

26) Count by 5 from 709 to 754

			724						

27) Count by 3 from 567 to 594

					582				

28) Count by 3 from 342 to 369

								363	

29) Count by 2 from 836 to 854

									854

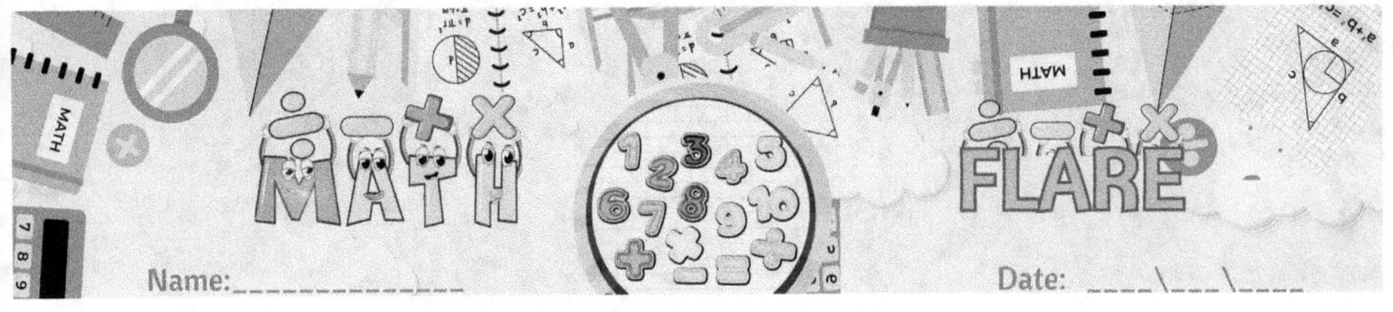

30) Count by 2 from 794 to 812

				802					

31) Count by 5 from 612 to 657

			627						

32) Count by 2 from 688 to 706

							702		

33) Count by 2 from 842 to 860

		848							

34) Count by 5 from 516 to 561

								561

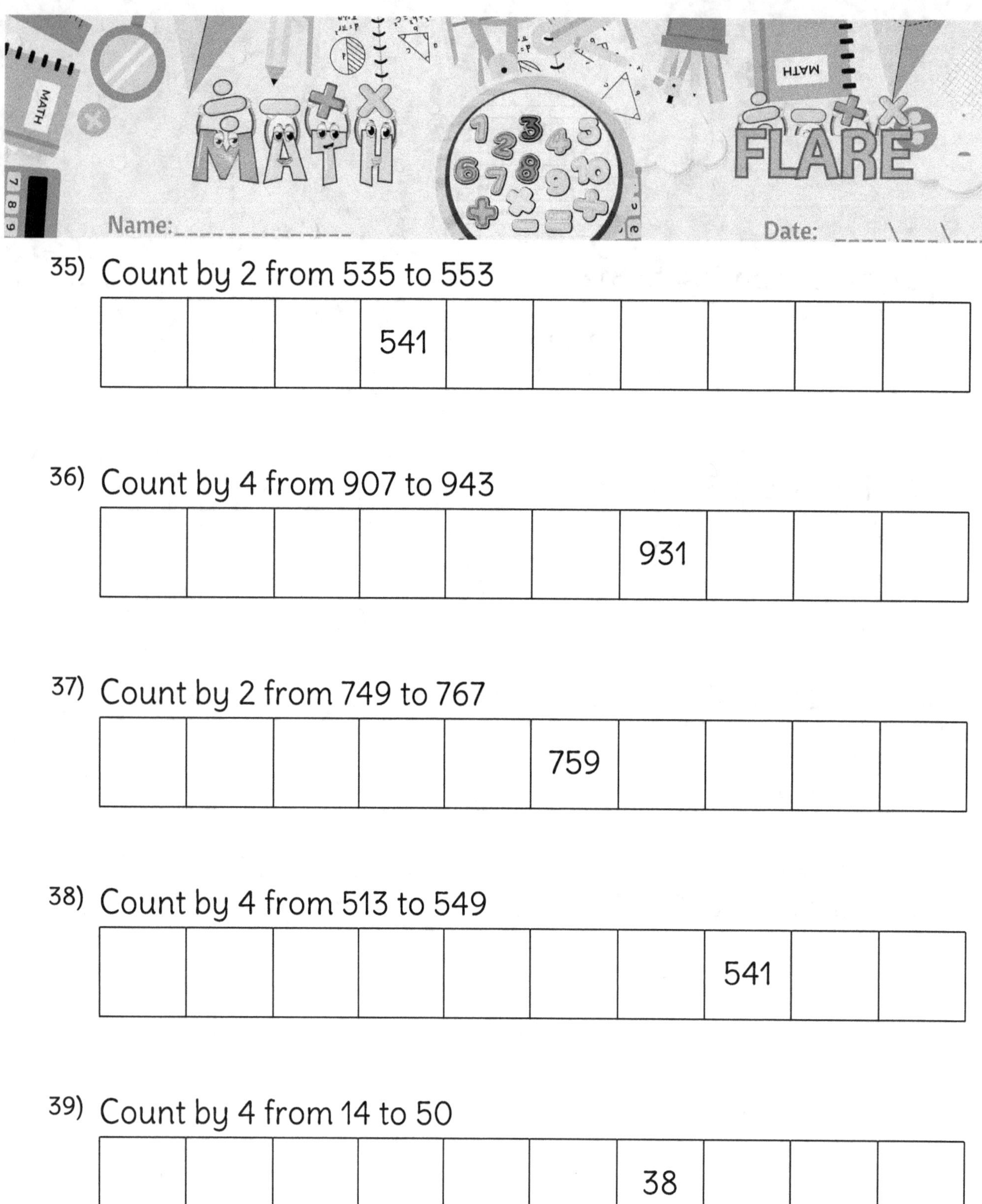

35) Count by 2 from 535 to 553

			541						

36) Count by 4 from 907 to 943

						931			

37) Count by 2 from 749 to 767

					759				

38) Count by 4 from 513 to 549

							541		

39) Count by 4 from 14 to 50

					38			

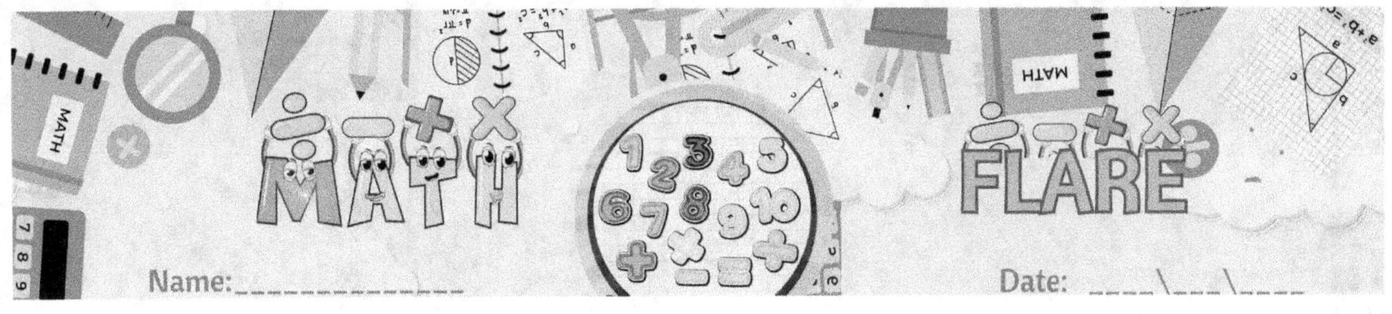

40) Count by 5 from 833 to 878

		843							

41) Count by 5 from 806 to 851

						836			

42) Count by 2 from 584 to 602

	586								

43) Count by 3 from 936 to 963

					951				

44) Count by 4 from 474 to 510

					494				

45) Count by 3 from 19 to 46

					37			

46) Count by 2 from 565 to 583

			573					

47) Count by 2 from 292 to 310

					304			

48) Count by 2 from 702 to 720

					714			

49) Count by 5 from 360 to 405

								405

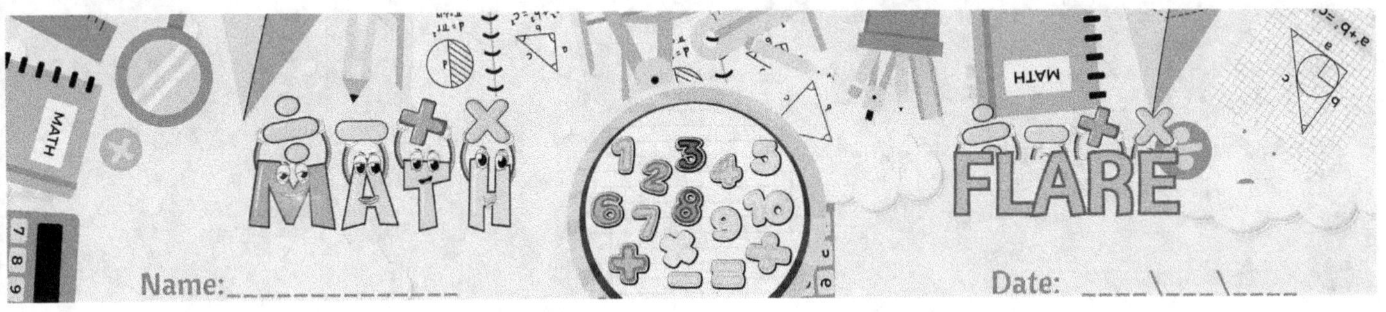

Compare the Numbers

Add: > or < or = to make the following statements true.

1) 269 < 940

2) 754 ___ 51

3) 165 ___ 721

4) 718 ___ 162

5) 233 ___ 835

6) 81 ___ 686

7) 466 ___ 233

8) 824 ___ 847

9) 686 ___ 904

10) 604 ___ 303

11) 488 ___ 421

12) 304 ___ 279

13) 6 ___ 979

14) 214 ___ 629

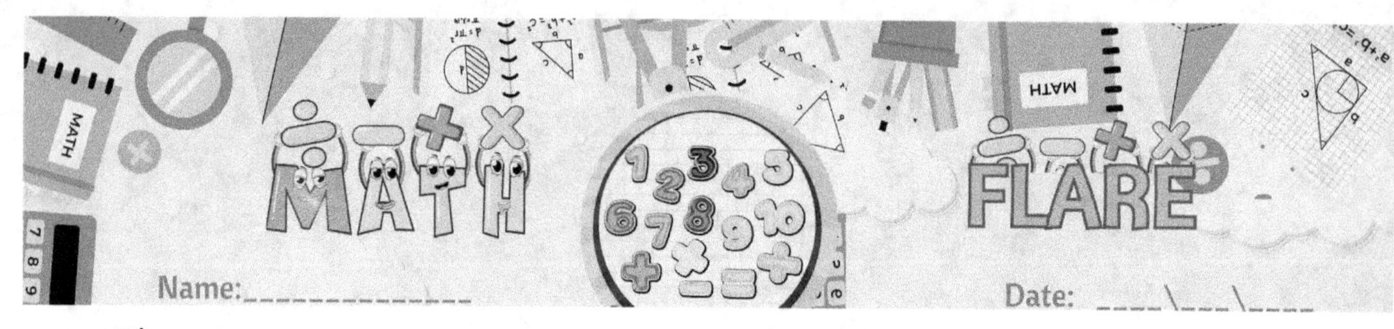

15) 319 ____ 750

16) 968 ____ 371

17) 907 ____ 398

18) 238 ____ 742

19) 819 ____ 982

20) 458 ____ 103

21) 959 ____ 434

22) 648 ____ 523

23) 50 ____ 272

24) 176 ____ 526

25) 704 ____ 631

26) 188 ____ 924

27) 731 ____ 380

28) 838 ____ 848

29) 637 ____ 475

30) 45 ____ 186

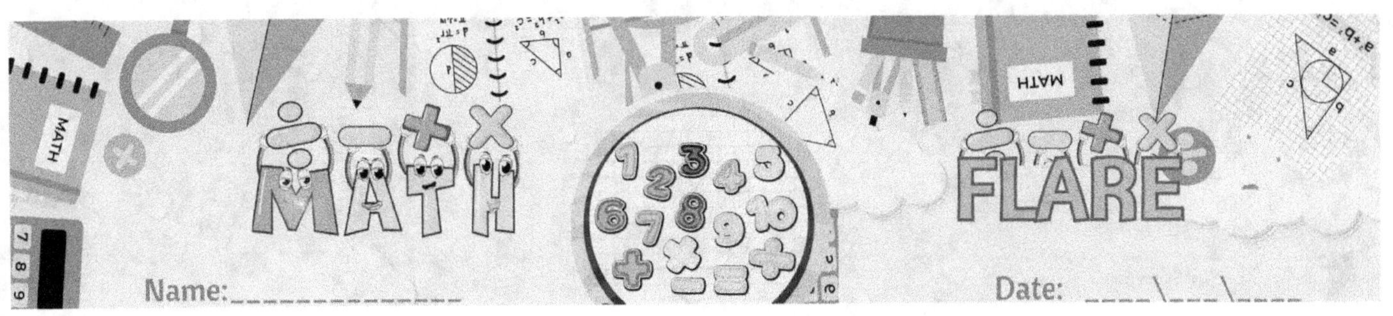

31) 508 ___ 90

32) 842 ___ 482

33) 867 ___ 710

34) 779 ___ 68

35) 995 ___ 82

36) 28 ___ 704

37) 446 ___ 501

38) 344 ___ 54

39) 772 ___ 780

40) 230 ___ 734

41) 803 ___ 687

42) 924 ___ 687

43) 563 ___ 45

44) 640 ___ 527

45) 560 ___ 390

46) 106 ___ 344

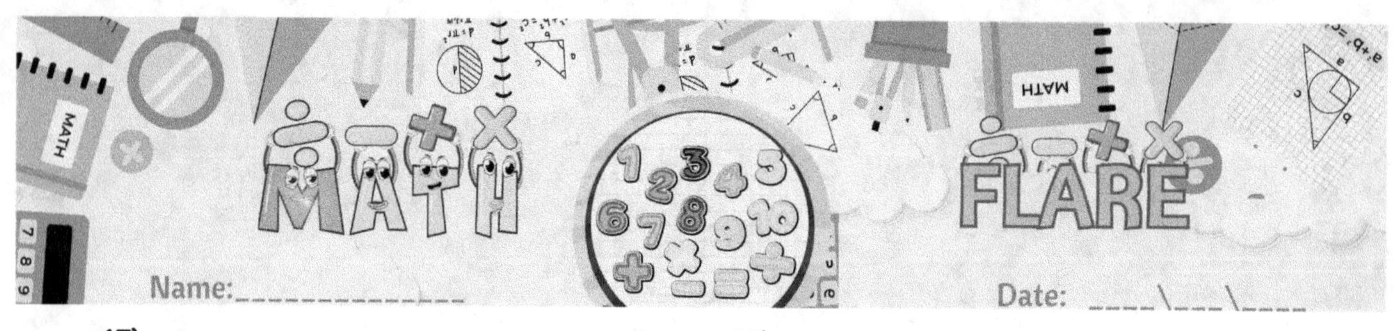

47) 938 ___ 273

48) 595 ___ 869

49) 592 ___ 167

50) 656 ___ 340

51) 493 ___ 109

52) 531 ___ 622

53) 603 ___ 484

54) 478 ___ 230

55) 37 ___ 784

56) 77 ___ 857

57) 246 ___ 310

58) 382 ___ 820

59) 165 ___ 155

60) 919 ___ 822

61) 70 ___ 252

62) 508 ___ 606

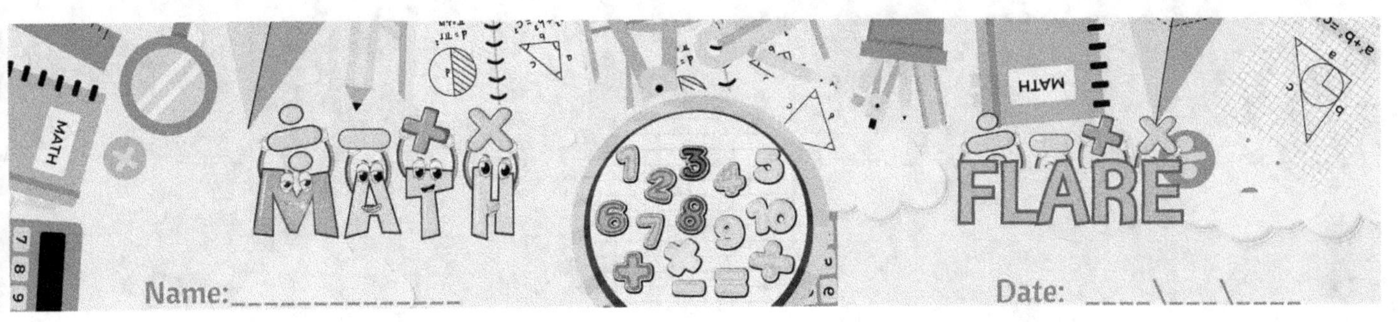

63) 976 ___ 684

64) 765 ___ 174

65) 905 ___ 474

66) 462 ___ 606

67) 124 ___ 889

68) 241 ___ 695

69) 157 ___ 303

70) 85 ___ 79

71) 566 ___ 410

72) 491 ___ 775

73) 313 ___ 248

74) 99 ___ 628

75) 890 ___ 775

76) 705 ___ 437

77) 247 ___ 834

78) 270 ___ 241

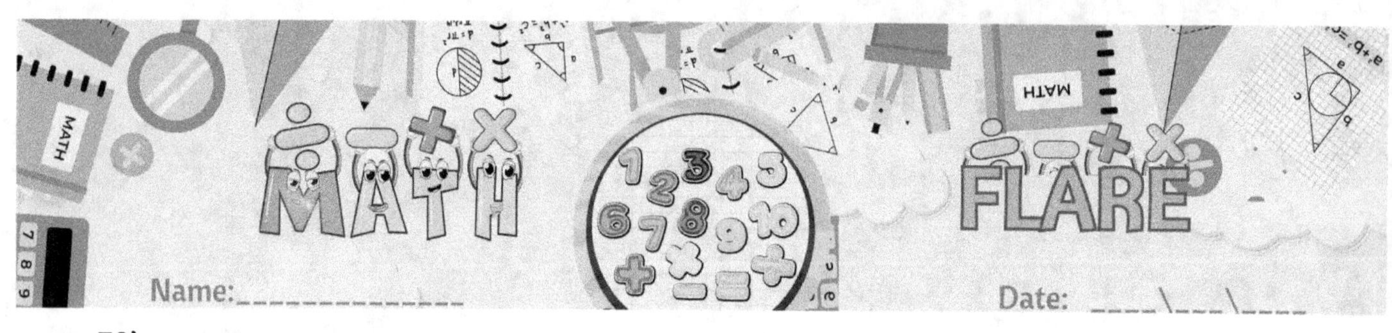

79) 600 ___ 925

80) 646 ___ 919

81) 718 ___ 305

82) 324 ___ 562

83) 323 ___ 470

84) 733 ___ 357

85) 70 ___ 687

86) 664 ___ 862

87) 71 ___ 840

88) 256 ___ 660

89) 761 ___ 732

90) 293 ___ 728

91) 586 ___ 138

92) 283 ___ 131

93) 768 ___ 26

94) 359 ___ 290

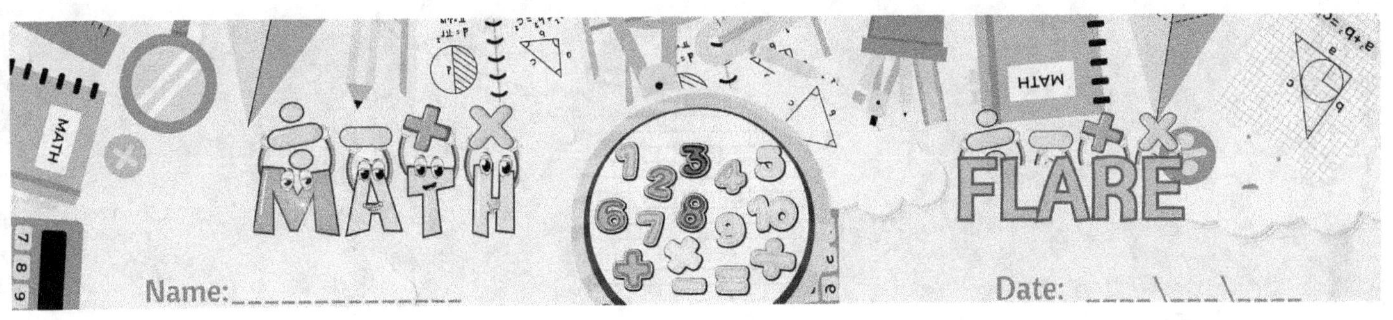

95) 619 ____ 1

96) 95 ____ 232

97) 657 ____ 165

98) 361 ____ 262

99) 86 ____ 928

100) 453 ____ 842

101) 515 ____ 741

102) 559 ____ 204

103) 112 ____ 843

104) 366 ____ 407

105) 578 ____ 610

106) 479 ____ 867

107) 633 ____ 917

108) 334 ____ 580

109) 22 ____ 194

110) 793 ____ 297

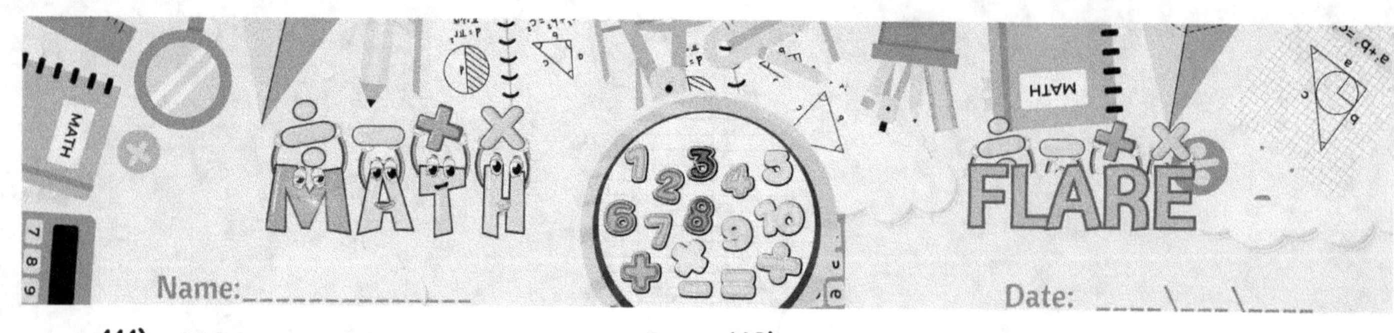

111) 112 ___ 444

112) 737 ___ 69

113) 592 ___ 432

114) 206 ___ 905

115) 480 ___ 994

116) 574 ___ 832

117) 280 ___ 450

118) 214 ___ 844

119) 579 ___ 79

120) 20 ___ 925

121) 659 ___ 952

122) 712 ___ 9

123) 521 ___ 227

124) 598 ___ 739

125) 831 ___ 780

126) 241 ___ 892

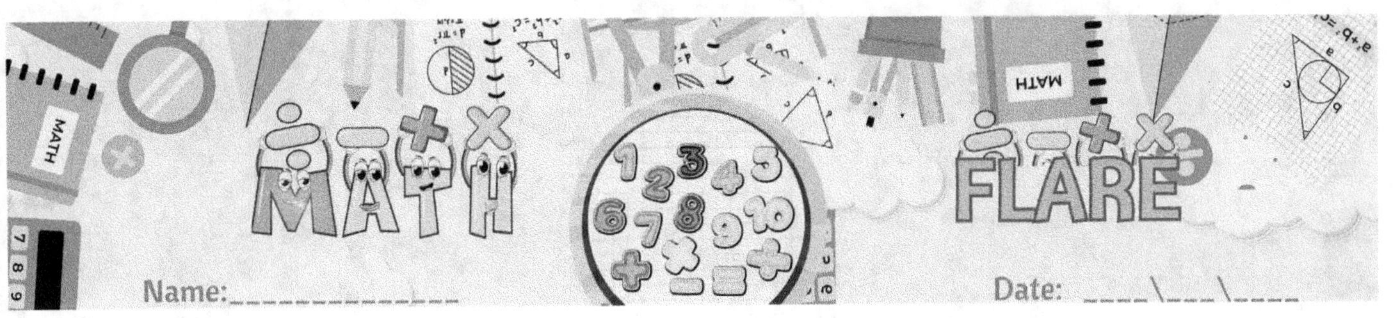

127) 136 ____ 156

128) 731 ____ 71

129) 5 ____ 490

130) 612 ____ 679

131) 638 ____ 461

132) 926 ____ 583

133) 36 ____ 647

134) 588 ____ 183

135) 703 ____ 489

136) 2 ____ 942

137) 174 ____ 868

138) 638 ____ 160

139) 732 ____ 728

140) 548 ____ 365

141) 834 ____ 466

142) 74 ____ 700

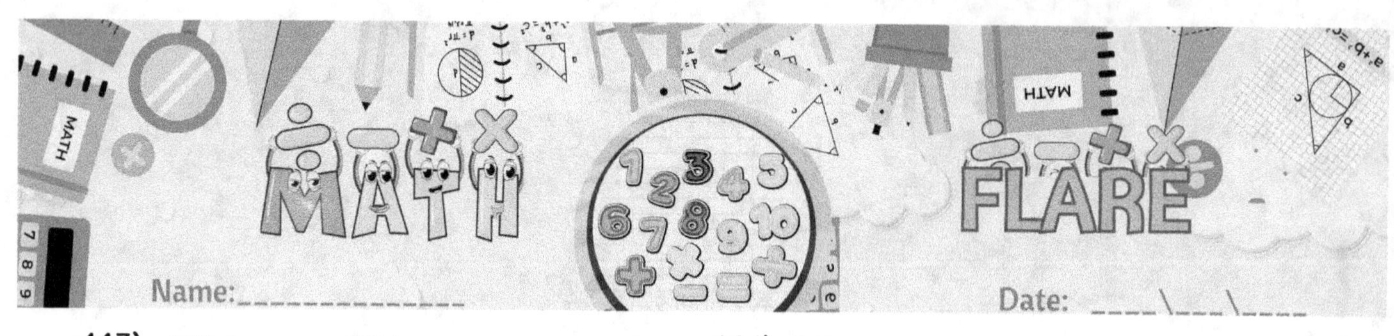

143) 754 ___ 682

144) 697 ___ 124

145) 718 ___ 144

146) 840 ___ 90

147) 467 ___ 341

148) 287 ___ 198

149) 27 ___ 129

150) 973 ___ 874

151) 639 ___ 416

152) 37 ___ 343

153) 779 ___ 298

154) 718 ___ 268

155) 517 ___ 572

156) 338 ___ 276

157) 941 ___ 247

158) 845 ___ 173

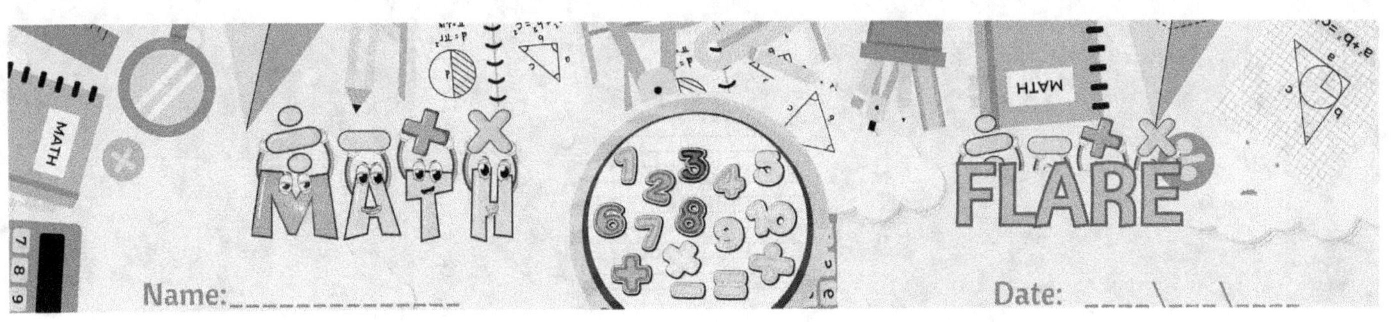

159) 387 ____ 227

160) 829 ____ 354

161) 949 ____ 464

162) 465 ____ 560

163) 649 ____ 911

164) 476 ____ 832

165) 581 ____ 440

166) 134 ____ 604

167) 755 ____ 674

168) 726 ____ 418

169) 429 ____ 731

170) 921 ____ 456

171) 963 ____ 430

172) 607 ____ 147

173) 805 ____ 565

174) 148 ____ 220

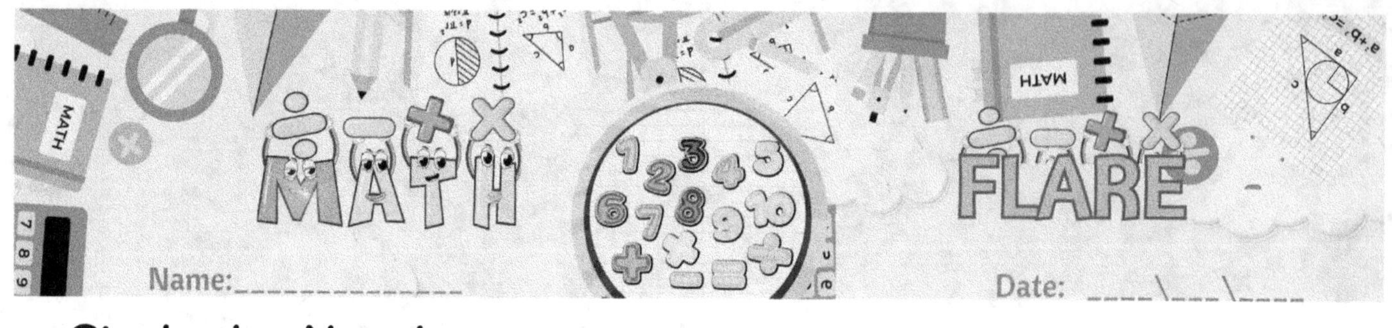

Circle the Numbers

Circle the smallest and biggest number in each group.

1)	2)	3)
(948)	602	111
(69)	642	581
529	661	538
523	363	242
82	729	186

4)	5)	6)
918	570	974
628	222	267
989	8	49
23	282	477
40	126	173

7)	8)	9)
735	670	41
125	782	378
560	254	520
191	246	828
304	8	157

10)	11)	12)
514	717	726
935	245	61
597	812	248
195	192	397
988	857	107

13) 336
594
184
190
993

14) 986
21
348
938
516

15) 136
374
743
15
998

16) 193
702
180
126
612

17) 40
669
854
489
455

18) 490
312
369
333
577

19) 609
535
856
140
672

20) 447
194
330
835
171

21) 494
588
658
679
852

22) 344
502
797
193
665

23) 25
881
123
785
68

24) 666
740
695
735
504

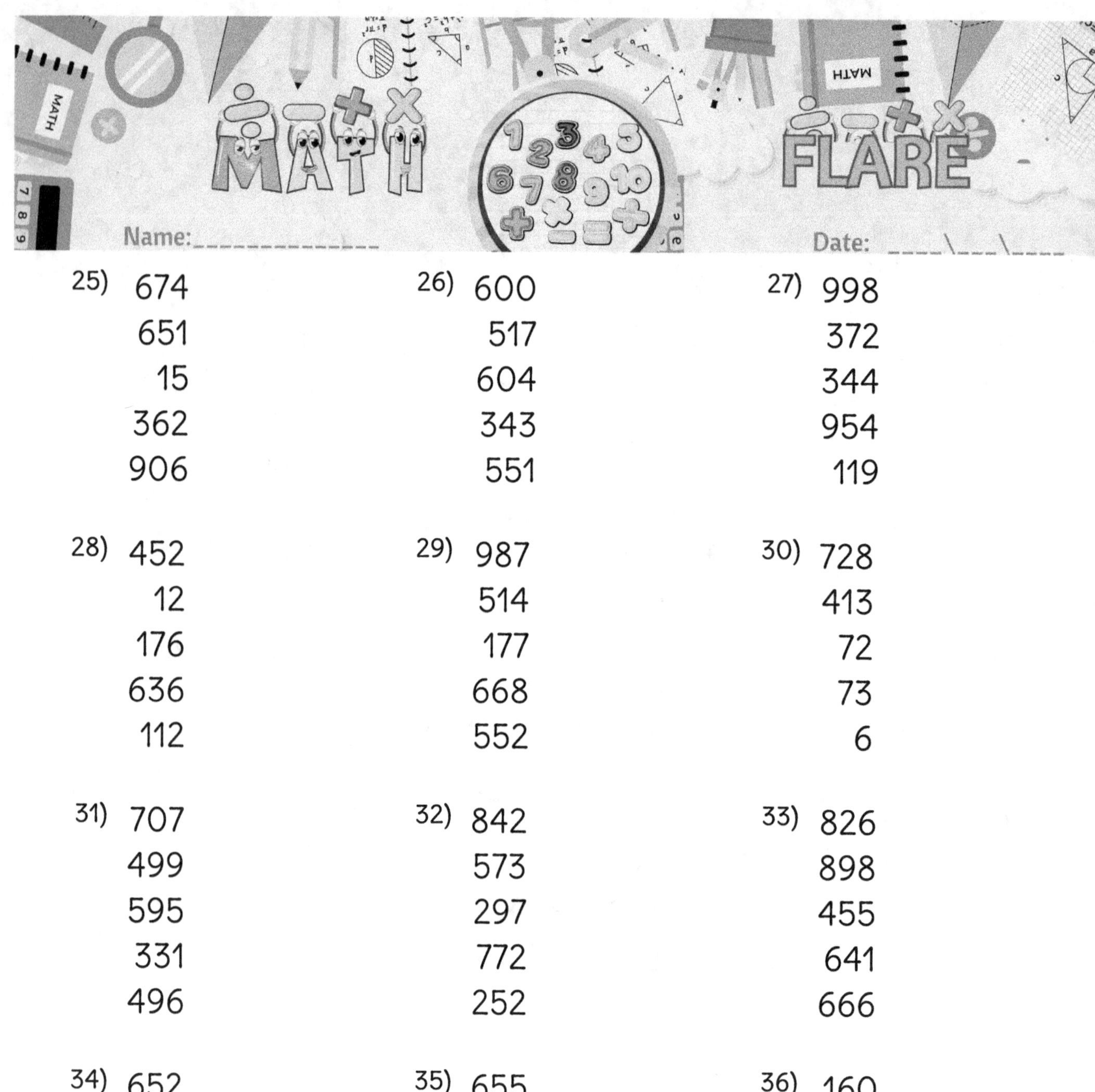

Name: _______________   Date: ___/___/___

25)	26)	27)
674	600	998
651	517	372
15	604	344
362	343	954
906	551	119

28)	29)	30)
452	987	728
12	514	413
176	177	72
636	668	73
112	552	6

31)	32)	33)
707	842	826
499	573	898
595	297	455
331	772	641
496	252	666

34)	35)	36)
652	655	160
537	564	475
168	59	347
667	624	809
616	516	179

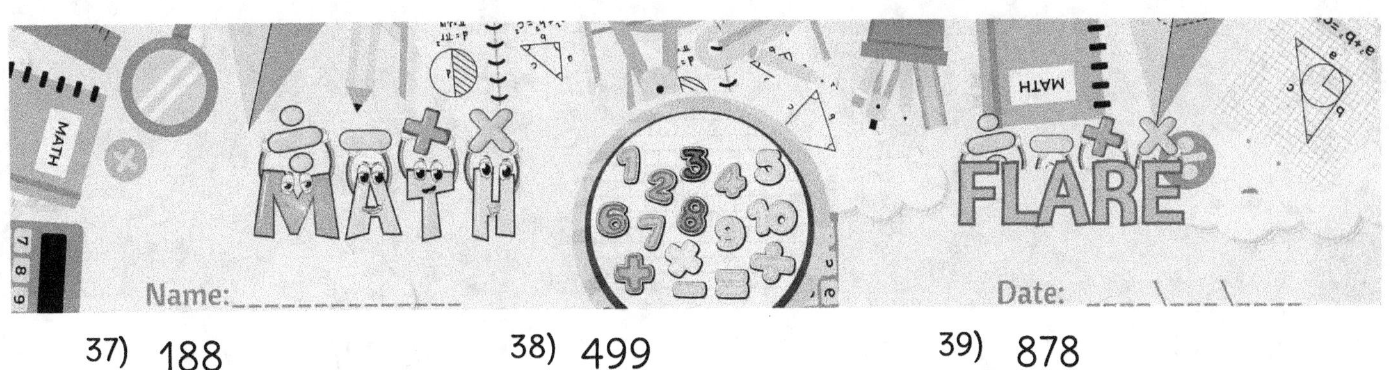

37) 188
446
532
337
844

38) 499
777
14
458
276

39) 878
715
403
384
285

40) 90
60
535
2
899

41) 191
246
404
457
350

42) 143
440
971
815
337

43) 367
227
487
594
65

44) 380
367
118
797
168

45) 875
524
709
392
737

46) 940
162
674
339
426

47) 101
940
345
909
988

48) 942
43
76
987
702

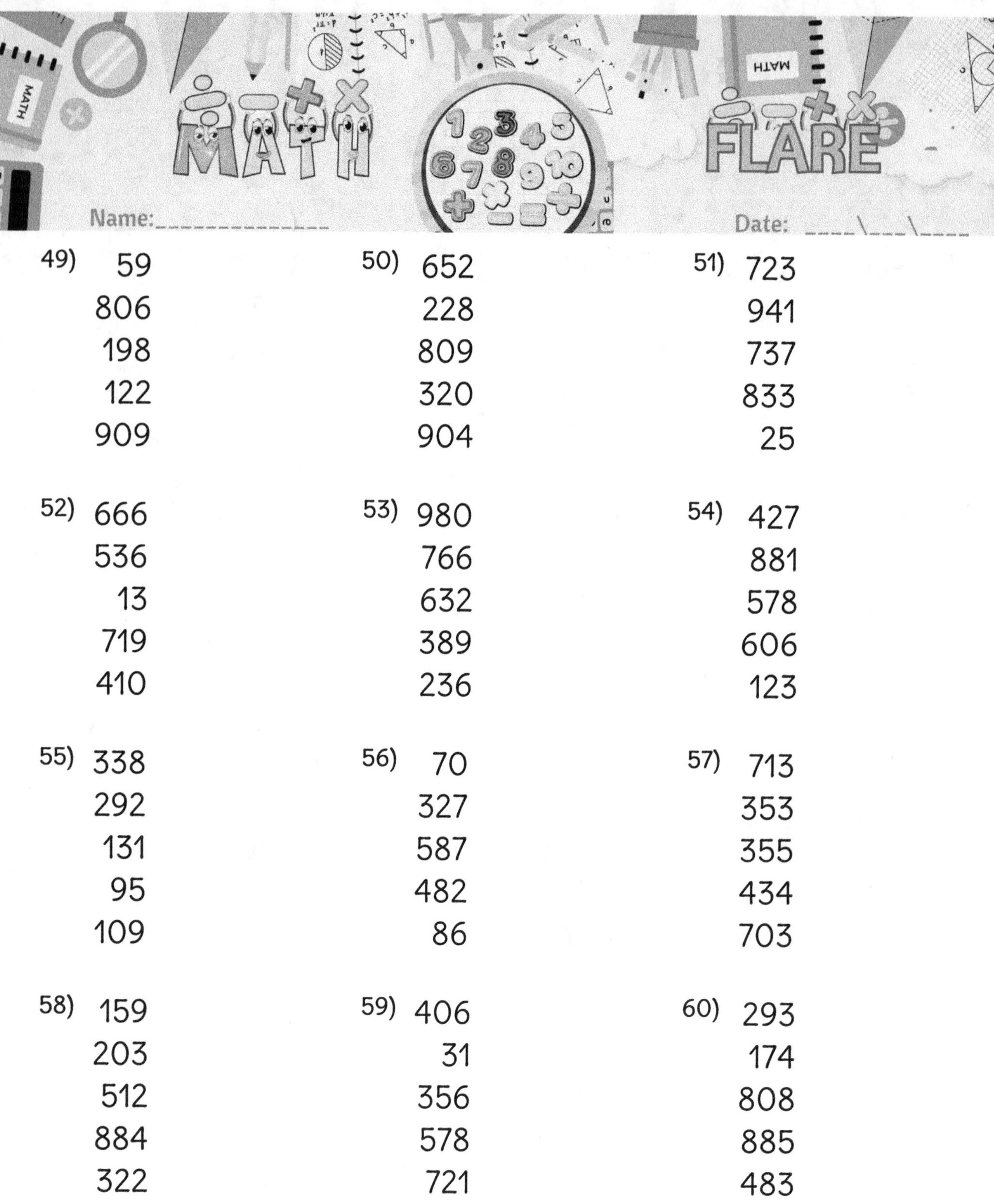

49)
59
806
198
122
909

50)
652
228
809
320
904

51)
723
941
737
833
25

52)
666
536
13
719
410

53)
980
766
632
389
236

54)
427
881
578
606
123

55)
338
292
131
95
109

56)
70
327
587
482
86

57)
713
353
355
434
703

58)
159
203
512
884
322

59)
406
31
356
578
721

60)
293
174
808
885
483

61) 770
649
203
198
567

62) 431
811
643
725
955

63) 340
949
530
634
696

64) 628
411
198
686
77

65) 224
370
693
284
716

66) 308
935
553
374
816

67) 895
518
701
999
315

68) 64
150
158
867
272

69) 348
560
786
929
982

70) 457
500
722
881
94

71) 881
975
123
809
259

72) 401
956
919
481
259

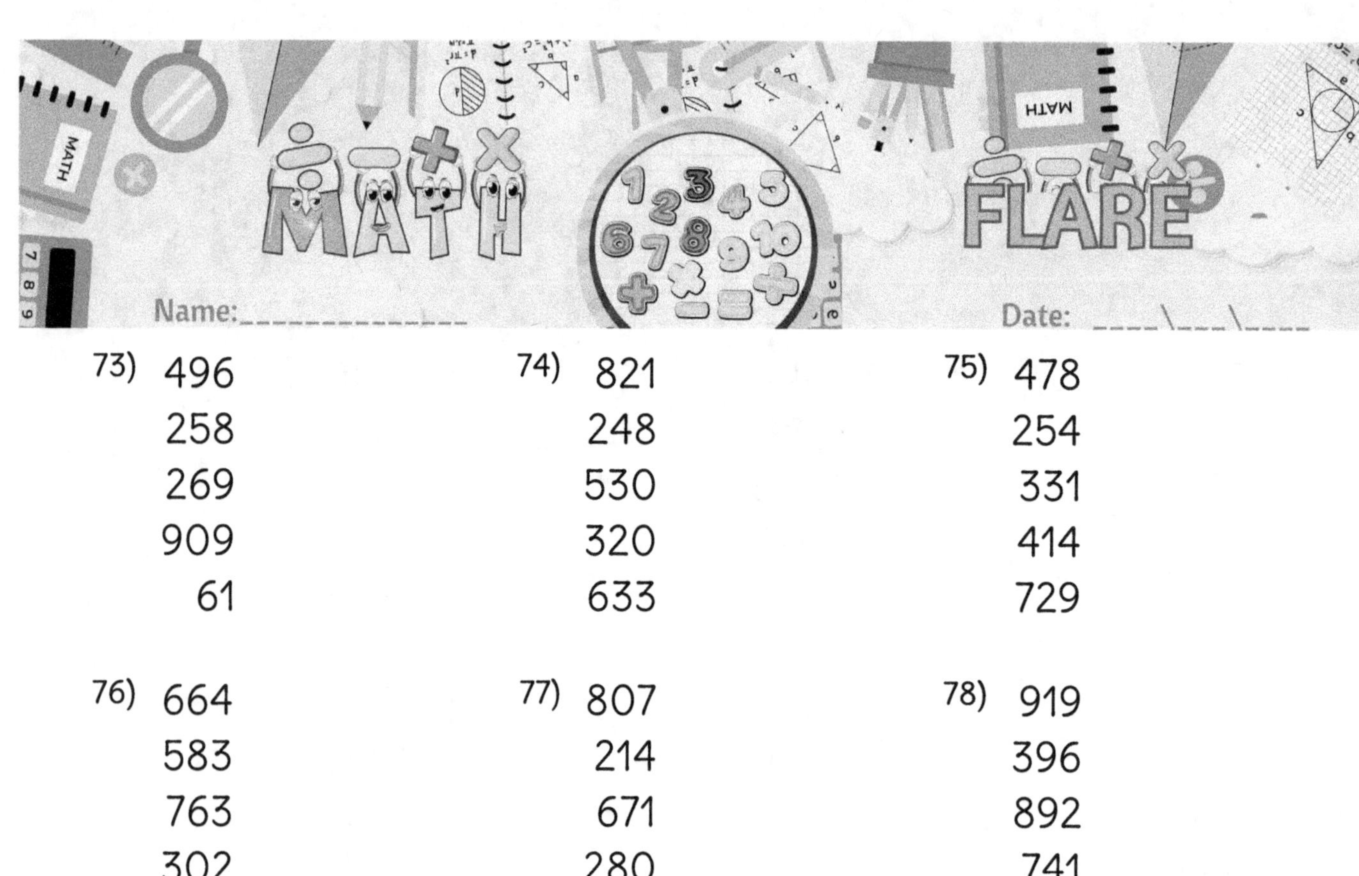

73)	74)	75)
496	821	478
258	248	254
269	530	331
909	320	414
61	633	729

76)	77)	78)
664	807	919
583	214	396
763	671	892
302	280	741
260	934	913

79)	80)	81)
108	90	210
231	291	970
677	877	403
608	869	249
776	162	615

82)	83)	84)
628	817	282
645	193	587
708	617	988
80	221	974
595	452	141

85) 425
355
788
406
526

86) 248
577
722
638
639

87) 373
706
894
141
51

88) 837
811
423
665
307

89) 274
687
812
147
96

90) 914
613
456
157
494

91) 503
302
902
728
736

92) 854
182
996
723
367

93) 51
923
71
441
222

94) 112
298
477
170
614

95) 470
164
324
668
867

96) 738
542
642
310
611

97)
635
121
565
144
136

98)
72
803
167
404
197

99)
655
815
700
298
256

100)
350
617
372
924
984

101)
616
136
286
543
24

102)
340
978
235
861
998

103)
312
539
687
112
732

104)
929
359
926
306
151

105)
309
132
74
973
958

106)
655
463
26
412
517

107)
121
171
718
326
994

108)
499
835
23
120
796

109) 94
      569
      306
      406
      884

110) 117
      128
      588
      566
      327

111) 991
      691
      66
      773
      675

112) 485
      63
      313
      584
      369

113) 876
      952
      822
      344
      877

114) 141
      820
      361
      117
      233

115) 95
      337
      806
      510
      58

116) 740
      826
      667
      90
      842

117) 527
      874
      460
      86
      525

118) 430
      105
      944
      650
      510

119) 437
      523
      438
      751
      919

120) 141
      746
      961
      528
      743

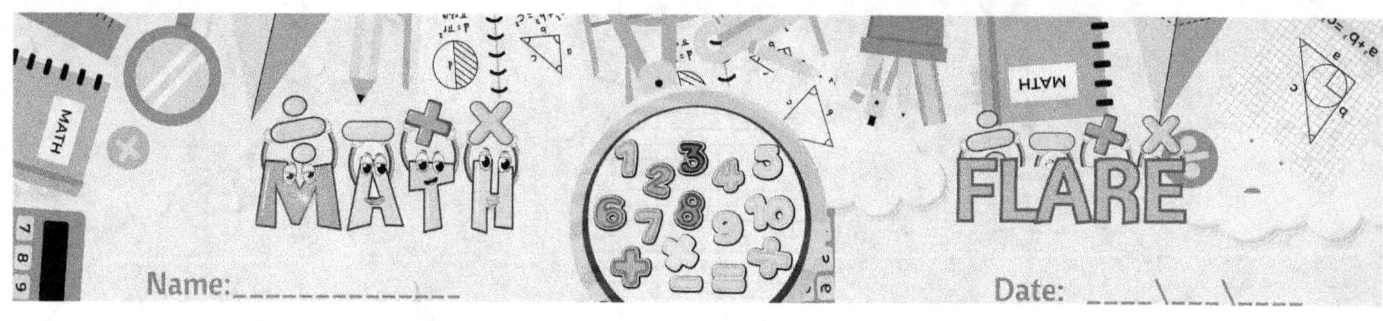

Missing Numbers

Fill in the missing numbers, before and after and between.

1) 296 __297__ 298

2) ______ 473

3) ______ 233 ______

4) ______ 885 ______

5) 716 ______ 718

6) ______ 660

7) ______ 224 ______

8) 841 ______

9) ______ 494 ______

10) ______ 819

11) 37 ______ 39

12) ______ 711 ______

13) ______ 797 ______

14) 898 ______

15) 590 ______ 592

16) 993 ______ 995

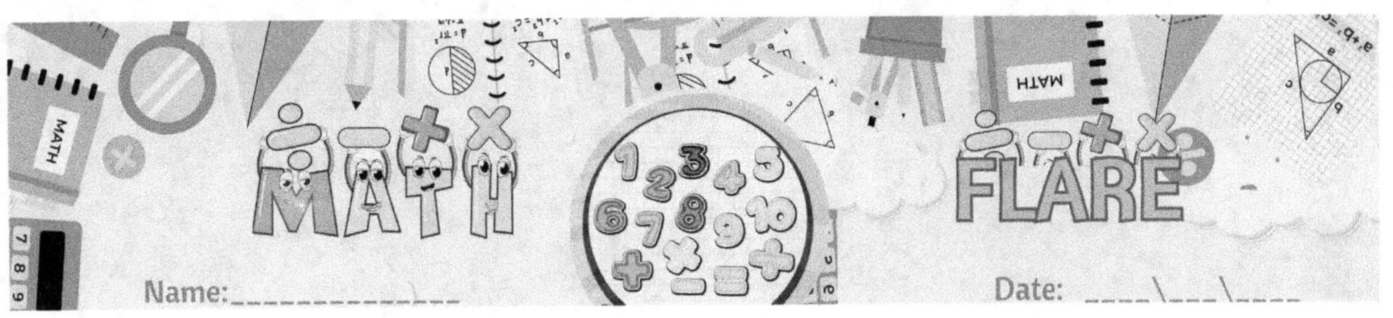

17) _______ 140

18) 546 _______ 548

19) 403 _______

20) 854 _______ 856

21) _______ 546 _______

22) _______ 230 _______

23) 850 _______

24) _______ 301 _______

25) 910 _______ 912

26) 648 _______

27) 143 _______

28) _______ 708

29) 57 _______ 59

30) _______ 537 _______

31) 756 _______ 758

32) 966 _______ 968

33) 942 _______ 944

34) 257 _______ 259

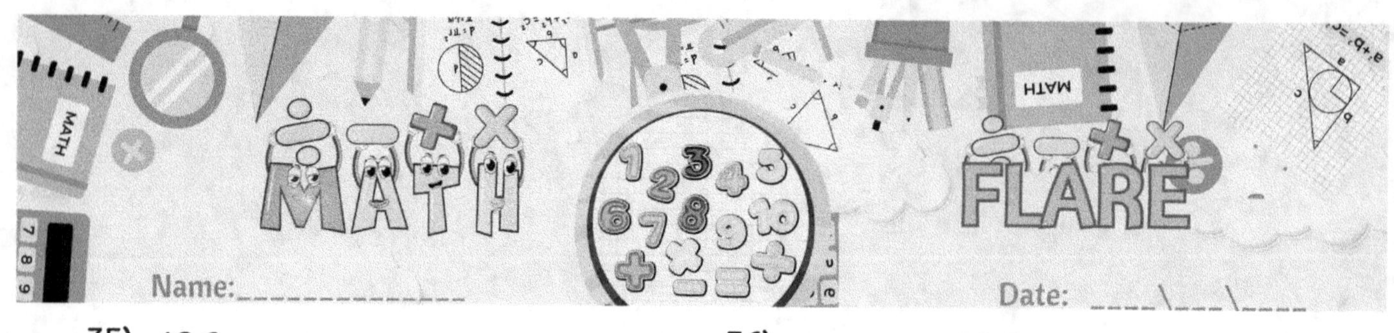

Name:____________________   Date:_____________

35) 196 ______   36) ______ 600

37) 882 ______ 884   38) ______ 904

39) 647 ______ 649   40) 272 ______

41) ______ 147 ______   42) 269 ______ 271

43) 721 ______   44) 639 ______

45) ______ 704 ______   46) 591 ______

47) ______ 115 ______   48) ______ 583

49) 772 ______   50) ______ 785

51) 501 ______ 503   52) ______ 319

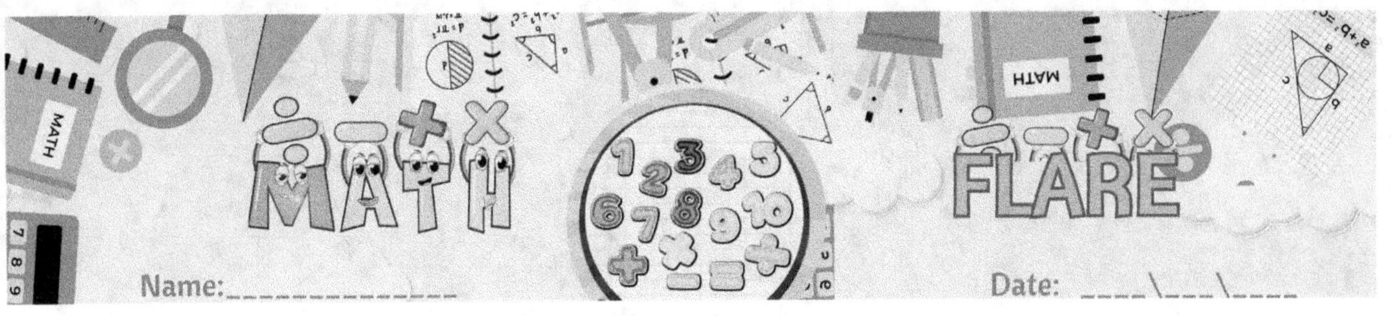

53) 128 ______

54) 178 ______

55) 773 ______

56) 108 ______ 110

57) ______ 389 ______

58) ______ 684

59) 530 ______ 532

60) 74 ______

61) 238 ______

62) 378 ______

63) ______ 776 ______

64) 835 ______

65) 905 ______

66) 970 ______ 972

67) ______ 701

68) 356 ______ 358

69) ______ 856 ______

70) ______ 882

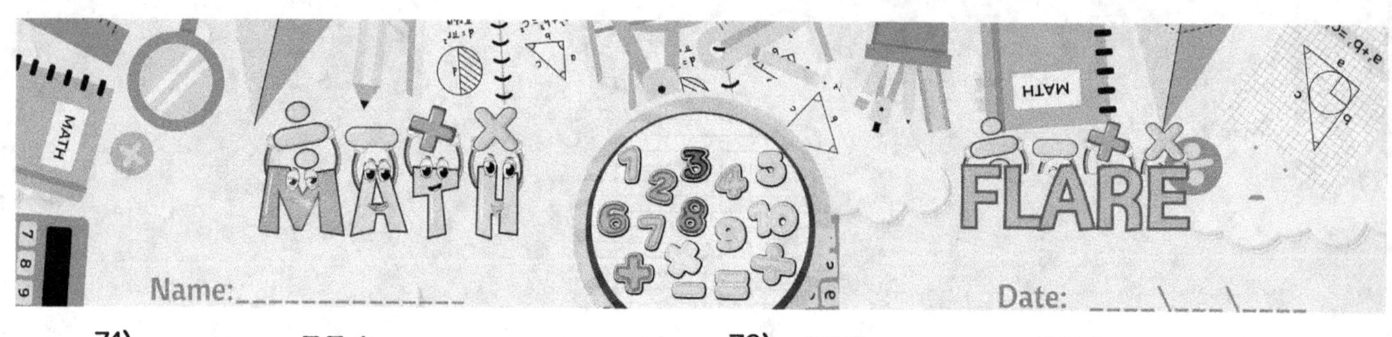

71) _______ 354 _______

72) 432 _______ 434

73) _______ 806 _______

74) _____ 34

75) 900 _______ 902

76) _______ 983 _______

77) _______ 186

78) _______ 453

79) _______ 508

80) 359 _______ 361

81) _______ 315 _______

82) _______ 839

83) _______ 812 _______

84) _______ 855

85) _______ 937 _______

86) _______ 105 _______

87) 318 _______ 320

88) _______ 717 _______

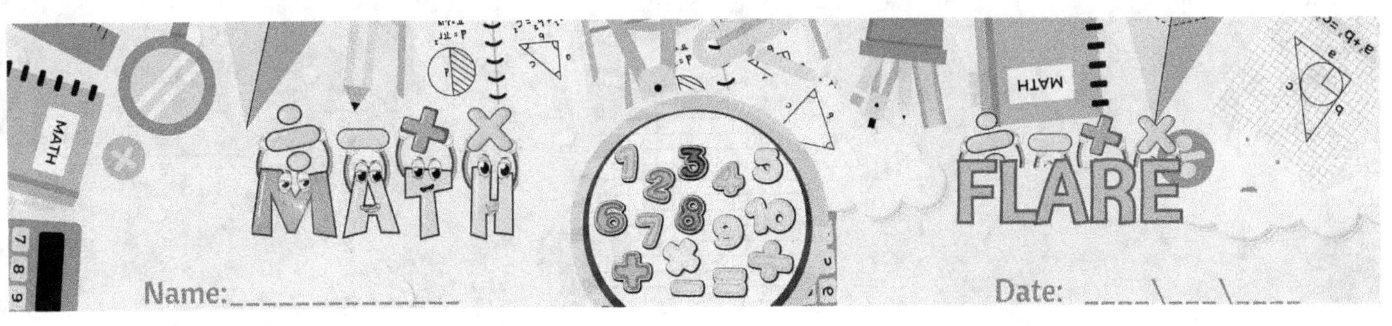

89) 629 _______ 631

90) _______ 884

91) _______ 155 _______

92) _______ 317

93) _______ 719

94) _______ 666

95) 864 _______

96) _______ 481

97) 168 _______ 170

98) 106 _______ 108

99) 803 _______

100) _______ 998

101) _______ 705 _______

102) _______ 355

103) _______ 711

104) _______ 270

105) _______ 629 _______

106) 555 _______

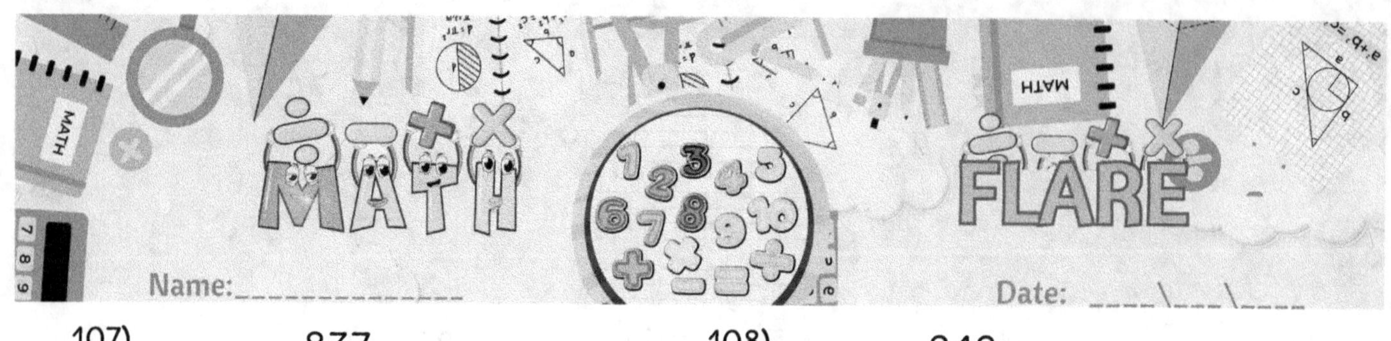

107) _______ 837 _______

108) _______ 242

109) _______ 689

110) _______ 875 _______

111) 503 _______ 505

112) _____ 64 _____

113) _______ 379

114) 713 _______ 715

115) _______ 933 _______

116) _______ 969 _______

117) _______ 574

118) 262 _______ 264

119) _______ 699

120) _____ 117

121) 553 _______

122) 470 _______ 472

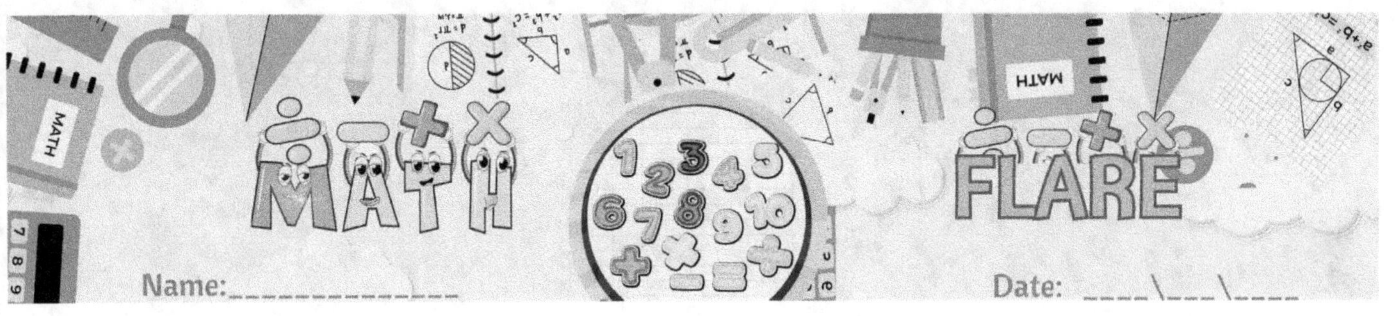

Addition 1 through 20

Find the Sum.

1) 17 + 3 **20**	2) 2 + 9 **11**	3) 12 + 8	4) 7 + 12	5) 8 + 3
6) 4 + 11	7) 7 + 1	8) 2 + 17	9) 13 + 16	10) 16 + 1
11) 12 + 19	12) 11 + 8	13) 9 + 6	14) 15 + 9	15) 2 + 8
16) 17 + 7	17) 8 + 7	18) 8 + 12	19) 6 + 9	20) 5 + 10
21) 7 + 15	22) 14 + 14	23) 5 + 6	24) 13 + 15	25) 8 + 9

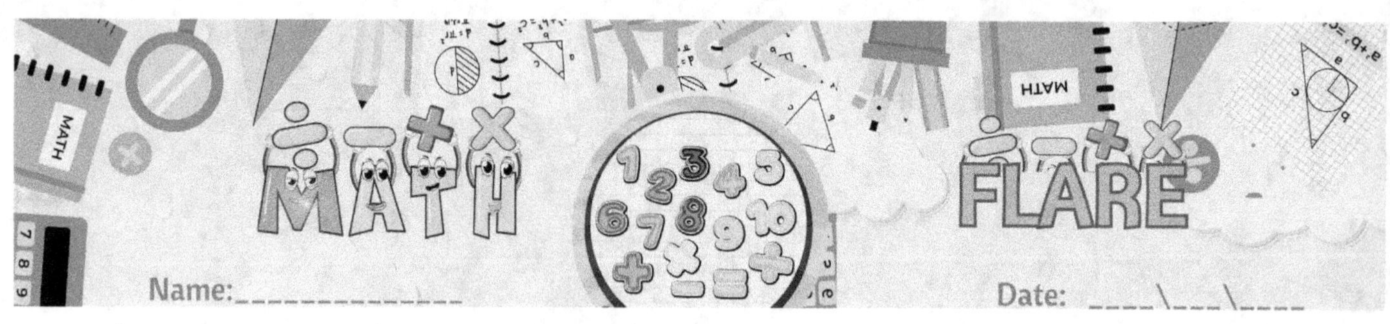

26) 8 + 19	27) 12 + 14	28) 19 + 6	29) 13 + 19	30) 6 + 17
31) 3 + 16	32) 4 + 4	33) 5 + 16	34) 10 + 8	35) 9 + 5
36) 15 + 4	37) 15 + 2	38) 1 + 14	39) 13 + 2	40) 4 + 2
41) 20 + 19	42) 15 + 18	43) 15 + 14	44) 7 + 3	45) 18 + 7
46) 4 + 9	47) 8 + 11	48) 12 + 10	49) 10 + 10	50) 16 + 7

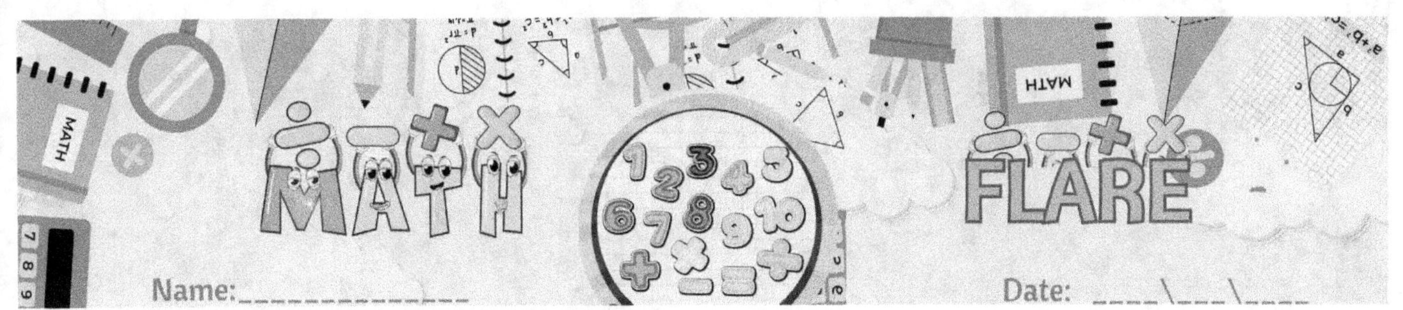

51) 7 + 4	52) 14 + 5	53) 5 + 11	54) 14 + 6	55) 13 + 12
56) 15 + 5	57) 18 + 16	58) 17 + 5	59) 9 + 7	60) 2 + 16
61) 1 + 7	62) 7 + 9	63) 2 + 7	64) 14 + 11	65) 3 + 3
66) 12 + 15	67) 5 + 13	68) 19 + 17	69) 5 + 12	70) 20 + 2
71) 11 + 12	72) 14 + 8	73) 3 + 4	74) 9 + 1	75) 6 + 20

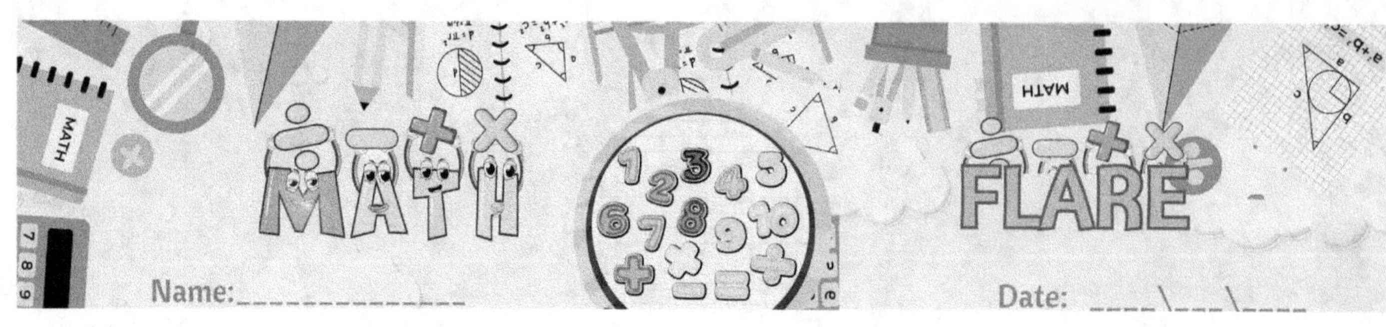

76) 17 + 6	77) 4 + 18	78) 17 + 4	79) 1 + 1	80) 20 + 6
81) 17 + 19	82) 20 + 17	83) 13 + 17	84) 18 + 20	85) 16 + 3
86) 16 + 15	87) 7 + 5	88) 1 + 19	89) 9 + 16	90) 8 + 16
91) 17 + 18	92) 14 + 15	93) 8 + 6	94) 12 + 12	95) 5 + 7
96) 3 + 17	97) 9 + 2	98) 3 + 15	99) 8 + 10	100) 10 + 12

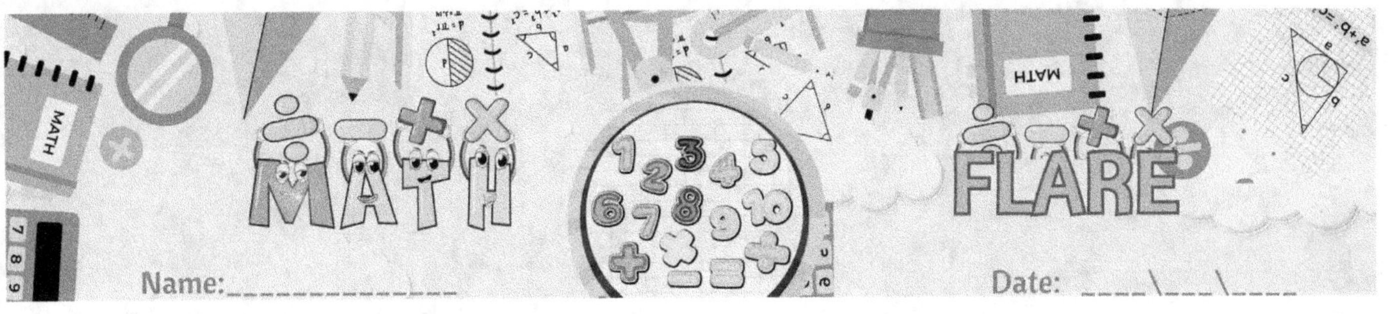

Addition 1 through 20

Find the unknown number.

1) 14 + __15__ = 29

2) 18 + ___ = 36

3) 19 + ___ = 20

4) 9 + ___ = 26

5) 10 + 1 = ___

6) 3 + ___ = 23

7) 13 + 6 = ___

8) 4 + 11 = ___

9) 9 + 2 = ___

10) 7 + 16 = ___

11) ___ + 15 = 32

12) 2 + 1 = ___

13) ___ + 4 = 22

14) 11 + 8 = ___

15) ___ + 13 = 27

16) 9 + 8 = ___

17) ___ + 15 = 24

18) 8 + ___ = 25

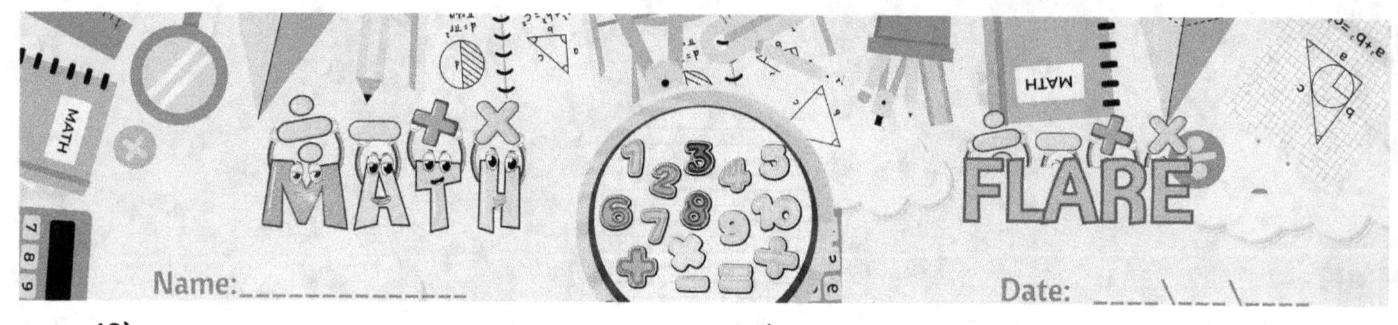

19) ___ + 8 = 24

20) 16 + 15 = ___

21) 2 + 4 = ___

22) ___ + 3 = 8

23) ___ + 4 = 9

24) 18 + 12 = ___

25) 7 + ___ = 14

26) ___ + 14 = 18

27) 15 + ___ = 34

28) 15 + 18 = ___

29) 1 + 16 = ___

30) ___ + 2 = 12

31) ___ + 17 = 21

32) ___ + 14 = 26

33) 12 + 19 = ___

34) 8 + ___ = 9

35) 4 + 12 = ___

36) 7 + ___ = 27

37) ___ + 3 = 23

38) 14 + ___ = 31

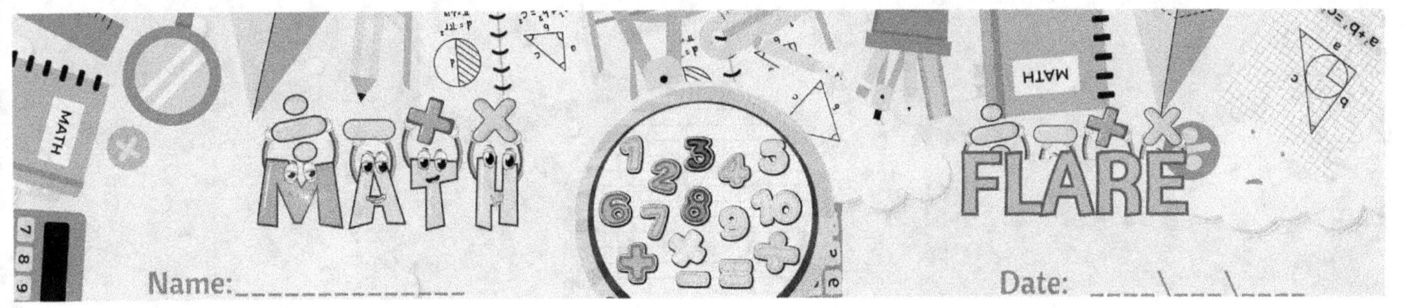

39) 16 + ____ = 32

40) 19 + 8 = ____

41) ____ + 4 = 11

42) 6 + 15 = ____

43) ____ + 19 = 38

44) 10 + ____ = 20

45) 16 + 20 = ____

46) 12 + ____ = 17

47) 12 + 11 = ____

48) 11 + ____ = 17

49) 16 + 18 = ____

50) 1 + ____ = 5

51) ____ + 14 = 28

52) ____ + 17 = 23

53) 3 + 5 = ____

54) 16 + ____ = 20

55) 12 + 3 = ____

56) 11 + ____ = 20

57) ____ + 16 = 25

58) 19 + 10 = ____

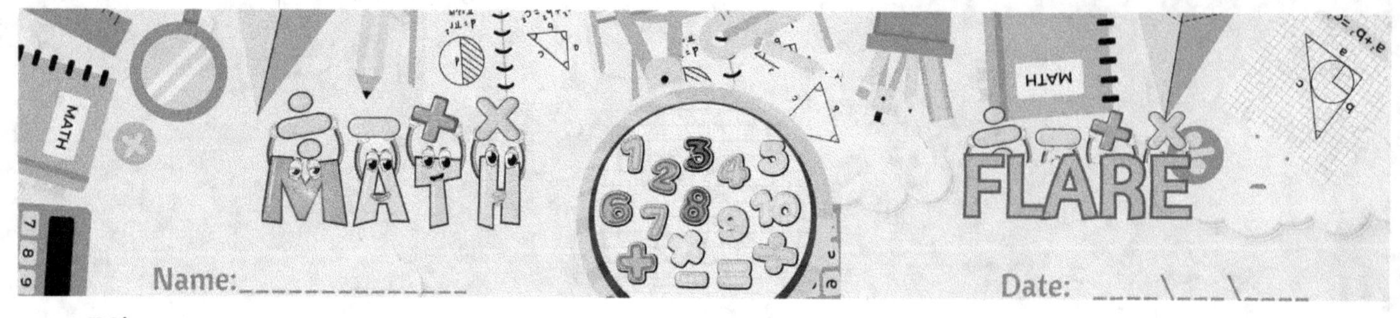

59) 11 + 14 = ____

60) 16 + 7 = ____

61) ____ + 6 = 9

62) ____ + 6 = 12

63) ____ + 14 = 20

64) 12 + 13 = ____

65) 13 + 13 = ____

66) ____ + 3 = 7

67) ____ + 7 = 9

68) 14 + 12 = ____

69) 8 + 12 = ____

70) 5 + 15 = ____

71) 14 + 4 = ____

72) 3 + ____ = 18

73) 7 + 15 = ____

74) 19 + ____ = 33

75) 2 + 9 = ____

76) ____ + 16 = 20

77) 12 + 18 = ____

78) 19 + 3 = ____

Name:_____________________   Date: ____________

79) ___ + 18 = 27

80) 7 + 8 = ___

81) 15 + ___ = 28

82) 16 + 19 = ___

83) 8 + 5 = ___

84) 3 + ___ = 11

85) ___ + 19 = 22

86) ___ + 3 = 19

87) 7 + ___ = 25

88) 14 + ___ = 23

89) 2 + 13 = ___

90) 3 + ___ = 21

91) ___ + 10 = 11

92) 13 + ___ = 15

93) 2 + ___ = 18

94) 20 + ___ = 34

95) 12 + ___ = 20

96) 8 + 15 = ___

97) 7 + 5 = ___

98) 20 + ___ = 30

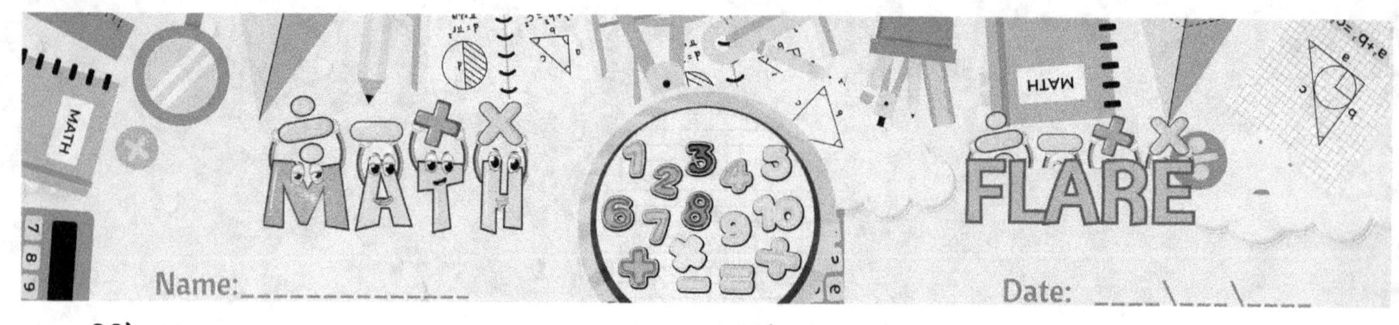

99) 15 + 9 = ___

100) 15 + ___ = 23

101) 14 + ___ = 25

102) 6 + 18 = ___

103) 7 + ___ = 10

104) ___ + 17 = 28

105) 19 + 18 = ___

106) 12 + ___ = 14

107) ___ + 20 = 38

108) ___ + 9 = 15

109) 13 + ___ = 31

110) 11 + ___ = 29

111) 17 + ___ = 25

112) 18 + ___ = 29

113) 15 + ___ = 20

114) 11 + 11 = ___

115) 11 + ___ = 30

116) ___ + 15 = 19

117) 9 + ___ = 19

118) 5 + 12 = ___

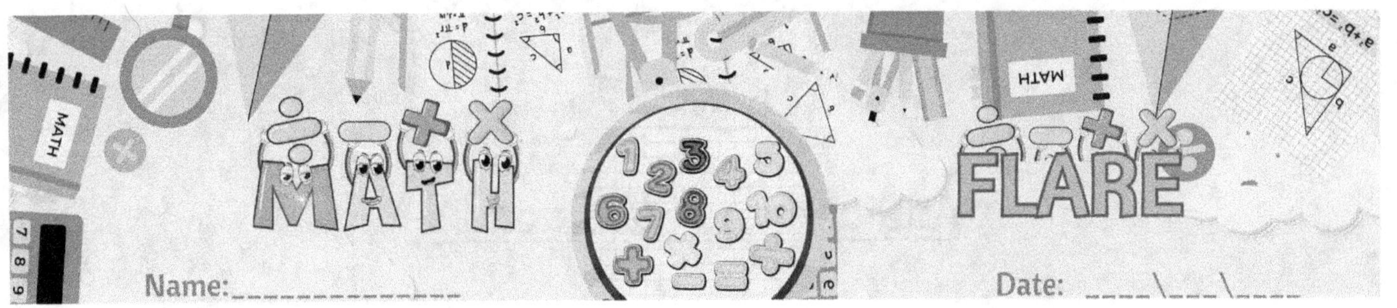

119) 9 + ___ = 18

120) 7 + 1 = ___

121) 5 + ___ = 12

122) 18 + 2 = ___

123) 15 + 15 = ___

124) ___ + 8 = 9

125) 2 + 18 = ___

126) ___ + 9 = 28

127) ___ + 8 = 16

128) ___ + 7 = 17

129) 14 + 6 = ___

130) ___ + 18 = 38

131) ___ + 9 = 16

132) 7 + ___ = 13

133) ___ + 4 = 15

134) 3 + ___ = 14

135) 16 + ___ = 17

136) 8 + ___ = 24

137) ___ + 18 = 35

138) 2 + ___ = 21

Chapter 2

Addition and Subtraction

Addition

Adding is like putting things together to see how many we have altogether.

For instance, imagine we have 2 colorful blocks. Then, we add 3 more blocks. How many blocks do we have in total?

Let's count them together. 1, 2, 3, 4, 5.

Exactly! We have 5 blocks altogether! We show this with a plus sign (+) like this:

$$2 + 3 = 5.$$

Now, let's try another one.

If we have 1 pencil and we add one more pencil, how many pencils do we have in total?

Right, we have 2 pencils! We can write it down like this:

$$1 + 1 = 2.$$

Let's solve a problem:

$$\begin{array}{r} 17 \\ +\ \ 3 \\ \hline 20 \end{array}$$

Subtraction

Subtraction is all about taking things away or finding out how much is left.

Imagine you have a basket of 5 apples. Now, let's pretend you ate 2 of those yummy apples. How many do you have left?

Let's count them together. 1, 2, 3. Yes, you got it! You have 3 apples left!

We use this special sign "-" to show that we're taking away some apples.

Now, let's try another one! Imagine you have a bag full of 8 colorful marbles. Now, let's say you give away 3 of them to your friend. How many marbles are still in your bag?

Let's count them together. 1, 2, 3, 4, 5. Yes, you're correct! You have 5 marbles left!

We can write it down like this: 8 - 3 = 5.

Subtraction helps us figure out what's left after we take some away.

Let's solve a problem:

$$
\begin{array}{r}
18 \\
-\ 16 \\
\hline
2 \\
\hline
\end{array}
$$

Commutative Property of Addition

The commutative property of addition tells us that it doesn't matter which order we add numbers together; we'll still get the same answer.

For instance: you have 3 blue blocks and 2 red blocks.

Now, if we add them together, we get 5 blocks total, right? 3 (blue) + 2 (red) = 5.

But guess what? We can also add them in a different order!

Let's try adding the red blocks first, then the blue ones.

So, we have 2 (red) + 3 (blue).

Let's count them together. 1, 2, 3, 4, 5. We still get 5 blocks in total!

It doesn't matter if we add the blue blocks first or the red ones first, we still end up with the same number of blocks.

Word Problems

Word problems are like little puzzles that help us use addition in real-life situations.

For instance:

1. Jake has 6 carrots. He gets 2 more carrots. How many carrots does he have now?

To find out how many carrots he has now, we add the number of carrots he started with (6) to the number of carrots he got (2).

So, we add 6 + 2, which equals 8.

Jake now has 8 carrots in total!

2. Jake saved up 4 dollars to buy pencils. He spent 2 dollars on it. How much money does he have left?

To solve this problem, we need to start with the number of dollars Jake started with and subtract the number of dollars he spent on the pencils.

So, we subtract 2 from 4, which equals 2:

Jake has 2 dollars left after buying the pencils.

We need to understand what the problem is asking and what information it provides. Then, we can use addition or subtraction, depending on whether we're combining or taking away objects, to find the answer.

Let's solve problems from the exercises:

There are 5 brushes on the shelf. Genesis puts 1 more brush on   the shelf. How many brushes are there on the shelf now?

$$
\begin{array}{rl}
5 & \text{five brushes on the shelf} \\
+\,1 & \underline{\text{Genesis Put one more}} \\
6 & \text{There are 6 brushes on the shelf now}
\end{array}
$$

Emma has 9 dresses. She gave 1 dress to Stephanie. How many   dresses does Emma have now?

$$
\begin{array}{rl}
9 & \text{Emma has 9 dresses} \\
-\,1 & \underline{\text{She gave away 1 dress}} \\
8 & \\
& \text{Emma has 8 dresses left}
\end{array}
$$

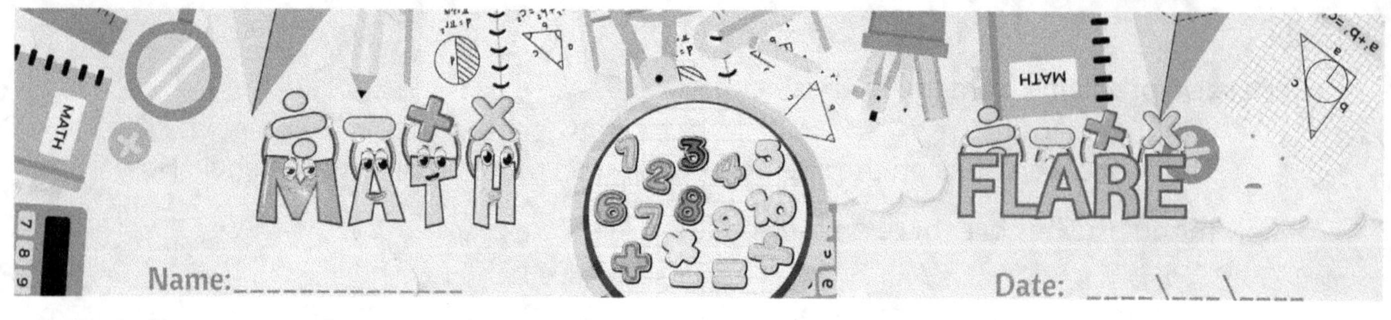

Addition 1 through 50

Find the Sum.

1) 28 + 43 — 71	2) 19 + 12 — 31	3) 26 + 41	4) 14 + 48	5) 33 + 38
6) 47 + 42	7) 3 + 2	8) 5 + 35	9) 5 + 21	10) 25 + 29
11) 42 + 15	12) 22 + 22	13) 27 + 2	14) 8 + 23	15) 35 + 45
16) 22 + 5	17) 43 + 31	18) 19 + 24	19) 5 + 5	20) 39 + 11
21) 27 + 29	22) 26 + 8	23) 30 + 15	24) 24 + 38	25) 47 + 34

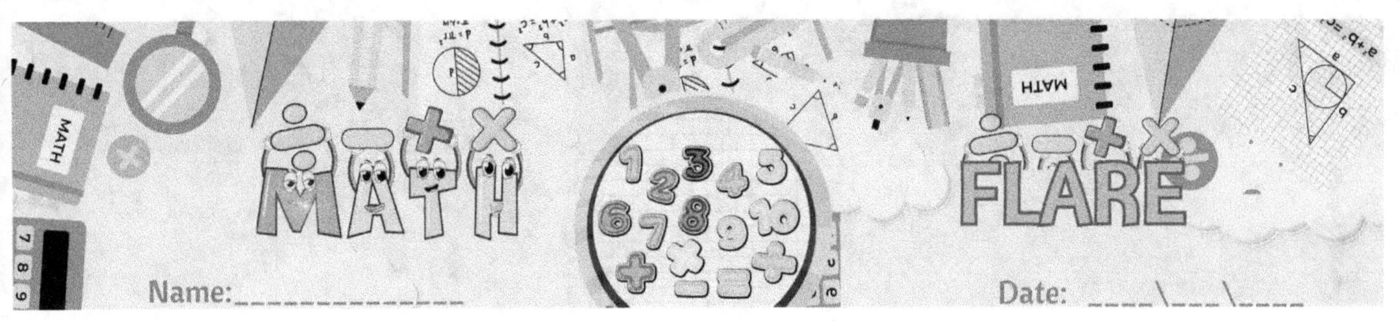

26)   37
   + 22

27)   21
   + 24

28)   8
   + 14

29)   23
   + 47

30)   35
   + 24

31)   34
   + 41

32)   14
   + 38

33)   17
   + 44

34)   49
   + 22

35)   33
   + 31

36)   31
   + 1

37)   32
   + 15

38)   3
   + 14

39)   39
   + 15

40)   42
   + 13

41)   28
   + 19

42)   26
   + 2

43)   9
   + 50

44)   33
   + 20

45)   25
   + 6

46)   2
   + 8

47)   20
   + 16

48)   26
   + 36

49)   15
   + 38

50)   41
   + 36

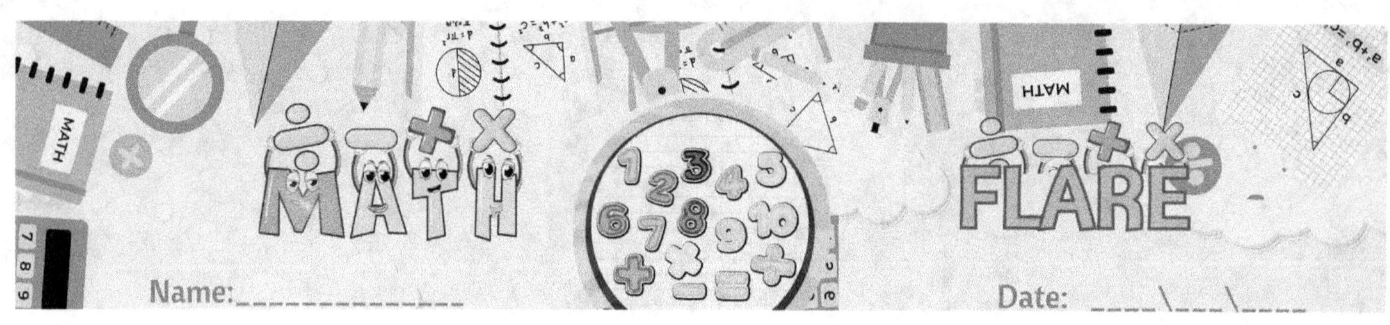

51)   16
  + 3

52)   6
  + 17

53)   3
  + 37

54)   40
  + 7

55)   22
  + 44

56)   25
  + 9

57)   5
  + 22

58)   47
  + 16

59)   16
  + 13

60)   31
  + 17

61)   11
  + 30

62)   47
  + 28

63)   30
  + 25

64)   39
  + 17

65)   48
  + 2

66)   24
  + 7

67)   48
  + 26

68)   15
  + 11

69)   11
  + 27

70)   48
  + 31

71)   31
  + 44

72)   4
  + 48

73)   19
  + 11

74)   21
  + 3

75)   8
  + 24

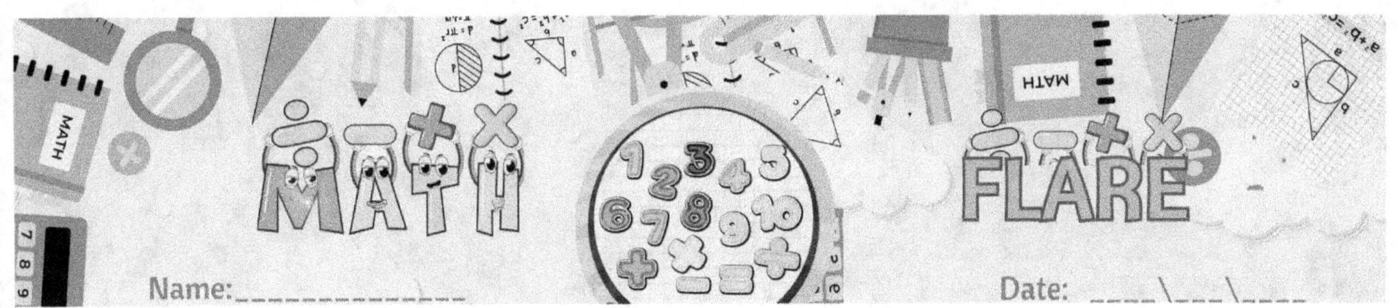

76) 6 + 28	77) 36 + 29	78) 6 + 24	79) 18 + 6	80) 45 + 25
81) 35 + 48	82) 25 + 22	83) 2 + 6	84) 14 + 10	85) 8 + 34
86) 32 + 17	87) 47 + 37	88) 22 + 33	89) 48 + 29	90) 46 + 46
91) 44 + 50	92) 31 + 13	93) 21 + 37	94) 24 + 22	95) 17 + 37
96) 10 + 43	97) 36 + 7	98) 10 + 5	99) 24 + 47	100) 10 + 16

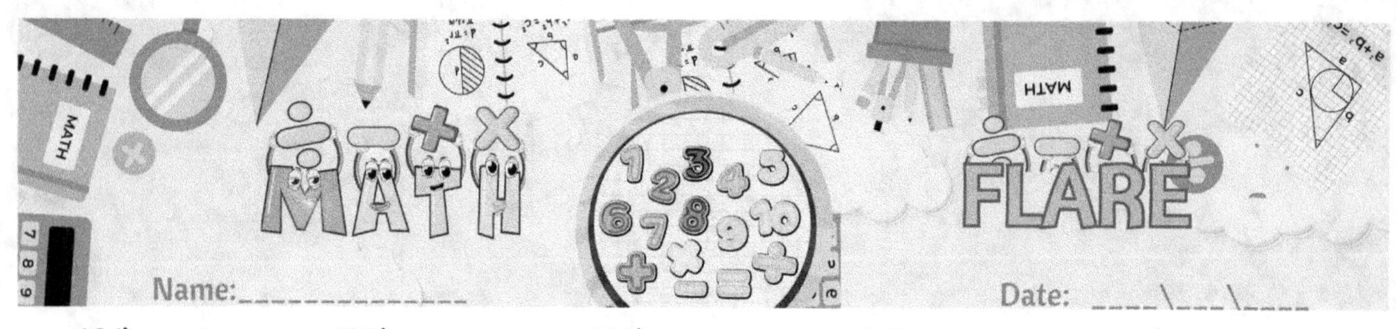

101)   39
+ 48

102)   18
+ 42

103)   5
+ 39

104)   30
+ 50

105)   26
+ 39

106)   10
+ 49

107)   31
+ 35

108)   18
+ 13

109)   3
+ 16

110)   32
+ 43

111)   43
+ 21

112)   25
+ 39

113)   32
+ 41

114)   28
+ 18

115)   10
+ 2

116)   20
+ 31

117)   8
+ 45

118)   33
+ 39

119)   9
+ 32

120)   7
+ 25

121)   15
+ 43

122)   12
+ 21

123)   35
+ 37

124)   26
+ 25

125)   38
+ 12

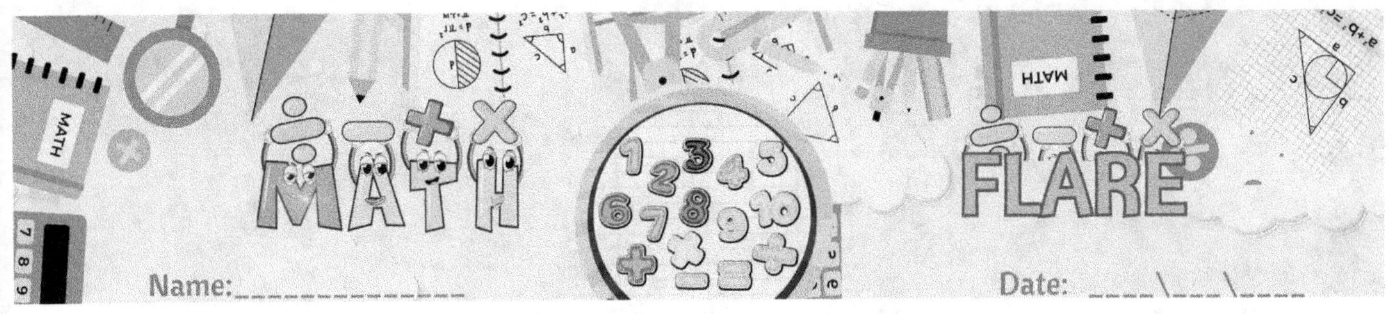

126) 46 + 44	127) 35 + 46	128) 6 + 47	129) 19 + 16	130) 8 + 40
131) 23 + 40	132) 14 + 25	133) 21 + 29	134) 42 + 36	135) 3 + 29
136) 9 + 8	137) 29 + 50	138) 6 + 45	139) 15 + 3	140) 30 + 48
141) 6 + 25	142) 46 + 12	143) 40 + 36	144) 21 + 43	145) 25 + 18
146) 2 + 25	147) 31 + 37	148) 50 + 7	149) 45 + 41	150) 23 + 10

Subtraction 1 through 20

Find the Difference.

1) 2
  − 2
  ‾‾0‾‾

2) 11
  − 4
  ‾‾7‾‾

3) 4
  − 4
  ‾‾‾‾

4) 19
  − 4
  ‾‾‾‾

5) 2
  − 1
  ‾‾‾‾

6) 9
  − 5
  ‾‾‾‾

7) 7
  − 5
  ‾‾‾‾

8) 12
  − 6
  ‾‾‾‾

9) 18
  − 4
  ‾‾‾‾

10) 3
  − 3
  ‾‾‾‾

11) 18
  − 11
  ‾‾‾‾

12) 4
  − 3
  ‾‾‾‾

13) 9
  − 9
  ‾‾‾‾

14) 1
  − 1
  ‾‾‾‾

15) 14
  − 4
  ‾‾‾‾

16) 16
  − 14
  ‾‾‾‾

17) 19
  − 2
  ‾‾‾‾

18) 20
  − 17
  ‾‾‾‾

19) 19
  − 19
  ‾‾‾‾

20) 9
  − 7
  ‾‾‾‾

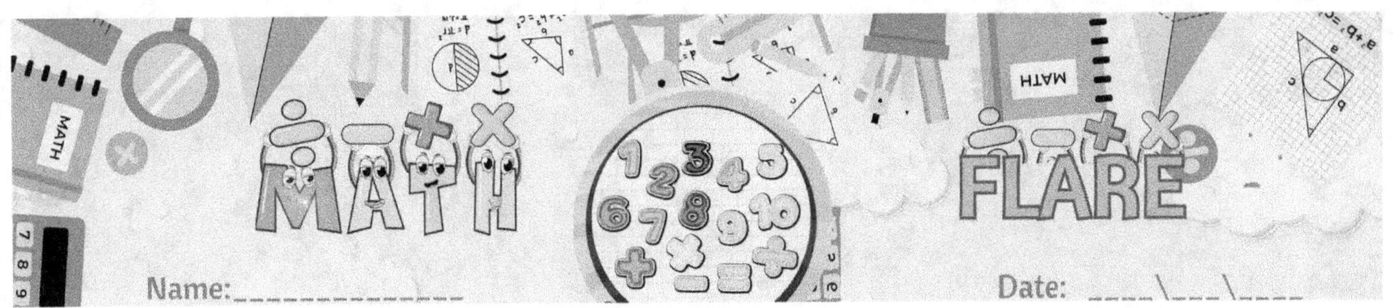

21) 5 − 1	22) 7 − 4	23) 16 − 13	24) 10 − 7	25) 15 − 4
26) 15 − 2	27) 17 − 3	28) 18 − 13	29) 11 − 9	30) 5 − 2
31) 4 − 2	32) 18 − 16	33) 5 − 3	34) 13 − 7	35) 18 − 3
36) 8 − 3	37) 6 − 6	38) 12 − 7	39) 17 − 9	40) 8 − 8
41) 11 − 8	42) 14 − 14	43) 15 − 8	44) 7 − 3	45) 13 − 6

46) 10 − 6	47) 9 − 6	48) 15 − 14	49) 17 − 4	50) 18 − 6
51) 11 − 2	52) 13 − 9	53) 6 − 3	54) 7 − 6	55) 10 − 1
56) 12 − 11	57) 3 − 2	58) 8 − 6	59) 18 − 9	60) 16 − 7
61) 16 − 10	62) 14 − 6	63) 13 − 12	64) 15 − 1	65) 12 − 4
66) 14 − 12	67) 8 − 5	68) 19 − 8	69) 14 − 7	70) 7 − 2

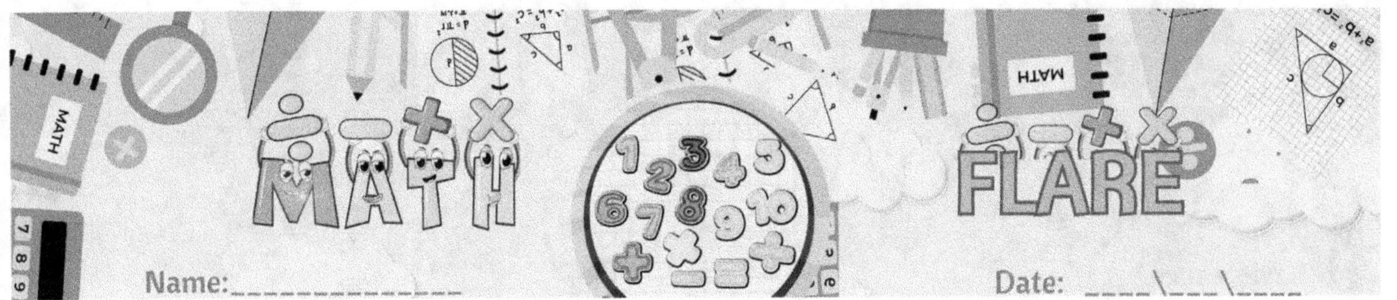

Name:______________________   Date:_____/_____/_____

71)   3
 - 1
_____

72)   12
 - 8
_____

73)   6
 - 2
_____

74)   12
 - 5
_____

75)   16
 - 4
_____

76)   6
 - 4
_____

77)   13
 - 4
_____

78)   15
 - 15
_____

79)   10
 - 9
_____

80)   5
 - 4
_____

81)   13
 - 11
_____

82)   4
 - 1
_____

83)   17
 - 14
_____

84)   17
 - 6
_____

85)   10
 - 10
_____

86)   20
 - 3
_____

87)   17
 - 15
_____

88)   11
 - 10
_____

89)   15
 - 5
_____

90)   19
 - 15
_____

91)   10
 - 5
_____

92)   12
 - 2
_____

93)   19
 - 3
_____

94)   5
 - 5
_____

95)   15
 - 13
_____

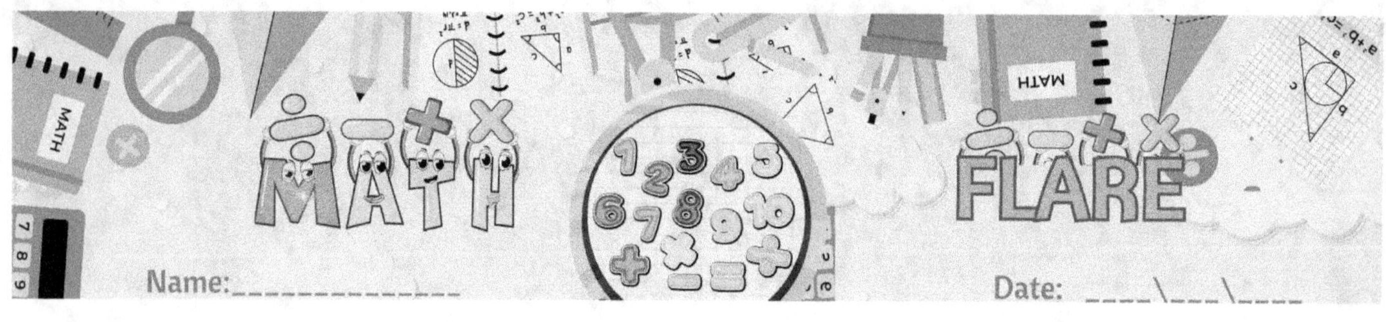

Subtraction 1 through 20

Find the unknown number.

1) 19 - 6 = __13__

2) 11 - ___ = 6

3) 14 - 13 = ___

4) ___ - 7 = 6

5) 16 - 9 = ___

6) ___ - 4 = 2

7) ___ - 1 = 4

8) 6 - 5 = ___

9) 12 - 7 = ___

10) 5 - 4 = ___

11) ___ - 5 = 10

12) 13 - ___ = 10

13) 2 - ___ = 1

14) ___ - 2 = 6

15) 17 - 12 = ___

16) 18 - 12 = ___

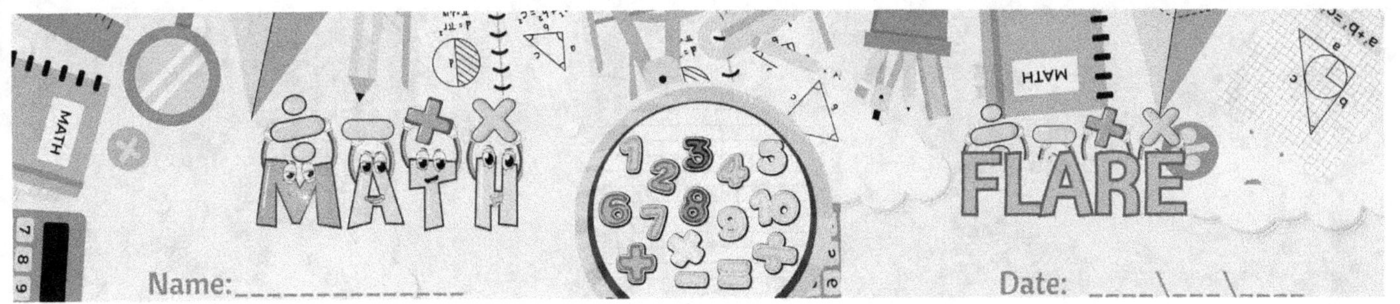

17) 3 - 1 = ___

18) 17 - 16 = ___

19) ___ - 8 = 2

20) 16 - ___ = 12

21) 13 - ___ = 2

22) 4 - ___ = 1

23) 17 - ___ = 9

24) 16 - 5 = ___

25) 7 - ___ = 2

26) 1 - ___ = 0

27) 3 - ___ = 1

28) 13 - 6 = ___

29) ___ - 3 = 4

30) ___ - 6 = 5

31) 14 - ___ = 11

32) ___ - 9 = 4

33) 8 - 1 = ___

34) 5 - 2 = ___

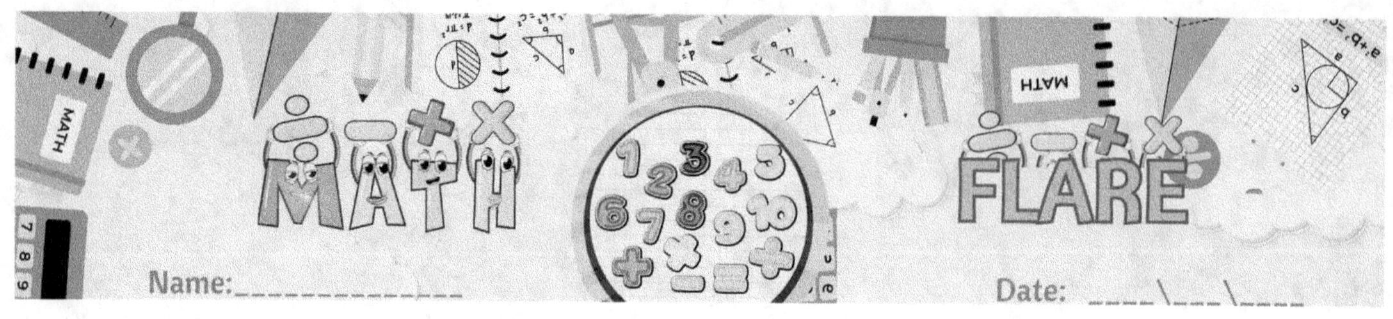

35) ___ − 6 = 1

36) ___ − 1 = 15

37) 3 − 3 = ___

38) 12 − ___ = 1

39) 8 − 5 = ___

40) 13 − 2 = ___

41) 7 − 2 = ___

42) 9 − 5 = ___

43) 4 − ___ = 3

44) ___ − 4 = 14

45) ___ − 3 = 3

46) 19 − ___ = 9

47) 17 − ___ = 16

48) ___ − 2 = 0

49) 13 − ___ = 5

50) ___ − 7 = 9

51) 19 − ___ = 17

52) 8 − ___ = 5

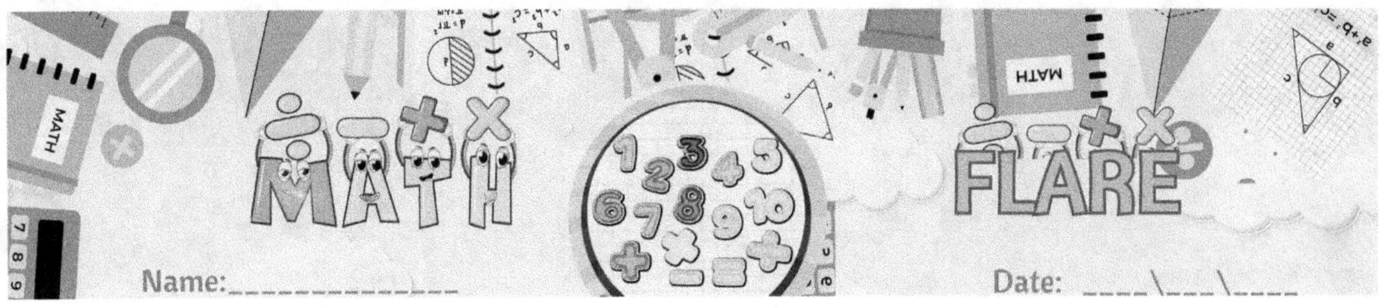

53) 7 - ___ = 0

54) 15 - 2 = ___

55) ___ - 14 = 0

56) ___ - 6 = 3

57) ___ - 5 = 0

58) 13 - 10 = ___

59) 18 - 2 = ___

60) 5 - ___ = 2

61) 17 - 4 = ___

62) 8 - ___ = 2

63) 10 - ___ = 4

64) 17 - 15 = ___

65) 19 - ___ = 16

66) 9 - 9 = ___

67) 19 - ___ = 10

68) 9 - 3 = ___

69) ___ - 4 = 0

70) 17 - 13 = ___

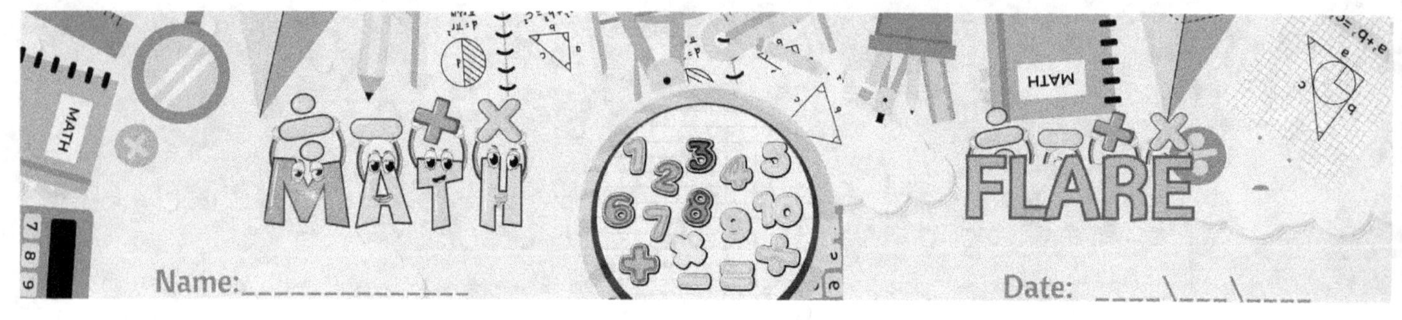

71) ___ - 3 = 17

72) 13 - ___ = 1

73) 14 - 12 = ___

74) ___ - 5 = 13

75) 9 - ___ = 7

76) 14 - ___ = 13

77) ___ - 4 = 9

78) ___ - 8 = 3

79) 19 - 15 = ___

80) 16 - 2 = ___

81) 12 - 4 = ___

82) ___ - 2 = 2

83) 14 - ___ = 5

84) ___ - 14 = 5

85) 18 - 9 = ___

86) 11 - 9 = ___

87) 13 - 5 = ___

88) ___ - 8 = 6

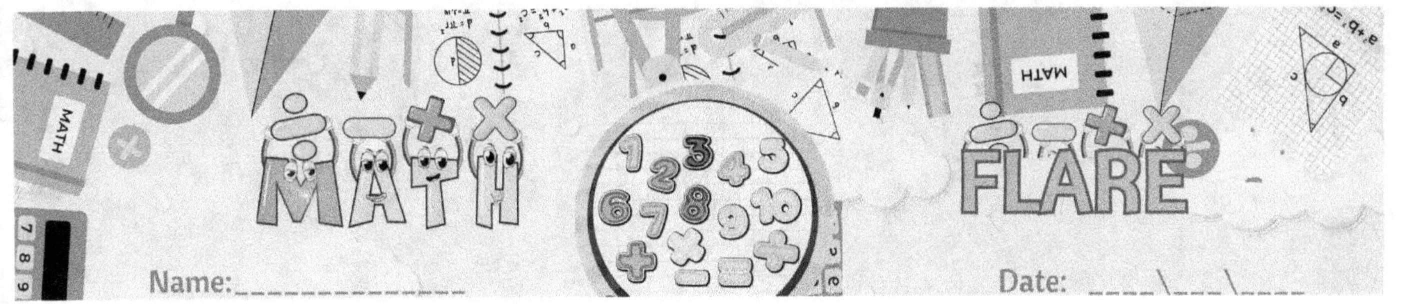

89) 8 - ___ = 4

90) 15 - 7 = ___

91) 9 - 8 = ___

92) ___ - 2 = 9

93) 9 - 7 = ___

94) 12 - ___ = 3

95) 16 - 15 = ___

96) 15 - ___ = 14

97) 17 - ___ = 11

98) 8 - ___ = 0

99) 14 - 10 = ___

100) ___ - 7 = 11

101) ___ - 11 = 7

102) 20 - 2 = ___

103) ___ - 10 = 1

104) 14 - ___ = 7

105) ___ - 4 = 7

106) ___ - 5 = 5

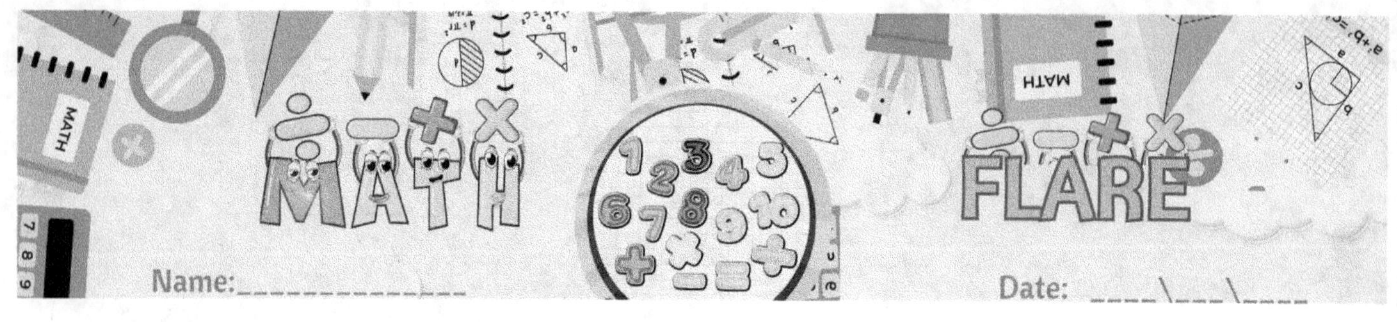

Subtraction 1 through 50

Find the Difference.

1)   19
   - 18
   ___
     1

2)   3
   - 2
   ___
     1

3)   13
   - 6
   ___

4)   18
   - 16
   ___

5)   11
   - 8
   ___

6)   19
   - 12
   ___

7)   13
   - 13
   ___

8)   14
   - 13
   ___

9)   15
   - 5
   ___

10)   5
   - 4
   ___

11)   9
   - 3
   ___

12)   17
   - 3
   ___

13)   19
   - 14
   ___

14)   18
   - 15
   ___

15)   14
   - 6
   ___

16)   12
   - 8
   ___

17)   2
   - 2
   ___

18)   10
   - 3
   ___

19)   17
   - 11
   ___

20)   8
   - 2
   ___

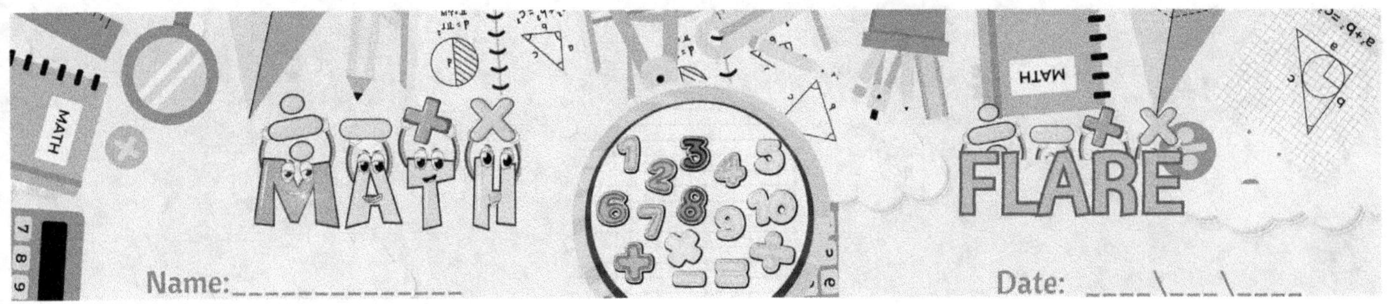

21) 17 − 14	22) 17 − 13	23) 15 − 4	24) 1 − 1	25) 3 − 3
26) 12 − 11	27) 11 − 2	28) 4 − 1	29) 13 − 4	30) 17 − 6
31) 18 − 14	32) 17 − 16	33) 16 − 13	34) 17 − 12	35) 6 − 2
36) 14 − 4	37) 13 − 12	38) 13 − 10	39) 13 − 5	40) 7 − 1
41) 8 − 5	42) 16 − 12	43) 10 − 4	44) 11 − 7	45) 16 − 1

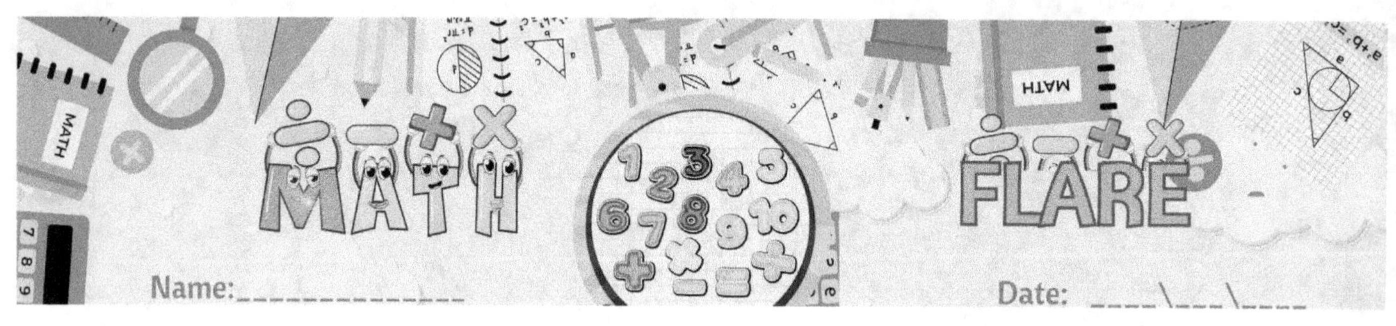

46) 15 − 8	47) 18 − 1	48) 2 − 1	49) 19 − 8	50) 14 − 7
51) 5 − 2	52) 9 − 7	53) 8 − 4	54) 8 − 3	55) 4 − 3
56) 7 − 5	57) 10 − 6	58) 11 − 6	59) 9 − 8	60) 8 − 7
61) 7 − 4	62) 14 − 3	63) 20 − 11	64) 13 − 2	65) 20 − 20
66) 18 − 8	67) 6 − 1	68) 15 − 9	69) 6 − 5	70) 12 − 12

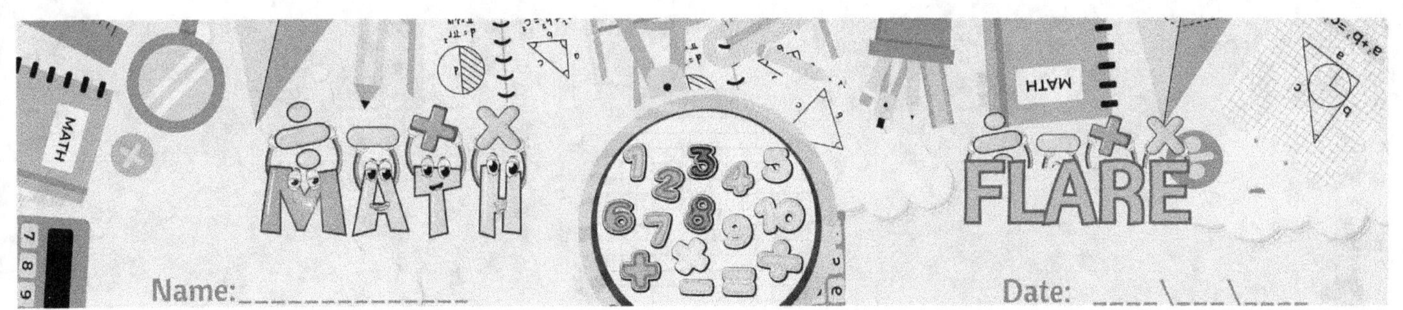

71) 9 − 5	72) 7 − 2	73) 14 − 11	74) 10 − 7	75) 11 − 1

76) 15 − 11	77) 16 − 4	78) 19 − 2	79) 11 − 9	80) 19 − 13

81) 5 − 3	82) 4 − 2	83) 14 − 10	84) 15 − 14	85) 12 − 7

86) 11 − 4	87) 15 − 13	88) 10 − 1	89) 17 − 4	90) 18 − 7

91) 13 − 9	92) 18 − 10	93) 10 − 9	94) 13 − 8	95) 18 − 12

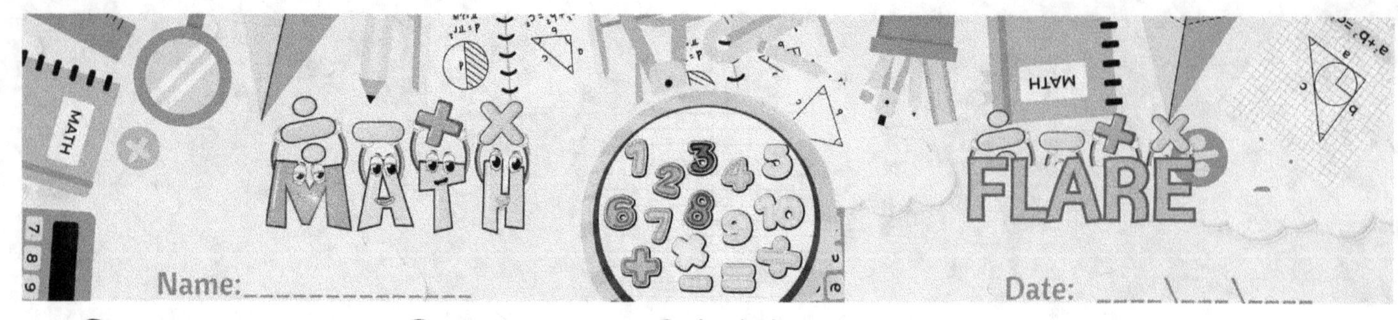

Commutative Property of Addition

Use the commutative property to fill the missing values.

1) 15 + 16 = __ + 15

2) __ + 8 = 8 + 4

3) 2 + __ = 12 + 2

4) 11 + 12 = __ + 11

5) __ + 5 = 5 + 7

6) 14 + 17 = 17 + __

7) __ + 17 = 17 + 4

8) 16 + 14 = 14 + __

9) 11 + __ = 7 + 11

10) 12 + 11 = __ + 12

11) 7 + 4 = 4 + __

12) __ + 9 = 9 + 14

13) __ + 20 = 20 + 18

14) 16 + 12 = __ + 16

15) __ + 2 = 2 + 9

16) 13 + __ = 4 + 13

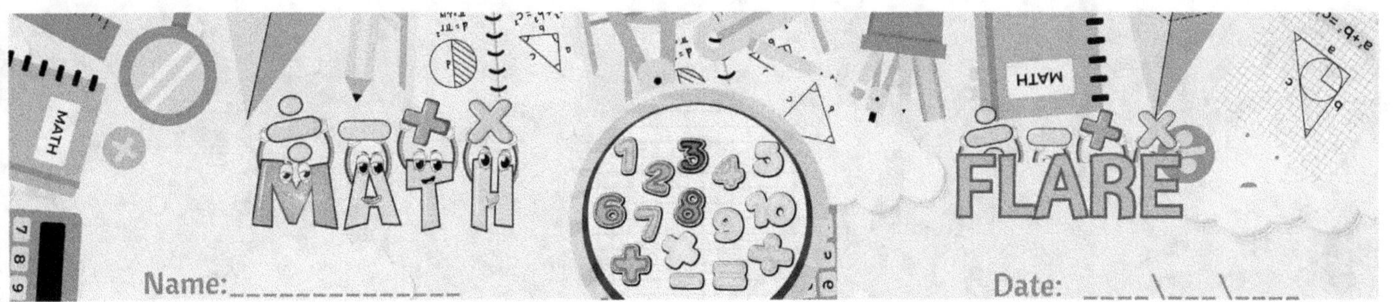

17) ___ + 9 = 9 + 12

18) ___ + 9 = 9 + 3

19) 1 + 18 = 18 + __

20) 19 + 20 = 20 + ___

21) 19 + ___ = 17 + 19

22) 16 + ___ = 17 + 16

23) 13 + __ = 2 + 13

24) ___ + 3 = 3 + 12

25) __ + 6 = 6 + 8

26) 19 + __ = 7 + 19

27) __ + 12 = 12 + 8

28) 3 + ___ = 15 + 3

29) 10 + 2 = __ + 10

30) 16 + ___ = 15 + 16

31) 1 + 17 = 17 + __

32) __ + 2 = 2 + 5

33) ___ + 12 = 12 + 14

34) 9 + 14 = ___ + 9

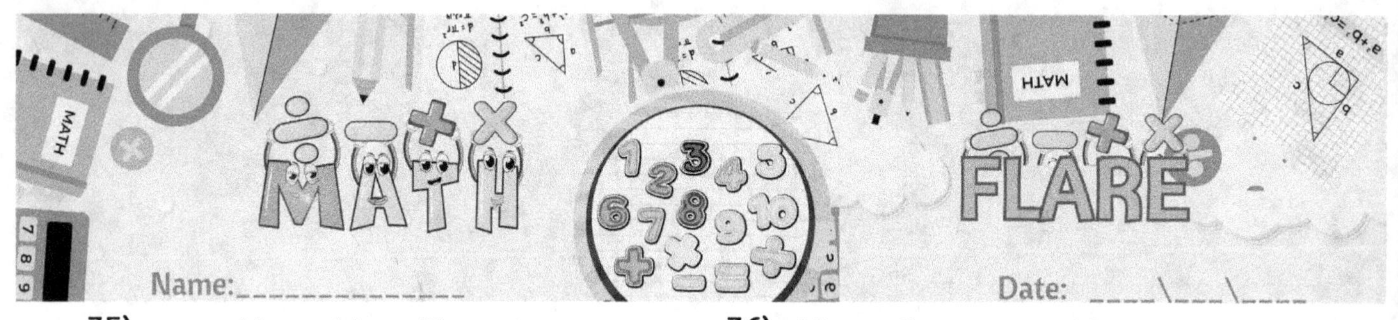

35) __ + 11 = 11 + 7

36) 12 + 8 = __ + 12

37) 7 + 19 = 19 + __

38) 12 + 7 = __ + 12

39) 18 + 5 = 5 + ___

40) 13 + 5 = 5 + ___

41) ___ + 16 = 16 + 14

42) __ + 17 = 17 + 5

43) 20 + 14 = ___ + 20

44) 11 + ___ = 17 + 11

45) 4 + 5 = __ + 4

46) ___ + 17 = 17 + 12

47) 18 + 10 = ___ + 18

48) 4 + 9 = __ + 4

49) __ + 17 = 17 + 2

50) 17 + 6 = __ + 17

51) ___ + 20 = 20 + 16

52) 6 + 4 = __ + 6

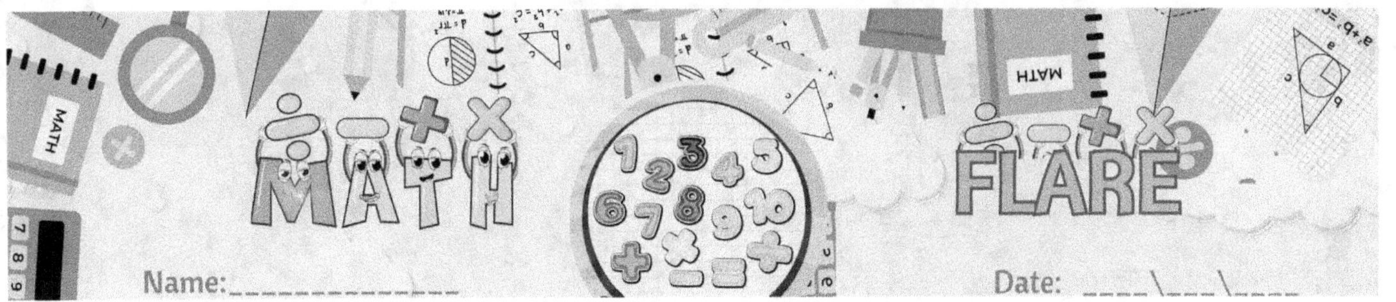

53) __ + 12 = 12 + 4

54) 3 + 17 = __ + 3

55) __ + 10 = 10 + 15

56) 7 + 18 = __ + 7

57) 14 + 13 = __ + 14

58) 19 + 13 = 13 + __

59) __ + 7 = 7 + 10

60) 8 + 15 = 15 + __

61) 8 + 9 = 9 + __

62) __ + 5 = 5 + 2

63) 4 + __ = 6 + 4

64) 18 + 9 = __ + 18

65) 1 + 5 = __ + 1

66) __ + 8 = 8 + 11

67) 3 + 6 = 6 + __

68) 3 + 11 = 11 + __

69) 1 + __ = 3 + 1

70) 13 + __ = 15 + 13

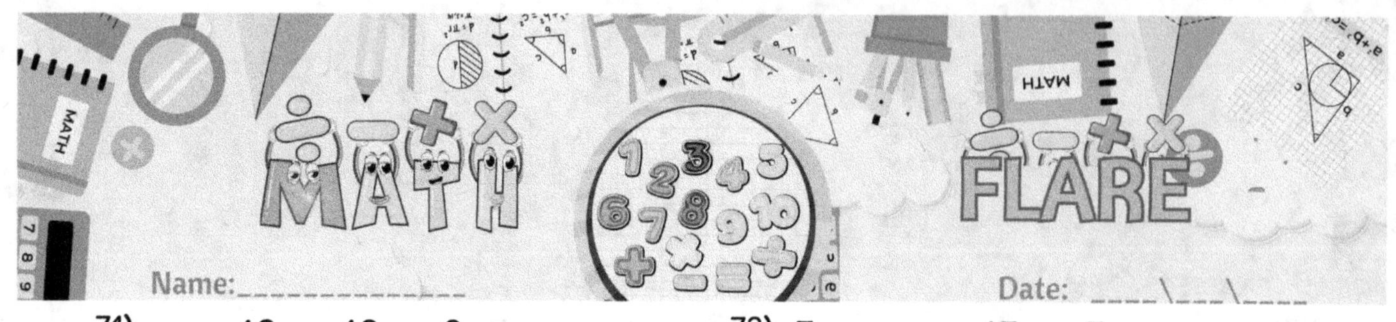

71) __ + 18 = 18 + 9

72) 5 + __ = 15 + 5

73) 10 + 11 = __ + 10

74) 8 + 16 = 16 + __

75) __ + 11 = 11 + 14

76) __ + 14 = 14 + 18

77) 18 + 3 = 3 + __

78) 19 + __ = 18 + 19

79) 19 + 5 = 5 + __

80) 8 + 2 = 2 + __

81) __ + 6 = 6 + 5

82) 8 + __ = 7 + 8

83) 9 + __ = 10 + 9

84) __ + 8 = 8 + 14

85) 1 + 4 = 4 + __

86) 12 + 20 = 20 + __

87) 2 + __ = 6 + 2

88) 9 + 15 = 15 + __

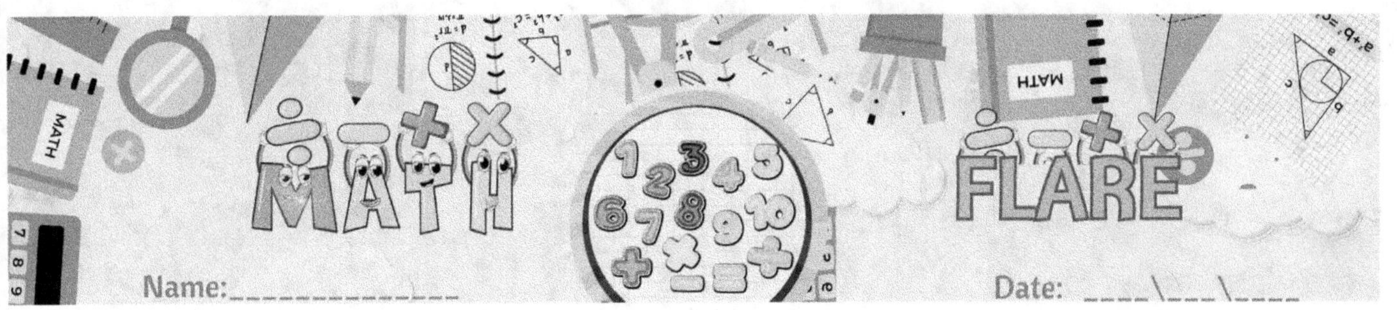

89) ___ + 13 = 13 + 20

90) 17 + 8 = __ + 17

91) 7 + 16 = ___ + 7

92) 18 + ___ = 12 + 18

93) 8 + 3 = __ + 8

94) __ + 19 = 19 + 8

95) 5 + 7 = 7 + __

96) 9 + __ = 7 + 9

97) 17 + 18 = 18 + ___

98) 20 + 19 = 19 + ___

99) 18 + 19 = 19 + ___

100) 13 + 6 = __ + 13

101) 13 + __ = 7 + 13

102) __ + 8 = 8 + 2

103) 18 + __ = 7 + 18

104) __ + 16 = 16 + 11

105) 9 + __ = 1 + 9

106) 9 + ___ = 13 + 9

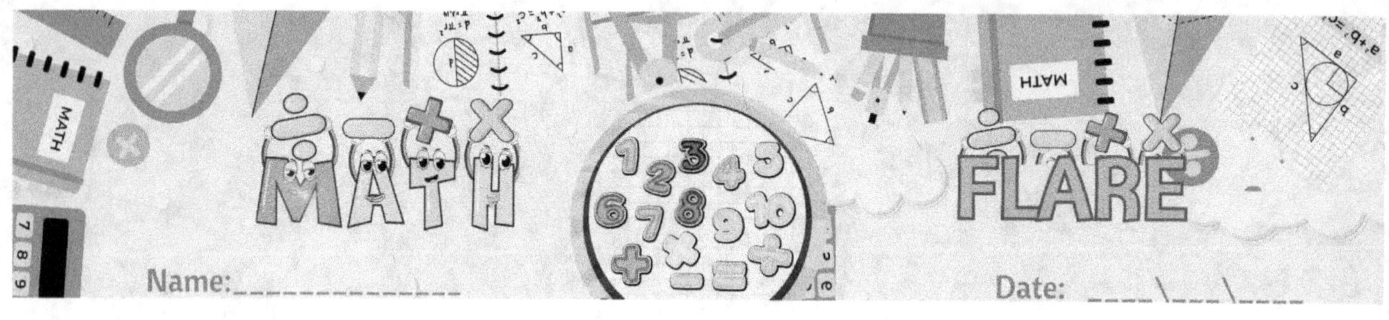

Make 50

Find the unknow number to make 50.

1) $16 + \underline{\quad} = 50$

2) $23 + \underline{\quad} = 50$

3) $40 + \underline{\quad} = 50$

4) $14 + \underline{\quad} = 50$

5) $37 + \underline{\quad} = 50$

6) $9 + \underline{\quad} = 50$

7) $39 + \underline{\quad} = 50$

8) $7 + \underline{\quad} = 50$

9) $26 + \underline{\quad} = 50$

10) $19 + \underline{\quad} = 50$

11) $2 + \underline{\quad} = 50$

12) $22 + \underline{\quad} = 50$

13) $36 + \underline{\quad} = 50$

14) $15 + \underline{\quad} = 50$

15) $4 + \underline{\quad} = 50$

16) $27 + \underline{\quad} = 50$

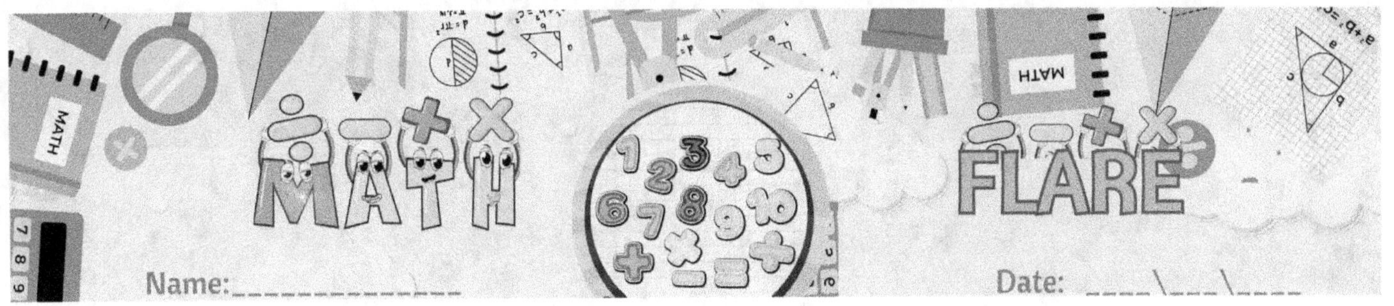

17) 10 + ___ = 50

18) 31 + ___ = 50

19) 29 + ___ = 50

20) 38 + ___ = 50

21) 18 + ___ = 50

22) 24 + ___ = 50

23) 32 + ___ = 50

24) 12 + ___ = 50

25) 33 + ___ = 50

26) 13 + ___ = 50

27) 5 + ___ = 50

28) 1 + ___ = 50

29) 25 + ___ = 50

30) 28 + ___ = 50

31) 3 + ___ = 50

32) 21 + ___ = 50

33) 11 + ___ = 50

34) 20 + ___ = 50

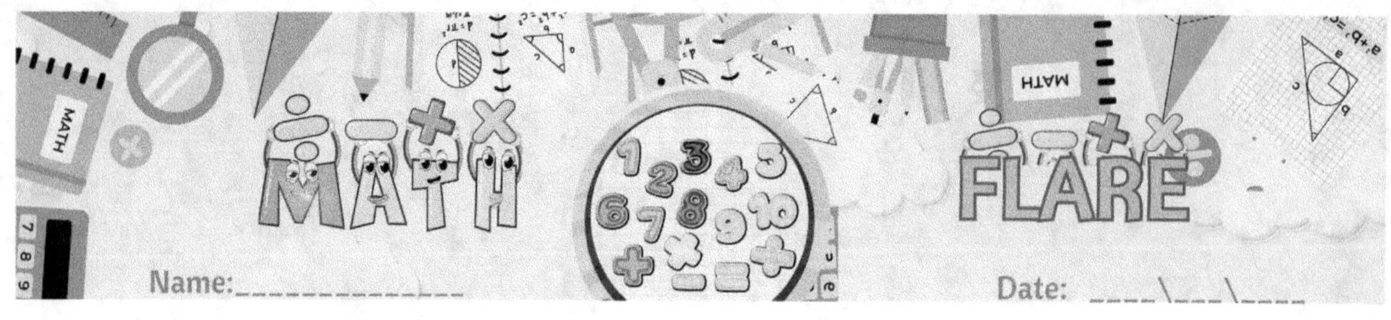

Matching the answers.

1)

a. 10 – 8 = ______ •	• J = 32
b. 19 – 11 = ______ •	• C = 7
c. 13 – 6 = ______ •	• I = 20
d. 5 – 5 = ______ •	• F = 8
e. 9 + 20 = ______ •	• H = 16
f. 6 + 10 = ______ •	• B = 26
g. 15 + 17 = ______ •	• D = 29
h. 13 + 7 = ______ •	• G = 0
i. 18 + 8 = ______ •	• E = 1
j. 3 – 2 = ______ •	• A = 2

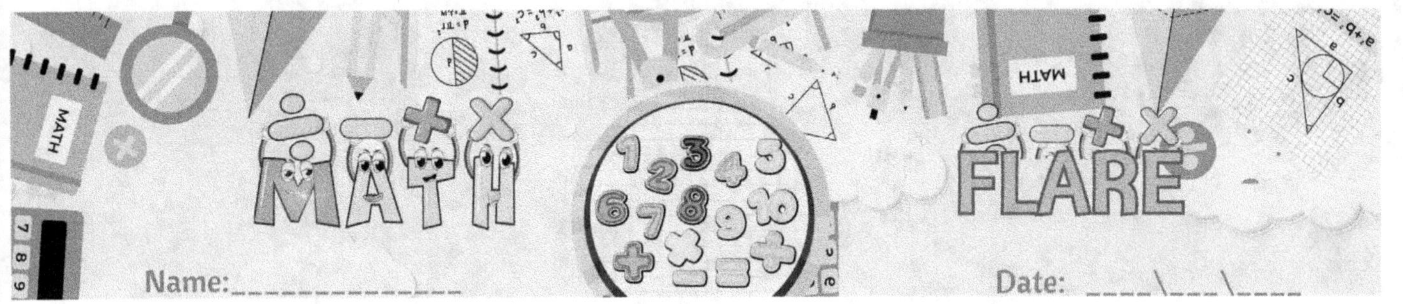

2)

a. 2 − 2 = _______ •	• F = 29
b. 19 + 9 = _______ •	• A = 27
c. 12 + 2 = _______ •	• G = 28
d. 20 + 7 = _______ •	• C = 19
e. 18 − 2 = _______ •	• H = 4
f. 18 + 1 = _______ •	• J = 32
g. 8 − 4 = _______ •	• E = 0
h. 13 + 19 = _______ •	• B = 12
i. 18 − 6 = _______ •	• I = 16
j. 13 + 16 = _______ •	• D = 14

3)

a. 20 - 11 = _______ •   • C = 36

b. 18 - 6 = _______ •   • D = 9

c. 6 + 3 = _______ •   • H = 7

d. 5 - 4 = _______ •   • G = 9

e. 20 + 16 = _______ •   • I = 0

f. 17 + 5 = _______ •   • A = 22

g. 1 + 6 = _______ •   • E = 1

h. 1 - 1 = _______ •   • B = 12

i. 3 + 12 = _______ •   • J = 20

j. 12 + 8 = _______ •   • F = 15

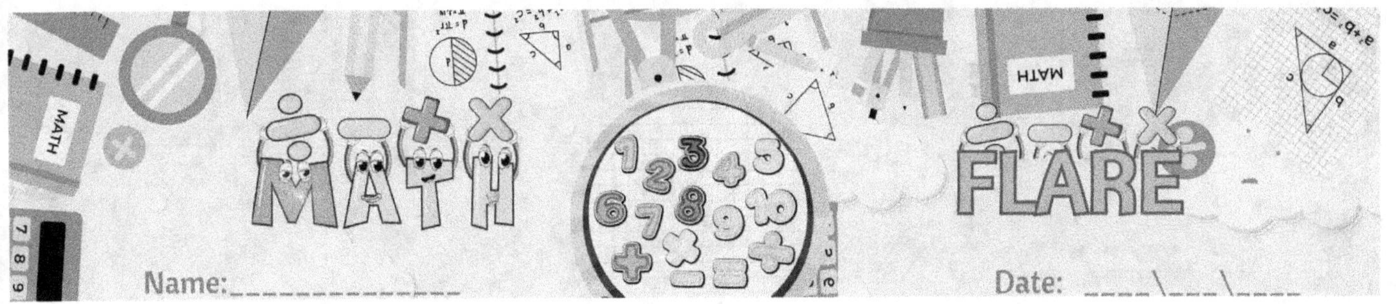

4)

a. 4 + 1 = _______ •	• B = 3
b. 1 + 17 = _______ •	• F = 24
c. 17 − 15 = _______ •	• A = 0
d. 7 − 7 = _______ •	• I = 5
e. 9 + 16 = _______ •	• J = 2
f. 10 + 14 = _______ •	• C = 18
g. 11 − 6 = _______ •	• D = 5
h. 6 − 3 = _______ •	• E = 3
i. 5 + 14 = _______ •	• G = 25
j. 14 − 11 = _______ •	• H = 19

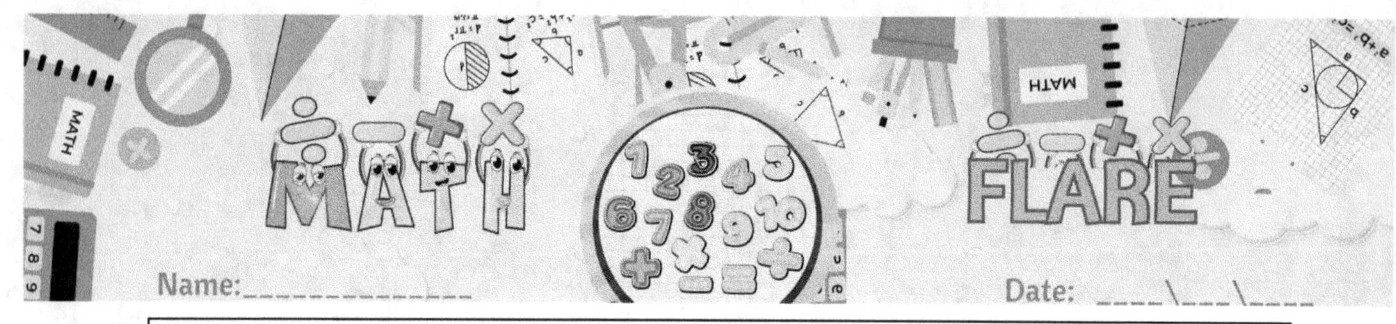

5)

a. 5 - 1 = _______ •

b. 9 + 18 = _______ •

c. 8 + 18 = _______ •

d. 11 - 3 = _______ •

e. 5 + 16 = _______ •

f. 4 - 2 = _______ •

g. 7 - 2 = _______ •

h. 12 - 4 = _______ •

i. 7 + 16 = _______ •

j. 7 - 3 = _______ •

• B = 8

• J = 27

• I = 4

• A = 5

• H = 2

• F = 4

• C = 23

• E = 8

• D = 26

• G = 21

Addition Word Problems

1) There are 5 brushes on the shelf. Genesis puts 1 more brush on the shelf. How many brushes are there on the shelf now?

$$\begin{array}{r} 5 \\ +\ 1 \\ \hline 6 \end{array}$$

    5   five brushes on the shelf
  +1   Genesis Put one more
    6   There are 6 brushes on the shelf now

2) Hudson bought 8 pencils and 2 pens. How many writing instruments did Hudson buy in total?

3) Elijah has 5 dollars and found 3 more dollars on the ground. How much money does Elijah have now?

4) Carter bought a bag of breads for 10 dollars. Later, Carter bought another bag of breads for 5 dollars. How much money did Carter spend in total?

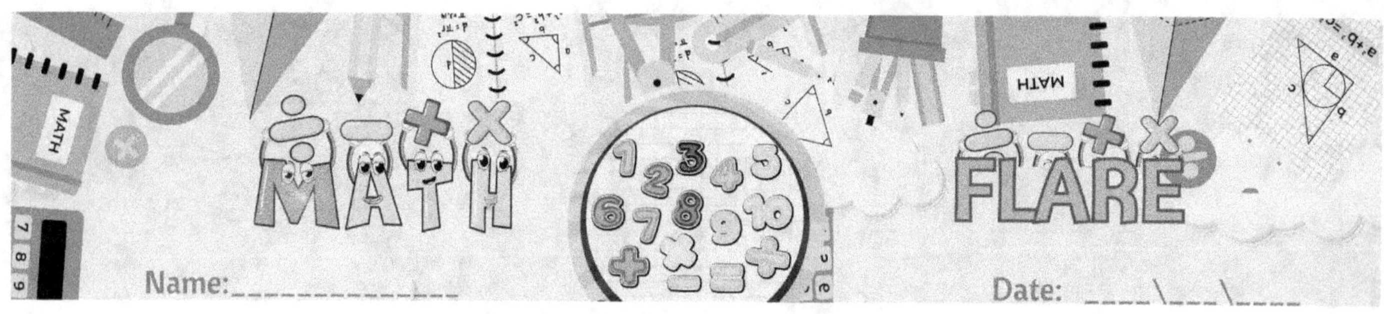

5) There are 2 kids playing on the playground. 2 more kids join them. How many kids are playing now?

6) Nathan has 10 shoes and 2 more shoes are added to the collection. How many shoes does Nathan have in total?

7) There are 7 tissues in the room. 8 more tissues are brought in. How many tissues are in the room now?

8) Jose has 5 pencils and 4 pens. If Jose puts all the writing utensils in a case, how many writing utensils are in the case in total?

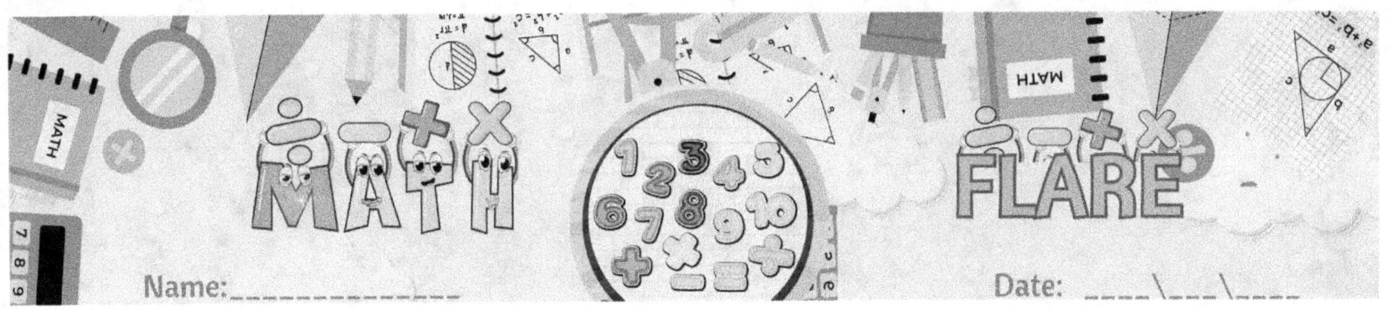

9) Bentley made 8 cookies and Molly made 6 cookies. How many cookies were made in total?

10) At the store, Christian bought 8 scrubs. Later, Gabriella bought 10 scrubs from the same store. How many scrubs were bought in total?

11) Kaylee has 4 watches. She gets 9 more watches. How many watches does Kaylee have now?

12) Scarlett wrote 10 pages of her book yesterday and 1 pages today. How many pages did she write in total?

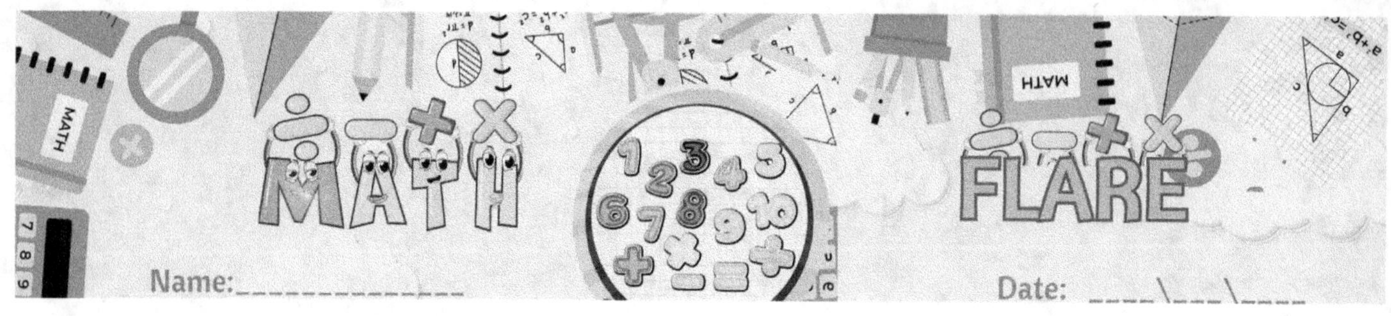

13) Jason has 3 flosses. He finds 6 more flosses. How many flosses does he have now?

14) An object has 10 parts. If 6 more parts are added, how many parts does the object have now?

15) A machine has 9 parts. If 4 more parts are added, how many parts does the machine have now?

16) On Monday, Mila read 5 pages, and on Tuesday, 9 pages. How many pages did Mila read altogether?

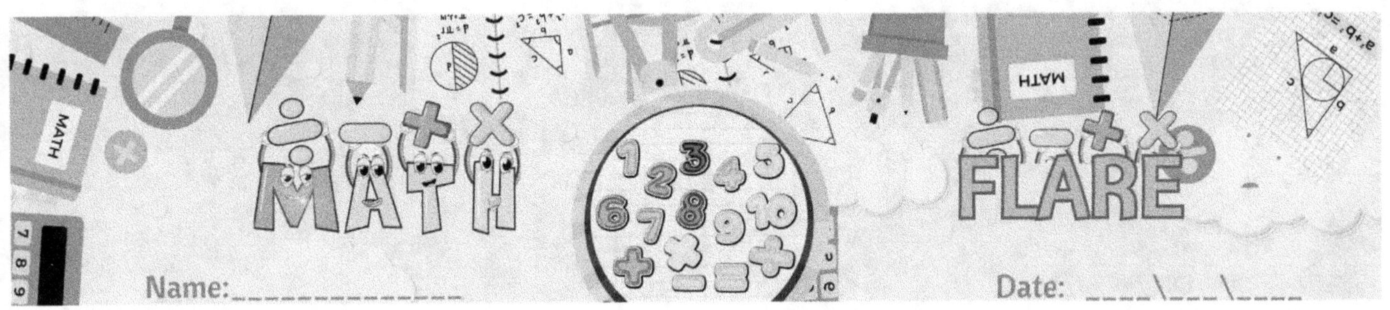

17) Oliver has 9 fish in an aquarium. If Oliver adds 1 more fish to the aquarium, how many fish will be in the aquarium in total?

18) Vincent has 3 pencils. He receives 8 more pencils. How many pencils does he have now?

19) Grayson has 4 calculators. He gets 8 more calculators. How many calculators does he have now?

20) Paisley has 9 pens in a bag. If Paisley adds 6 more pens to the bag, how many pens does Paisley have in total?

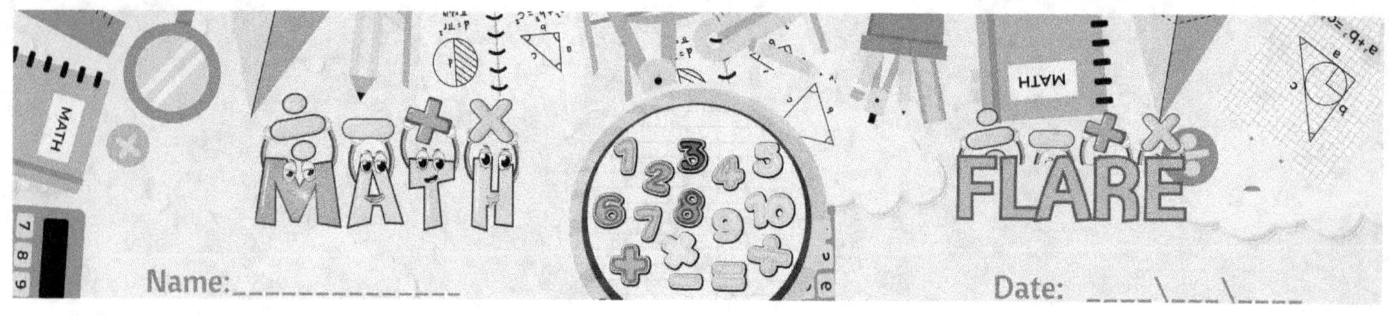

21) A bakery sold 2 cupcakes in the morning and 4 cupcakes in the afternoon. How many cupcakes did the bakery sell in total?

22) Jayden has 5 clocks. His sister gives him 9 more clocks . How many clocks does Jayden have now?

23) Jade has 3 liters of water in a container. She pours in 1 more liters of water. How much water is in the container now?

24) Thomas had 7 dollars in the morning and earned 10 more dollars in the afternoon. How many dollars Thomas have in total?

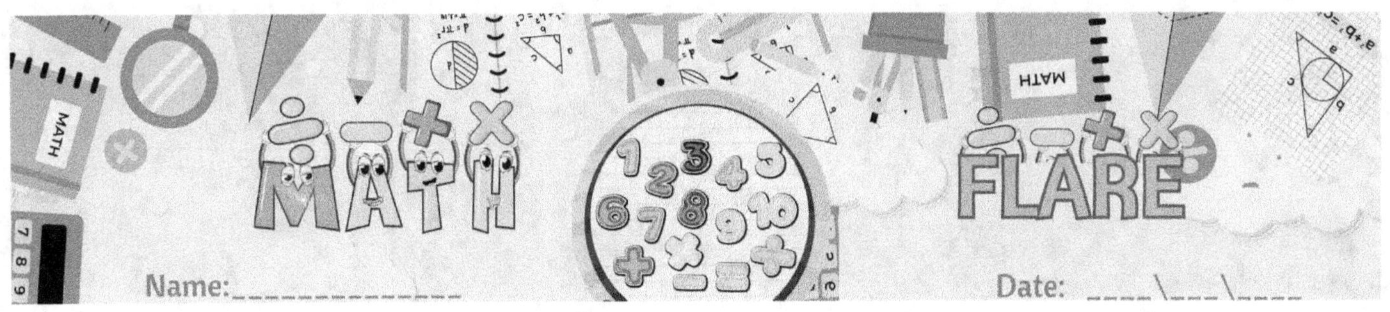

25) David has 6 deodorants. He finds 10 more deodorants on the ground. How many deodorants does David have now?

26) Wesley has 1 syringe. He gets 2 more syringes as a gift. How many syringes does Wesley have now?

27) Ethan has a basket with 2 erasers in it. After buying 8 more erasers, how many erasers does Ethan have in total?

28) A company produced 8 phones on Monday and 6 phones on Tuesday. How many phones did the company produce in total?

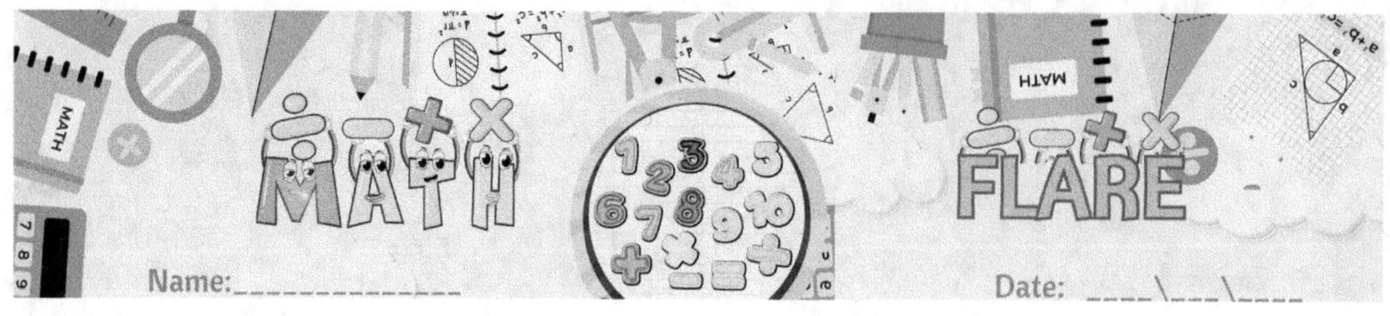

29) Diego has 1 apples and 8 oranges in a basket. How many fruits does Diego have in total?

30) Tristan has 10 shampoos. He buys 9 more shampoos. How many shampoos does she have now?

31) On Monday, Aurora caught 4 fish, and on Tuesday, Aurora caught 4 fish. How many fish did Aurora catch in total?

32) There are 7 fishes in the pond. 8 more fishes join them. How many fishes are in the pond now?

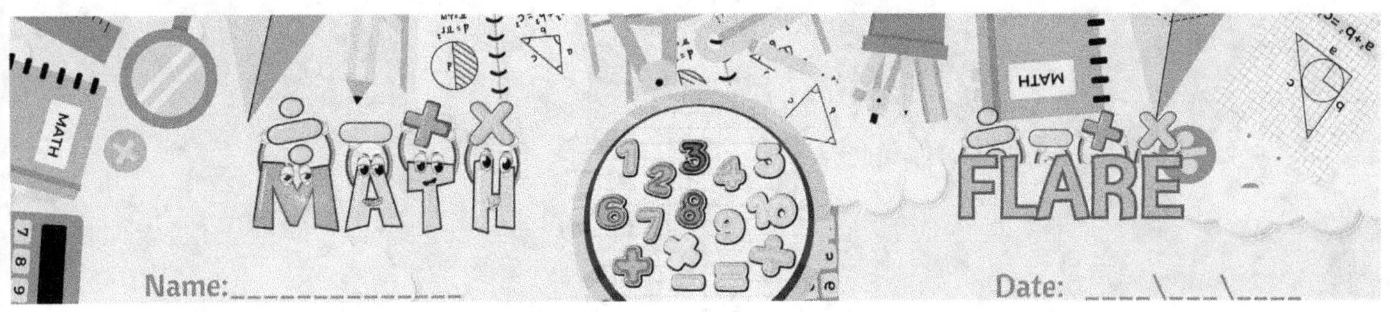

33) Logan has 7 red marbles and 1 blue marbles in a jar. How many marbles does Logan have in total?

34) There are 3 trees in the garden. 6 more trees are planted. How many trees are in the garden now?

35) Lydia baked 6 cakes yesterday and 7 cakes today. How many cakes did Lydia bake in total?

36) Lucas baked 10 cookies and 1 cupcakes. How many desserts did Lucas bake in total?

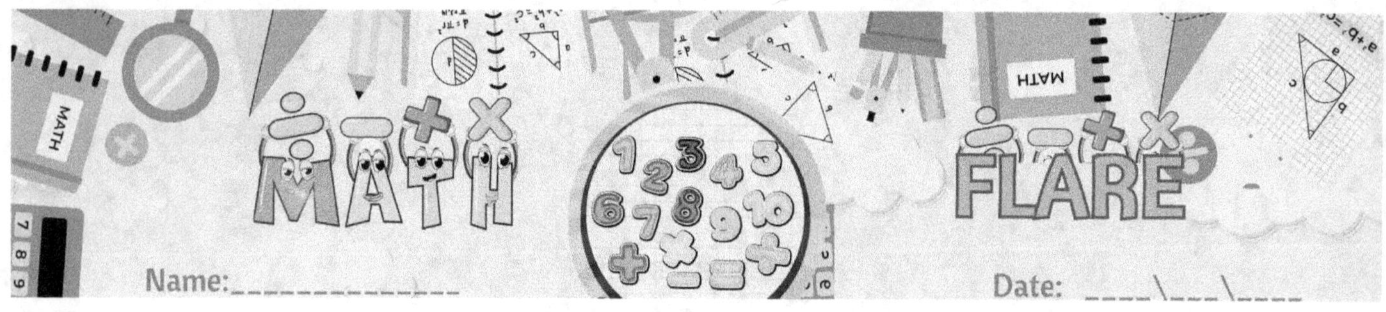

37) Olivia has 8 soaps. She buys 3 more soaps at the store. How many soaps does Olivia have now?

38) Kingston had 9 dollars and earned 10 more dollars. How much money does Kingston have now?

39) There are 4 socks in the bag. If 2 more socks are added, how many socks are in the bag now?

40) Harper planted 8 flowers in the morning and 2 flowers in the afternoon. How many flowers did Harper plant?

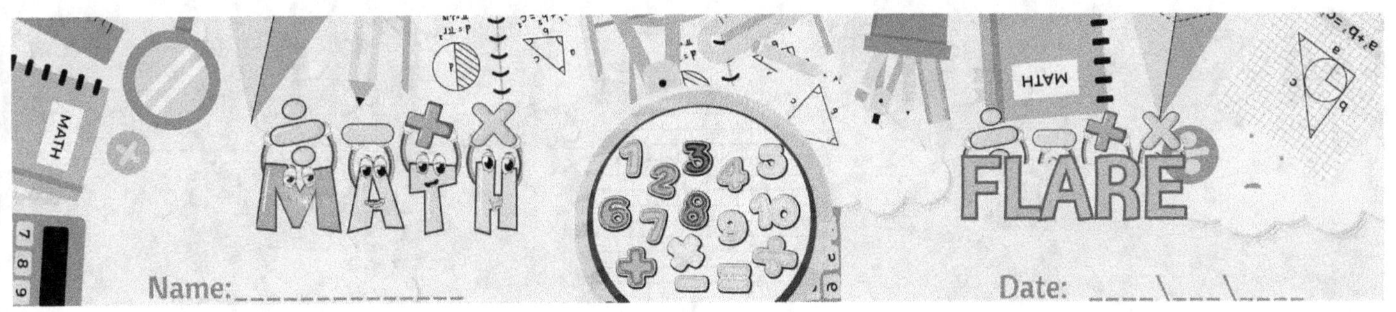

Subtraction Word Problems

1) Emma has 9 dresses. She gave 1 dress to Stephanie. How many dresses does Emma have now?

$$\begin{array}{r} 9 \\ -1 \\ \hline 8 \end{array}$$

Emma has 9 dresses

She gave away 1 dress

Emma has 8 dresses left

2) Matthew has 9 red radios and 3 green radios. How many more red radios does Matthew have than green radios?

3) Barbara bought trees for 8 dollars. She later returned some trees and received a refund of 3 dollars. How much money did she end up spending on trees?

4) Billy saved up 7 dollars to buy shoes. He spent 5 dollars on it. How much money does he have left?

5) Andrew had 8 pants. He gave 2 pants to Elizabeth. How many pants does Andrew have left?

6) Michele has 8 medicines. She lost 6 of them. How many medicines does Michele have left?

7) Christine bought towels for 2 dollars. She received 2 dollars in change. How much did towels cost?

8) Linda had 1 dollars. She spent 1 dollars on desks. How much money does Linda have left?

9) Karen and Sharon went on a shopping spree and bought 10 socks. After returning home, they realized that they didn't need 5 of them. How many socks did they end up keeping?

10) There are 10 dogs in a park. If 8 leave, how many dogs are left in the park?

11) There are 3 turtles in a pond. If 3 leave, how many turtles are left in the pond?

12) Debra bought needles for 8 dollars but later found out it was on sale for 3 dollars less. How much did she overpay for needles?

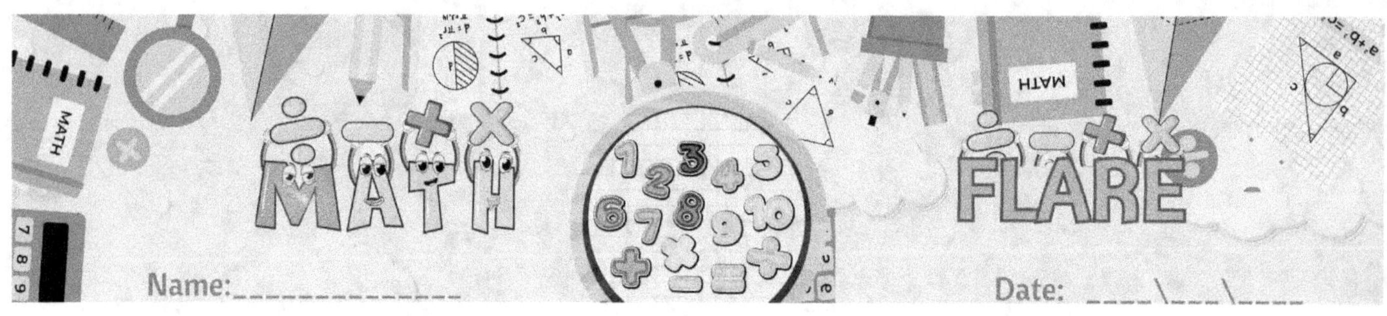

Name:_______________ Date:____________

13) There were 3 students in a class. 2 of them were absent. How many students were present in the class?

14) A cake recipe requires 4 cups of sugar. Samantha only has 1 cups of sugar. How many more cups of sugar does Samantha need?

15) Nicholas has 4 dollars. He wants to buy toothpastes that costs 4 dollars. How much more money does he need to buy the toothpastes?

16) There are 4 fish in a tank. If 3 leave, how many fish are left in the tank?

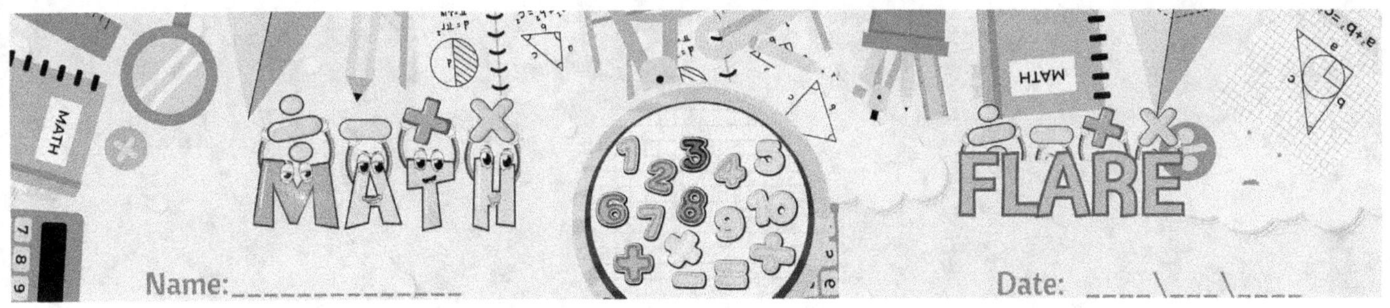

17) A pack of gum had 10 pieces. Sarah took 3 pieces of gum. How many pieces of gum are left in the pack?

18) A box of cotton swabs weighs 7 pounds. If you remove 5 pounds from it, how much does it weigh now?

19) William is 5 years old and Thomas is 3 years old. What is the difference in their ages?

20) If you have 3 stethoscopes and you give away 1, how many stethoscopes do you have left?

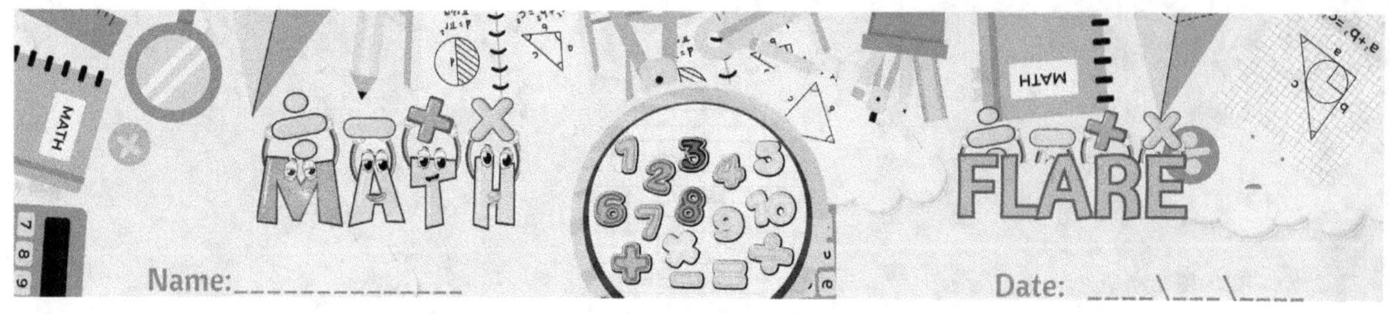

21) Susan has 9 candies in her collection. She gave 3 of them to her friend. How many candies does Susan have now?

22) Adam had 5 dollars. He spent 4 dollars on a carrots. How much money does Adam have left?

23) Amy has 1 dollars. She wants to buy chairs, which costs 7 dollars. How much more money does she need to buy it?

24) Sharon baked a 9 cookies. 9 of them were chocolate chip cookies and the rest were oatmeal raisin cookies. How many oatmeal raisin cookies did Sharon bake?

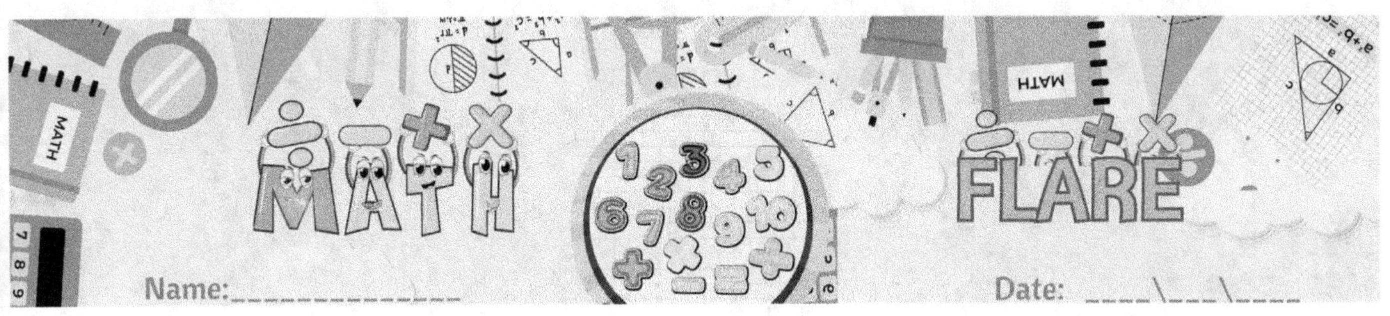

25) Marin and Elizabeth went shopping for cups. They had 3 dollars to spend but 3 dollars ended up being spent. How much money do they have left?

26) Jennifer and Amanda had 6 bats altogether. Amanda gave 3 bats to Andrew. How many bats do they have left?

27) Mirrors originally cost 9 dollars, but it is now on sale for 8 dollars. How much money can you save by buying it on sale?

28) Calendars costs 8 dollars. If you paid $7. How much change will you get back?

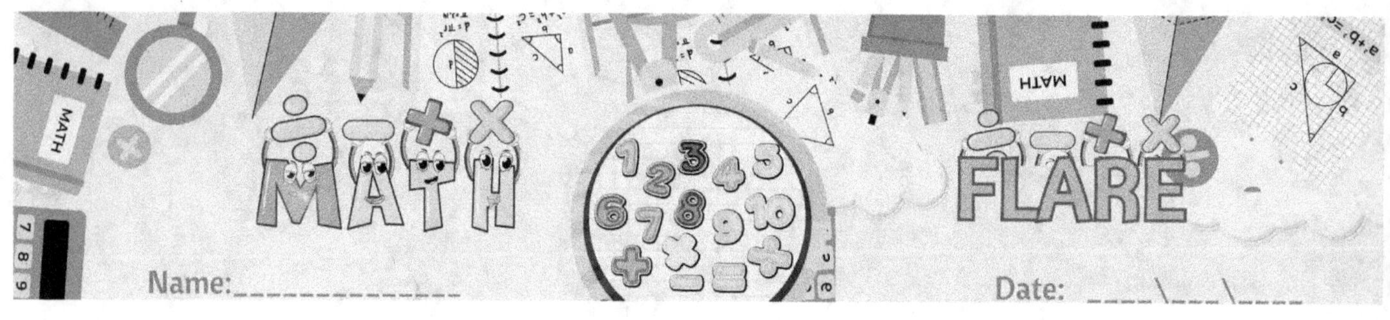

29) A cake recipe calls for 6 cups of flour. 1 cups of flour have already been added. How many more cups of flour are needed?

30) There are 4 pens in a bag. Ashley took 1 pen out of the bag. How many pens are still in the bag?

31) A pizza has 8 slices. Susan ate 8 slices. How many slices of pizza are left?

32) A small bag of chips has 4 chips in it. Charles ate 2 chips. How many chips are left in the bag?

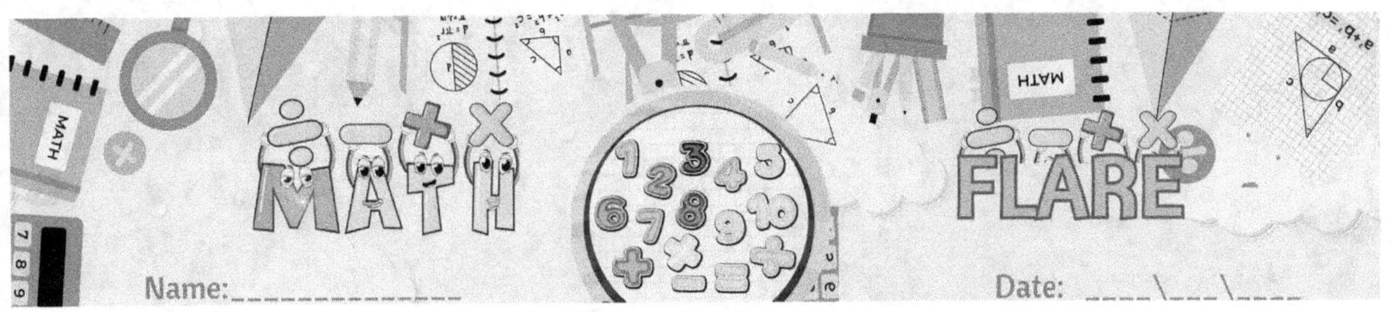

33) James has 6 dollars. He needs to buy sticks that costs 10 dollars. How much money will he have left after buying the sticks?

34) A recipe needs 3 cups of sugar. Debra added 1 cups of sugar. How many cups of sugar are still needed?

35) Anthony has 7 bagels in his collection. He sold 5 of them at a sale. How many bagels does he have left in his collection?

36) There are 3 fish in a pond. Lisa caught 1 fish. How many fish are left in the pond?

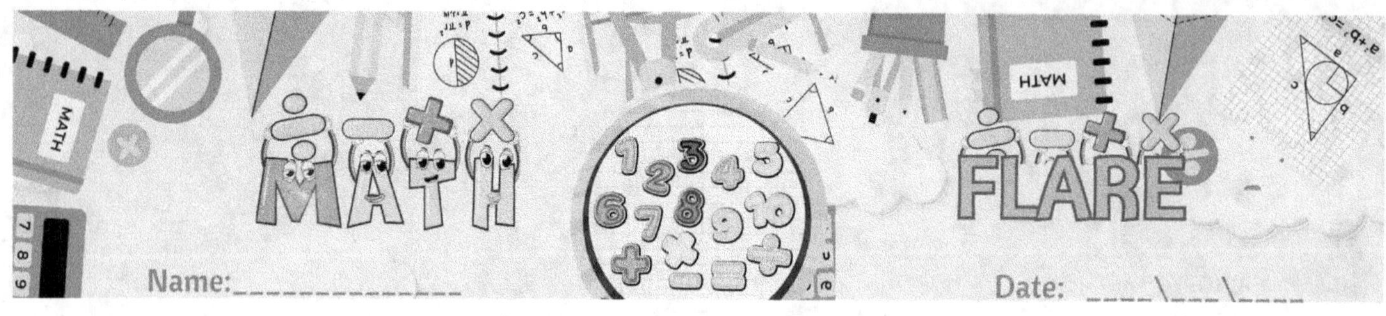

37) If thermometers costs 7 dollars and you have 1 dollars, how much more money do you need to buy it?

38) A box had 2 chocolates. Amanda ate 1 chocolates. How many chocolates are left in the box?

39) A flosses costs $4 and a pen costs $4. How much more expensive is the flosses than the pen?

40) Jackie wants to buy clocks, which costs 5 dollars. She has 4 dollars and plans to save the rest. How much more money does she need to save to buy clocks?

Chapter. 03

Place Value

Place value tells us the value of a digit in a number based on where it's placed.

Imagine we have the number 753. It has three digits: 7, 5, and 3.

Now, each digit holds a special place:

The digit 7 is in the hundreds place. It means it represents seven groups of 100.

The digit 5 is in the tens place. It means it's representing five groups of 10.

The digit 3 is in the ones place. It means it represents three single units.

So, when we want to know the total value of the number 753, we add up the values of each digit based on its place value:

The digit 7 in the hundreds place is worth 700.

The digit 5 in the tens place is worth 50.

The digit 3 in the ones place is worth 3.

When we add these values together, we find the value of the entire number:

700 + 50 + 3 = 753

Let's solve problems from the exercises:

Place value of the underlined digit:

125 = __1 hundred__

Expanded notations:

260   2 hundreds + 6 tens

124   1 hundred + 2 tens + 4 ones

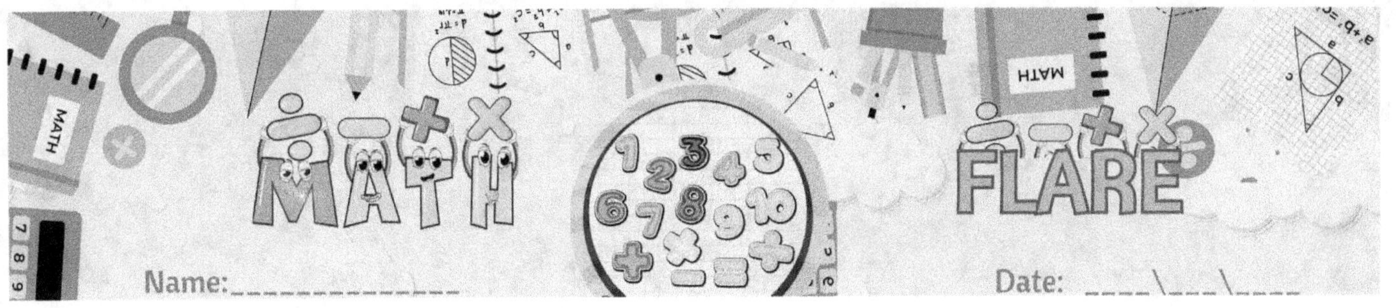

Place Value

Determine the place value of the underlined digit.

1) 1̲25 = __1 hundred__

2) 71̲8 = __________

3) 9̲80 = __________

4) 7̲27 = __________

5) 1,00̲0 = __________

6) 1̲21 = __________

7) 2̲6 = __________

8) 2̲93 = __________

9) 8̲65 = __________

10) 90̲8 = __________

11) 9̲88 = __________

12) 5̲75 = __________

13) 8̲26 = __________

14) 12̲8 = __________

15) 6̲86 = __________

16) 19̲5 = __________

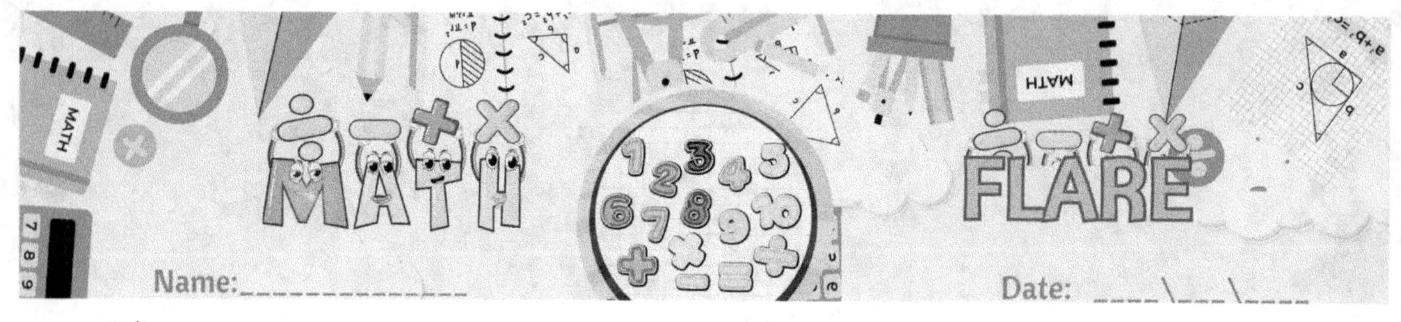

17) 7̲1 = _______________

18) 2̲12 = _______________

19) 59̲3 = _______________

20) 63̲ = _______________

21) 553̲ = _______________

22) 9̲1 = _______________

23) 7̲2 = _______________

24) 1̲57 = _______________

25) 284̲ = _______________

26) 948̲ = _______________

27) 2̲21 = _______________

28) 75̲0 = _______________

29) 9̲50 = _______________

30) 8̲9 = _______________

31) 291̲ = _______________

32) 30̲2 = _______________

33) 187̲ = _______________

34) 3̲49 = _______________

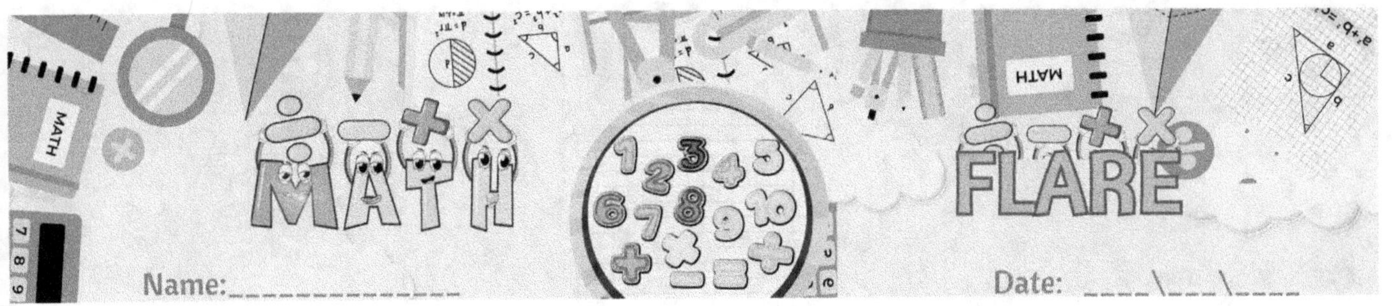

35) 827 = _______________

36) 894 = _______________

37) 90 = _______________

38) 232 = _______________

39) 567 = _______________

40) 2 = _______________

41) 678 = _______________

42) 484 = _______________

43) 386 = _______________

44) 343 = _______________

45) 862 = _______________

46) 858 = _______________

47) 876 = _______________

48) 629 = _______________

49) 25 = _______________

50) 878 = _______________

51) 767 = _______________

52) 630 = _______________

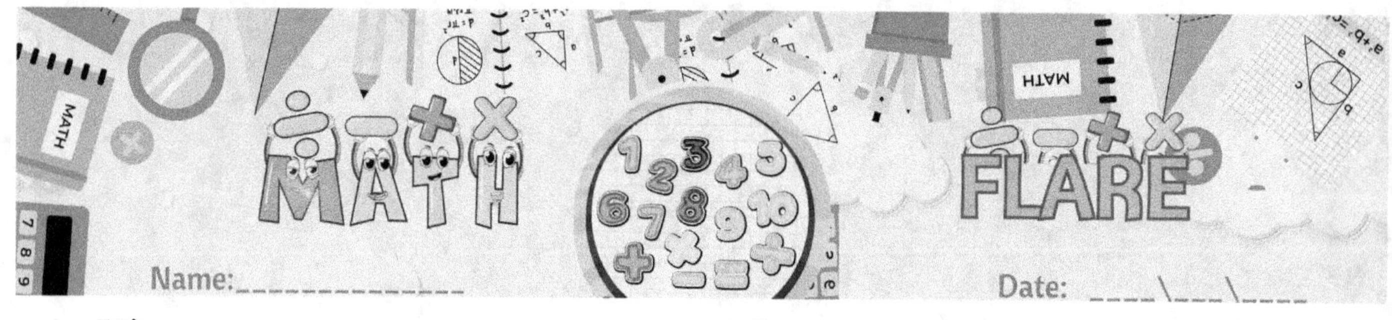

53) 2̲73 = _______________

54) 93̲7 = _______________

55) 1̲45 = _______________

56) 3̲6 = _______________

57) 647̲ = _______________

58) 82̲4 = _______________

59) 4̲44 = _______________

60) 5̲3 = _______________

61) 9̲00 = _______________

62) 2̲76 = _______________

63) 777̲ = _______________

64) 6̲18 = _______________

65) 6̲88 = _______________

66) 3̲89 = _______________

67) 47̲8 = _______________

68) 7̲92 = _______________

69) 1̲06 = _______________

70) 8̲39 = _______________

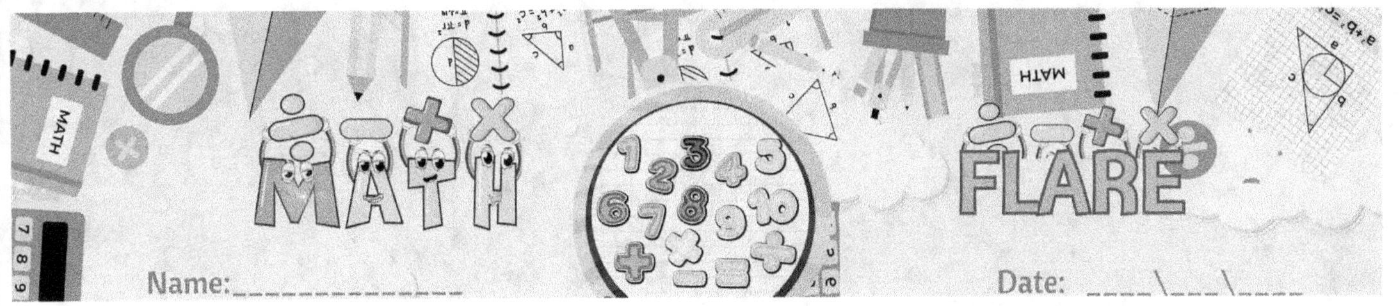

71) 645 = ___________________

72) 592 = ___________________

73) 385 = ___________________

74) 70 = ___________________

75) 705 = ___________________

76) 729 = ___________________

77) 295 = ___________________

78) 426 = ___________________

79) 73 = ___________________

80) 726 = ___________________

81) 74 = ___________________

82) 322 = ___________________

83) 661 = ___________________

84) 30 = ___________________

85) 250 = ___________________

86) 205 = ___________________

87) 248 = ___________________

88) 266 = ___________________

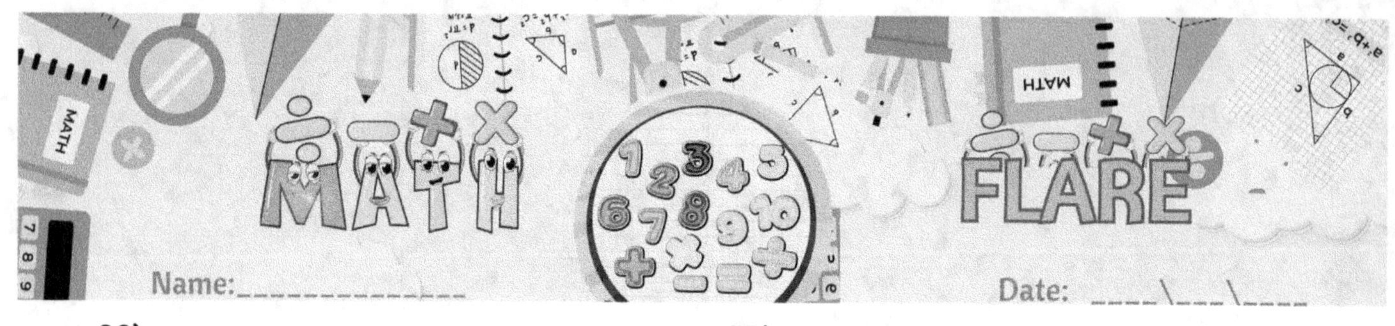

89) 787 = _______________

90) 515 = _______________

91) 101 = _______________

92) 403 = _______________

93) 143 = _______________

94) 608 = _______________

95) 724 = _______________

96) 175 = _______________

97) 470 = _______________

98) 399 = _______________

99) 329 = _______________

100) 233 = _______________

101) 772 = _______________

102) 927 = _______________

103) 985 = _______________

104) 681 = _______________

105) 554 = _______________

106) 76 = _______________

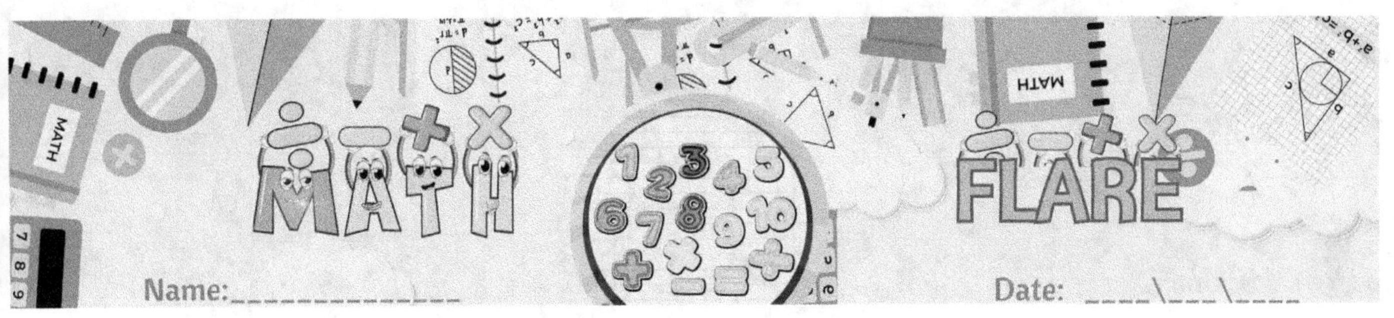

Place Value: Expanded Notation

Provide the expanded notation for each value.

1) _260_ 2 hundreds + 6 tens

2) _______ 4 hundreds + 9 tens

3) _______ 4 hundreds + 4 tens + 3 ones

4) _______ 9 tens + 4 ones

5) _______ 2 hundreds + 9 tens

6) _______ 6 hundreds + 7 tens + 4 ones

7) _______ 8 hundreds + 8 ones

8) _______ 4 hundreds + 3 tens + 8 ones

9) _______ 7 hundreds + 5 tens + 6 ones

10) _______ 6 hundreds

11) _______ 2 hundreds + 5 tens + 2 ones

12) _______ 5 hundreds + 4 tens + 3 ones

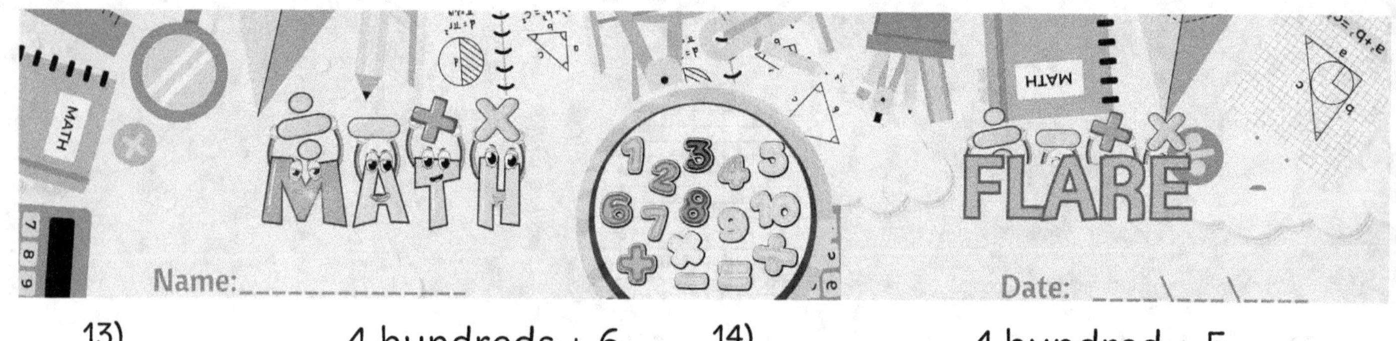

13) __________ 4 hundreds + 6 tens + 2 ones

14) __________ 1 hundred + 5 tens + 2 ones

15) __________ 3 hundreds + 1 ten + 9 ones

16) __________ 1 hundred + 6 tens + 5 ones

17) __________ 8 hundreds + 2 tens + 1 one

18) __________ 7 hundreds + 9 tens + 6 ones

19) __________ 7 hundreds + 8 tens + 2 ones

20) __________ 5 hundreds + 7 tens + 7 ones

21) __________ 3 hundreds + 6 tens + 6 ones

22) __________ 9 hundreds + 5 tens + 2 ones

23) __________ 3 hundreds + 3 tens + 2 ones

24) __________ 8 hundreds + 5 tens + 3 ones

25) __________ 7 hundreds + 5 tens + 5 ones

26) __________ 3 hundreds + 9 tens + 8 ones

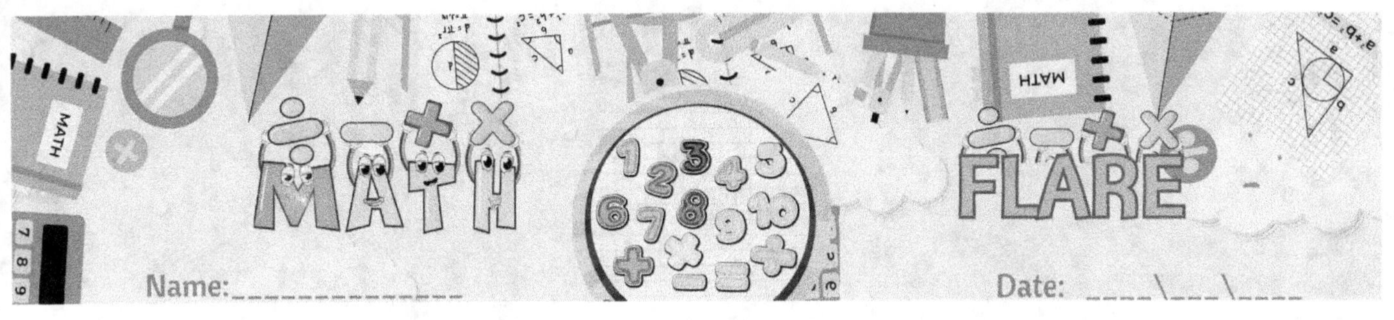

Name:____________________   Date: ____________

27) __________ 7 hundreds + 3 tens + 9 ones

28) __________ 5 hundreds + 7 tens + 2 ones

29) __________ 6 hundreds + 7 tens + 5 ones

30) __________ 3 hundreds + 3 tens

31) __________ 9 hundreds + 2 tens + 7 ones

32) __________ 5 hundreds + 6 tens + 2 ones

33) __________ 6 hundreds + 7 tens

34) __________ 6 hundreds + 8 tens + 2 ones

35) __________ 8 hundreds + 8 tens + 8 ones

36) __________ 9 hundreds + 3 tens + 8 ones

37) __________ 7 hundreds + 4 tens + 4 ones

38) __________ 5 hundreds + 1 ten + 7 ones

39) __________ 2 hundreds + 7 tens

40) __________ 4 hundreds + 7 tens + 5 ones

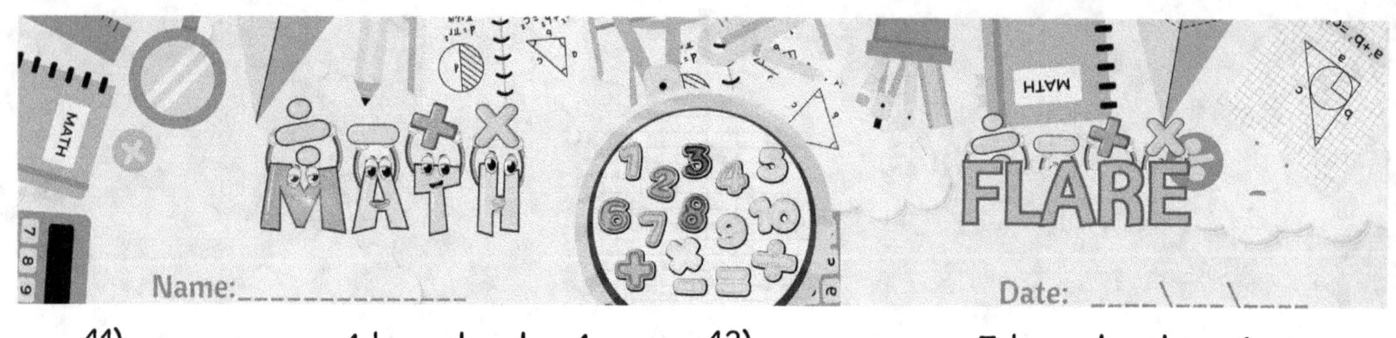

41) __________ 1 hundred + 4 tens + 8 ones

42) __________ 5 hundreds + 4 tens + 7 ones

43) __________ 3 hundreds + 5 ones

44) __________ 5 hundreds + 5 tens

45) __________ 2 tens + 4 ones

46) __________ 5 tens + 6 ones

47) __________ 5 hundreds + 6 tens + 9 ones

48) __________ 8 hundreds + 1 ten + 5 ones

49) __________ 9 hundreds + 5 tens

50) __________ 6 hundreds + 7 tens + 9 ones

51) __________ 4 tens + 6 ones

52) __________ 1 ten + 6 ones

53) __________ 8 hundreds + 9 tens + 4 ones

54) __________ 5 hundreds + 3 tens + 8 ones

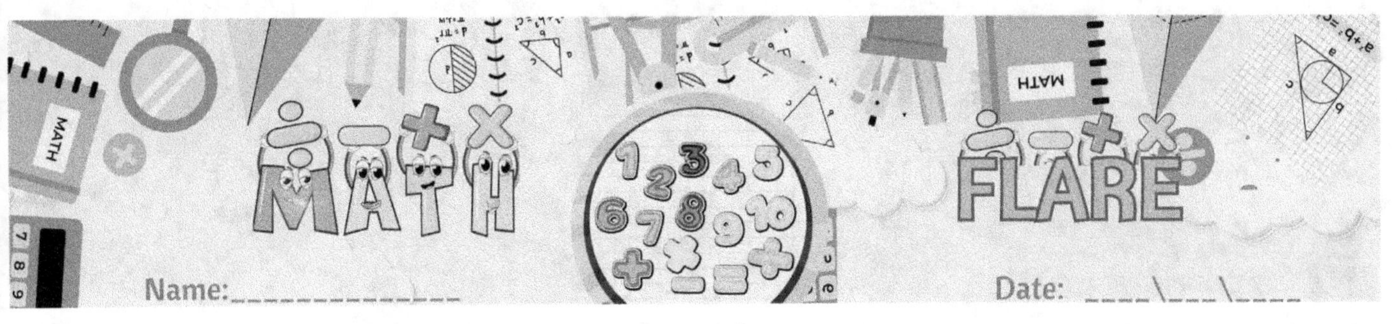

55) __________ 1 hundred + 1 ten + 2 ones

56) __________ 9 hundreds + 4 tens + 2 ones

57) __________ 9 hundreds + 1 ten + 9 ones

58) __________ 4 hundreds + 1 ten + 1 one

59) __________ 6 hundreds + 9 tens + 9 ones

60) __________ 1 hundred + 8 tens + 5 ones

61) __________ 9 hundreds + 2 tens + 5 ones

62) __________ 9 hundreds + 2 tens + 1 one

63) __________ 5 tens + 8 ones

64) __________ 6 hundreds + 1 ten + 5 ones

65) __________ 9 hundreds

66) __________ 4 hundreds + 8 tens + 2 ones

67) __________ 6 hundreds + 3 tens + 7 ones

68) __________ 2 hundreds + 7 tens + 7 ones

69) __________ 8 hundreds + 8 tens + 3 ones

70) __________ 5 tens + 3 ones

71) __________ 2 hundreds + 6 tens + 6 ones

72) __________ 3 hundreds + 8 ones

73) __________ 8 hundreds + 9 tens + 2 ones

74) __________ 8 hundreds + 5 ones

75) __________ 7 hundreds + 8 tens + 5 ones

76) __________ 8 hundreds + 4 tens + 7 ones

77) __________ 3 hundreds + 4 ones

78) __________ 7 hundreds + 3 tens + 2 ones

79) __________ 3 hundreds + 4 tens + 3 ones

80) __________ 1 hundred + 7 tens + 1 one

81) __________ 7 hundreds + 5 tens + 7 ones

82) __________ 7 hundreds + 2 tens + 5 ones

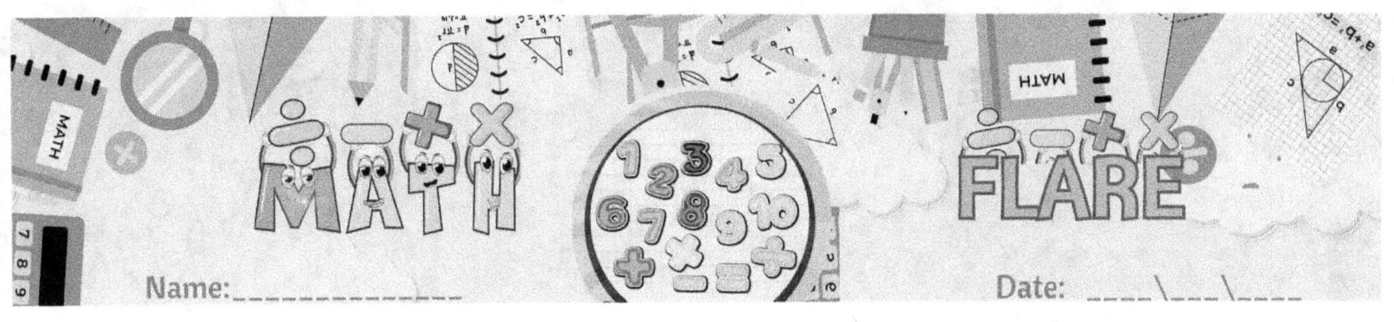

83) __________ 6 hundreds + 5 tens + 1 one

84) __________ 4 hundreds + 9 tens + 8 ones

85) __________ 9 hundreds + 1 ten + 3 ones

86) __________ 6 hundreds + 6 tens + 8 ones

87) __________ 1 hundred + 3 tens + 3 ones

88) __________ 5 hundreds + 7 tens + 1 one

89) __________ 9 hundreds + 4 tens + 6 ones

90) __________ 5 hundreds + 1 one

91) __________ 8 hundreds + 2 tens + 5 ones

92) __________ 1 hundred + 7 ones

93) __________ 2 hundreds + 2 tens + 3 ones

94) __________ 6 hundreds + 2 tens + 6 ones

95) __________ 2 hundreds + 4 tens + 8 ones

96) __________ 9 hundreds + 3 tens + 5 ones

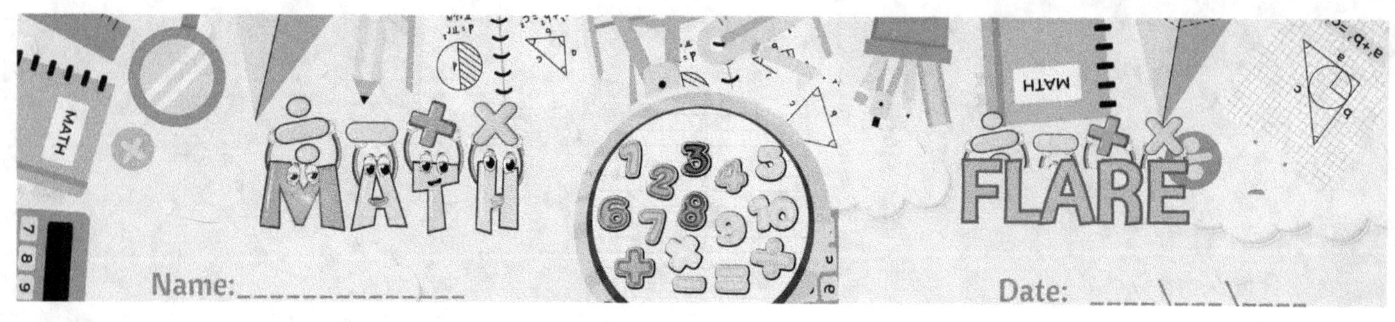

Place Value: Expanded Notation

Provide the expanded notation for each value.

1) 124   <u>1 hundred + 2 tens</u>
     <u>+ 4 ones</u>

2) 574 ___________________
____

3) 932 ___________________
____

4) 539 ___________________
____

5) 68 ___________________
____

6) 628 ___________________
____

7) 780 ___________________
____

8) 707 ___________________
____

9) 3 ___________________
____

10) 734 ___________________
____

11) 328 ___________________
____

12) 96 ___________________
____

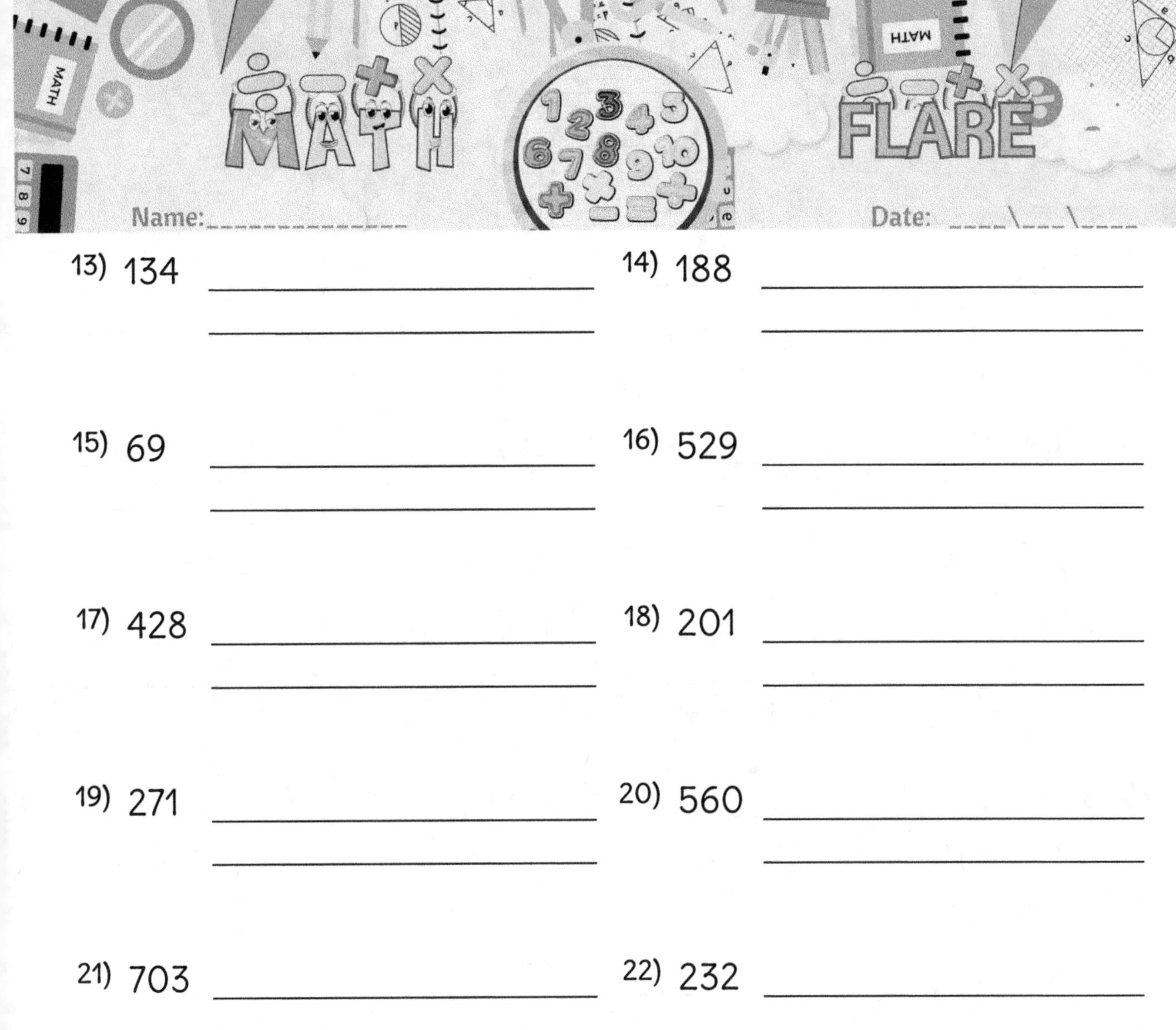

13) 134 _______________________

14) 188 _______________________

15) 69 _______________________

16) 529 _______________________

17) 428 _______________________

18) 201 _______________________

19) 271 _______________________

20) 560 _______________________

21) 703 _______________________

22) 232 _______________________

23) 350 _______________________

24) 67 _______________________

25) 331 _______________________

26) 383 _______________________

27) 228 ___________________

28) 160 ___________________

29) 738 ___________________

30) 602 ___________________

31) 583 ___________________

32) 600 ___________________

33) 370 ___________________

34) 609 ___________________

35) 769 ___________________

36) 239 ___________________

37) 219 ___________________

38) 658 ___________________

39) 24 ___________________

40) 718 ___________________

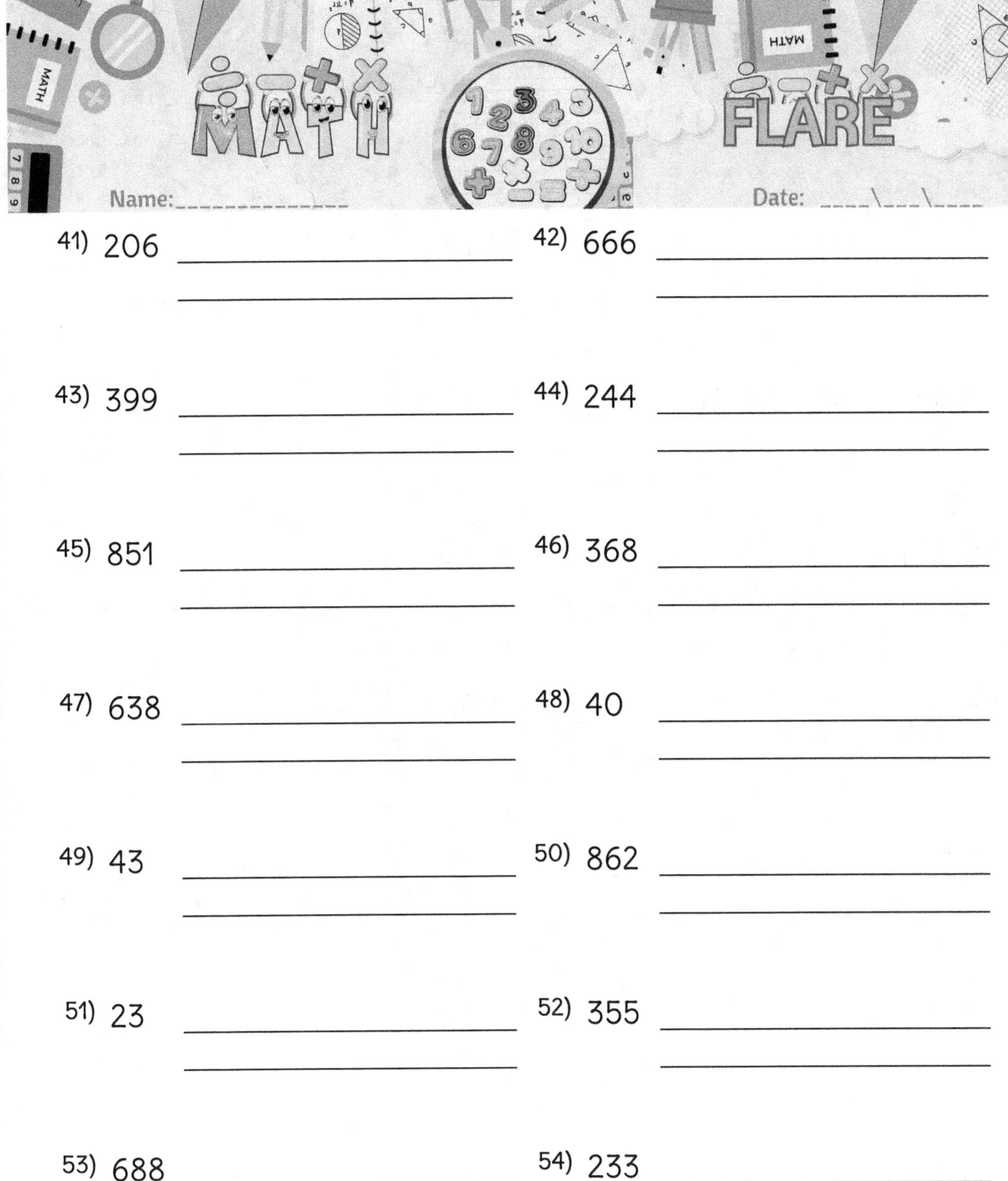

41) 206 _______________________
____

42) 666 _______________________
____

43) 399 _______________________
____

44) 244 _______________________
____

45) 851 _______________________
____

46) 368 _______________________
____

47) 638 _______________________
____

48) 40 _______________________
____

49) 43 _______________________
____

50) 862 _______________________
____

51) 23 _______________________
____

52) 355 _______________________
____

53) 688 _______________________
____

54) 233 _______________________
____

55) 891 _______________________

56) 225 _______________________

57) 866 _______________________

58) 209 _______________________

59) 685 _______________________

60) 401 _______________________

61) 621 _______________________

62) 970 _______________________

63) 152 _______________________

64) 169 _______________________

65) 496 _______________________

66) 765 _______________________

67) 579 _______________________

68) 300 _______________________

69) 291 _______________________

70) 210 _______________________

71) 543 _______________________

72) 248 _______________________

73) 842 _______________________

74) 497 _______________________

75) 566 _______________________

76) 951 _______________________

77) 823 _______________________

78) 480 _______________________

79) 16 _______________________

80) 590 _______________________

81) 121 _______________________

82) 696 _______________________

83) 740 _______________________

84) 561 _______________________

85) 804 _______________________

86) 913 _______________________

87) 137 _______________________

88) 544 _______________________

89) 373 _______________________

90) 11 _______________________

91) 974 _______________________

92) 623 _______________________

93) 98 _______________________

94) 236 _______________________

95) 267 _______________________

96) 247 _______________________

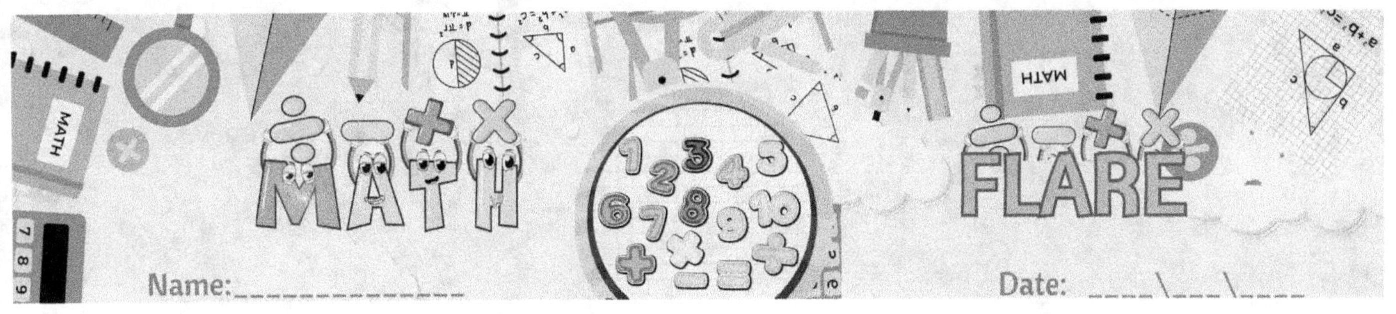

Understanding Time

1)
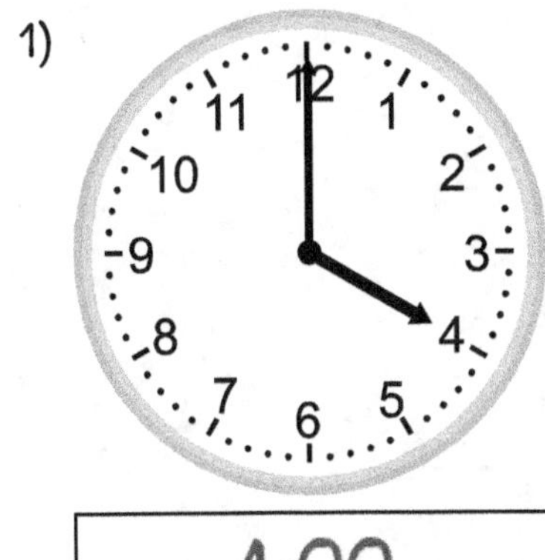

| 4:00 |

2)
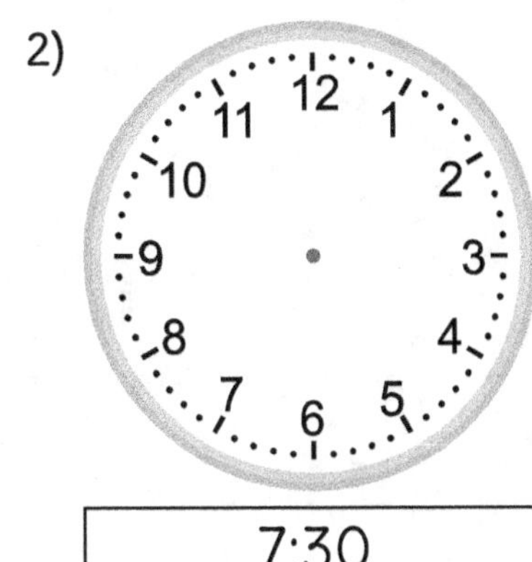

| 7:30 |

3)
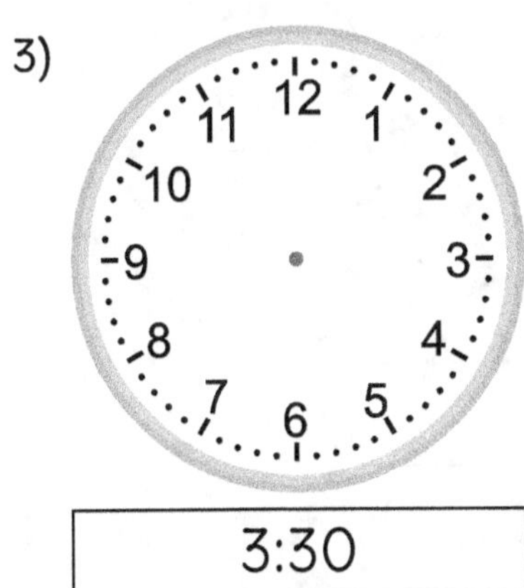

| 3:30 |

4)
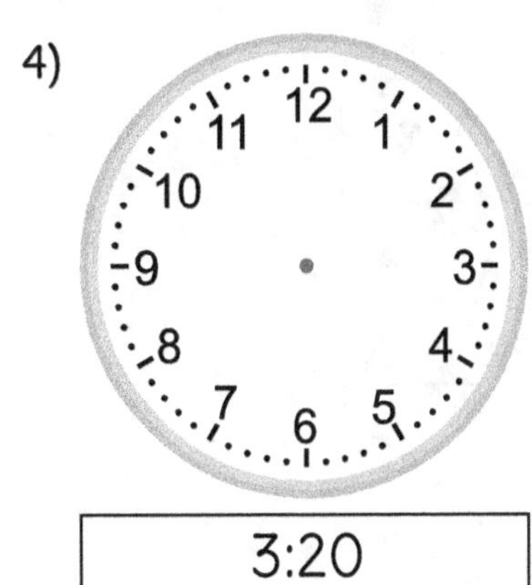

| 3:20 |

5)

| 11:55 |

6)

| |

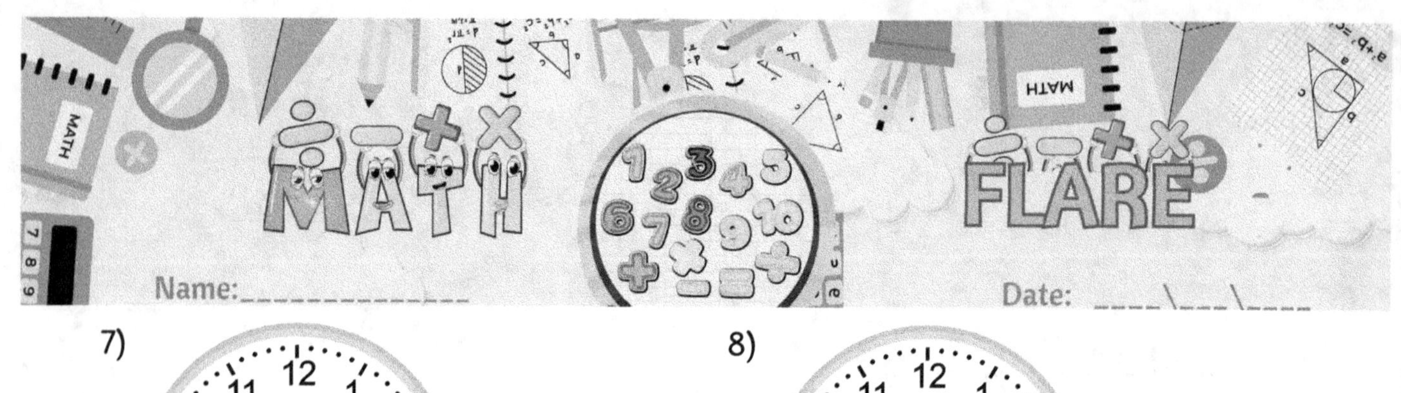

7)

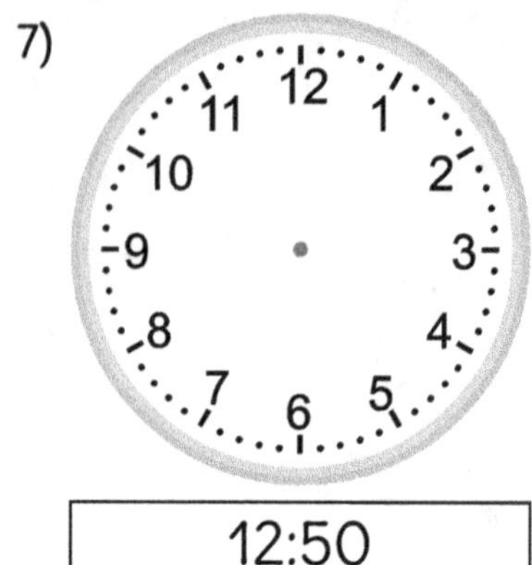

| 12:50 |

8)

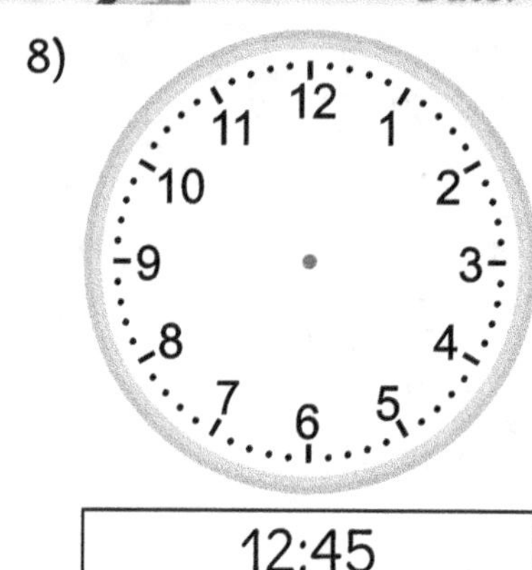

| 12:45 |

9)

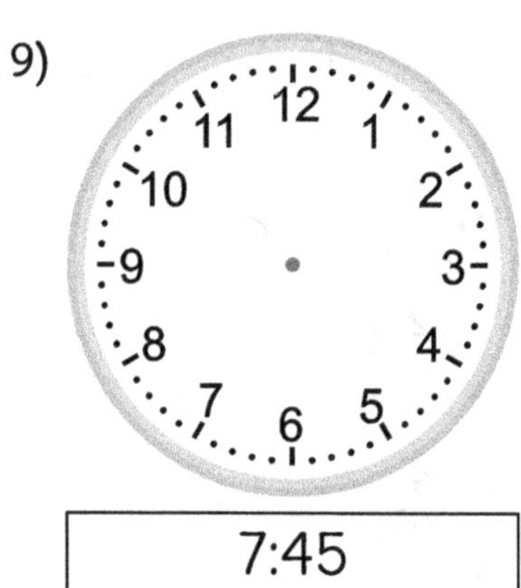

| 7:45 |

10)

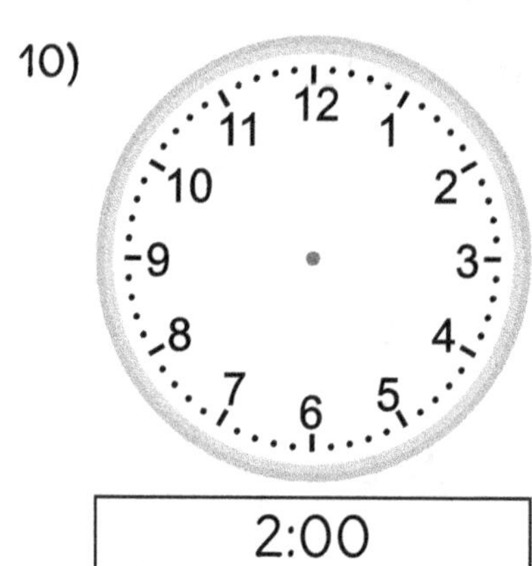

| 2:00 |

11)

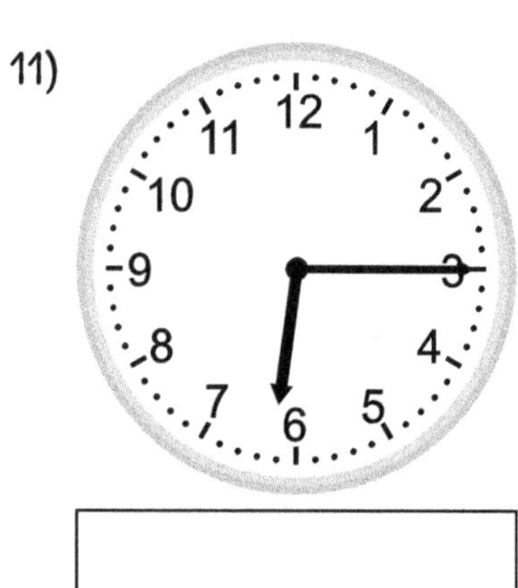

| |

12)

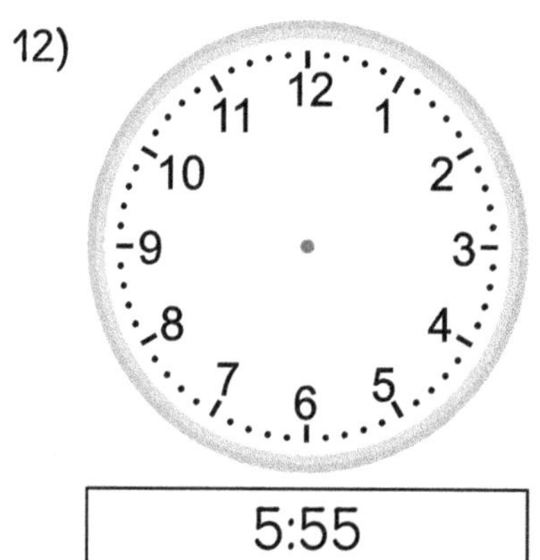

| 5:55 |

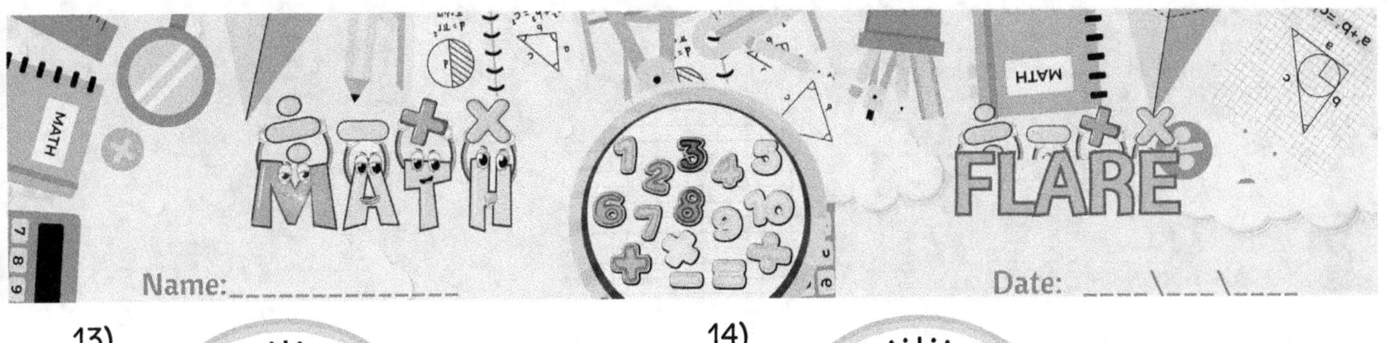

13)

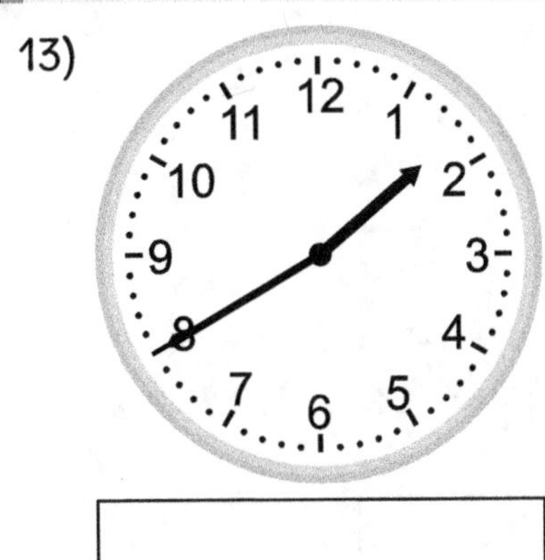

14)

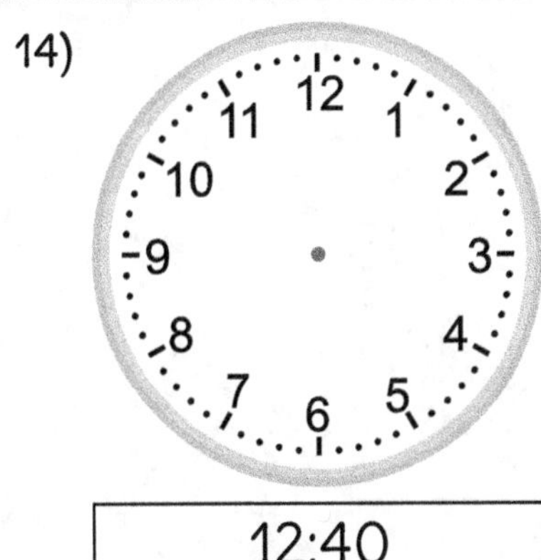

12:40

15)

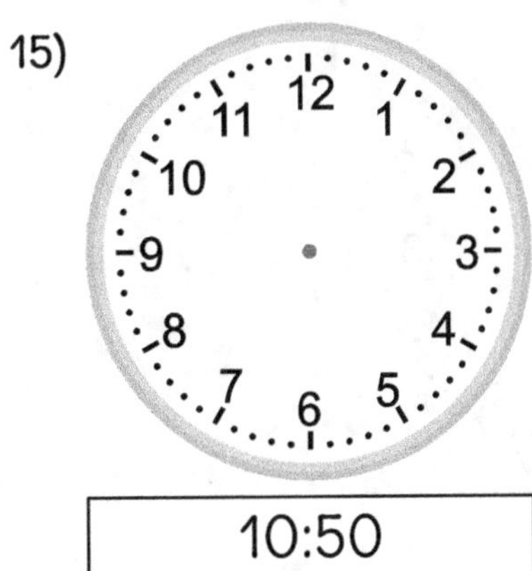

10:50

16)

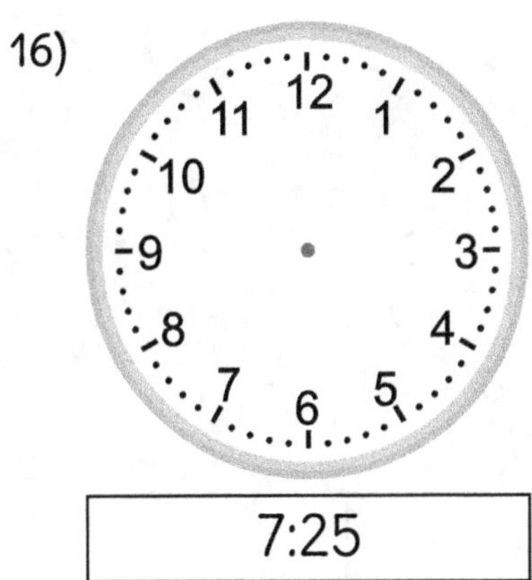

7:25

17)

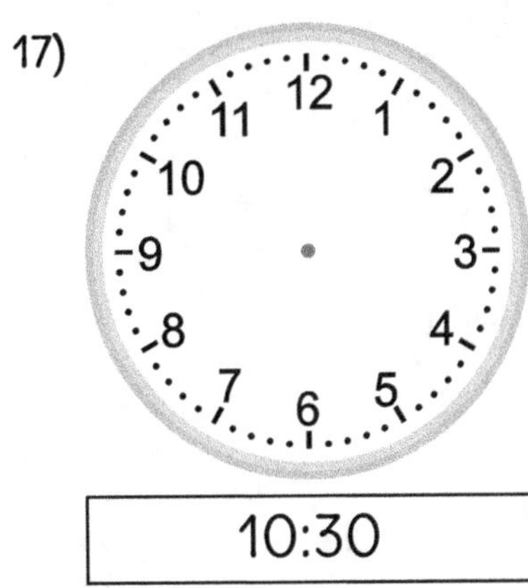

10:30

18)

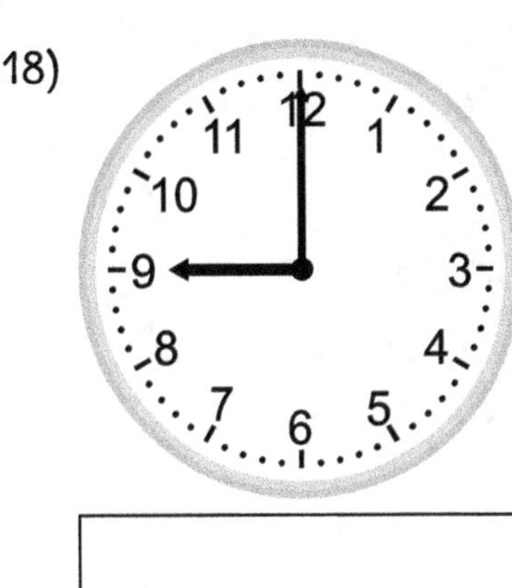

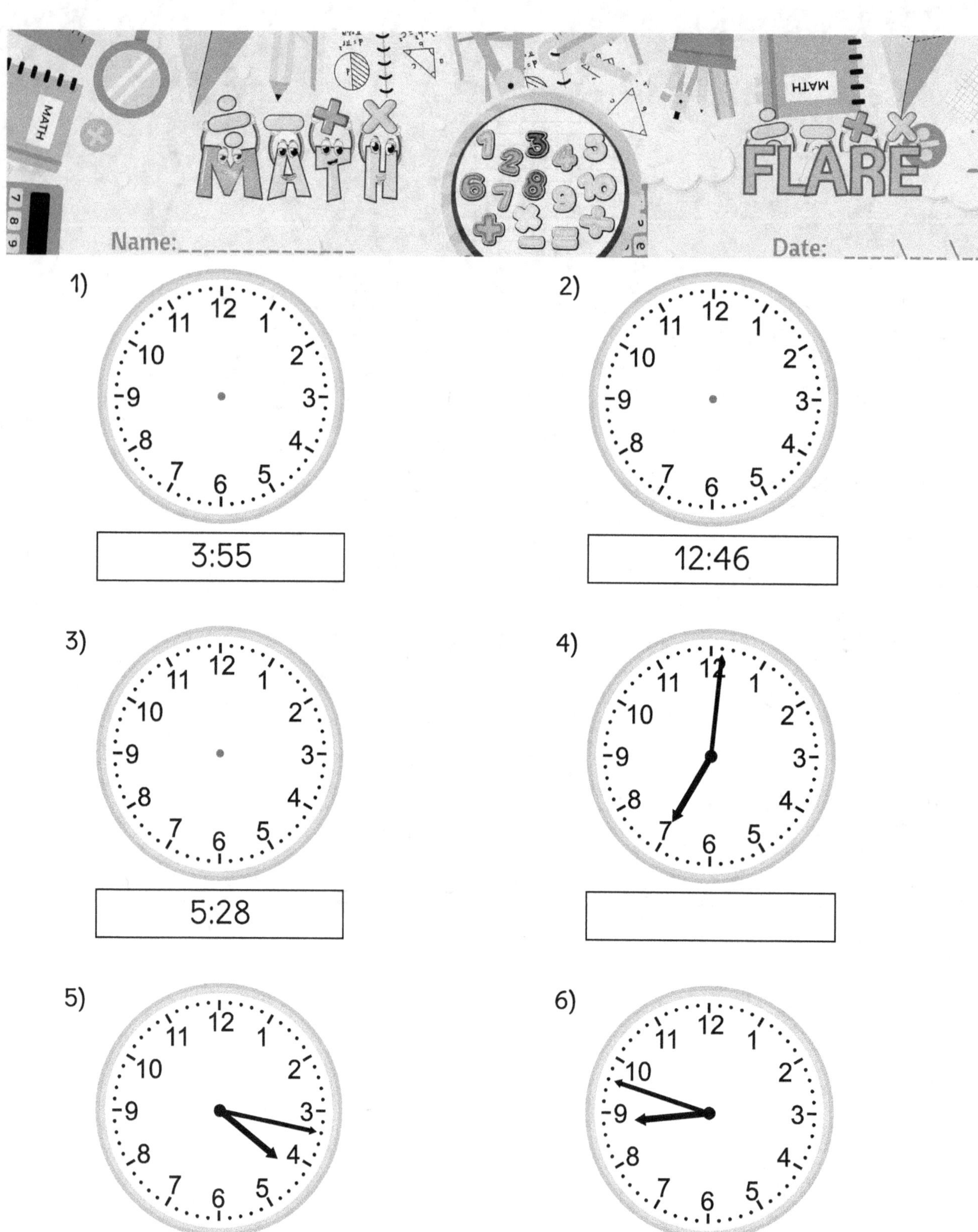

1)

3:55

2)

12:46

3)

5:28

4)

5)

6)

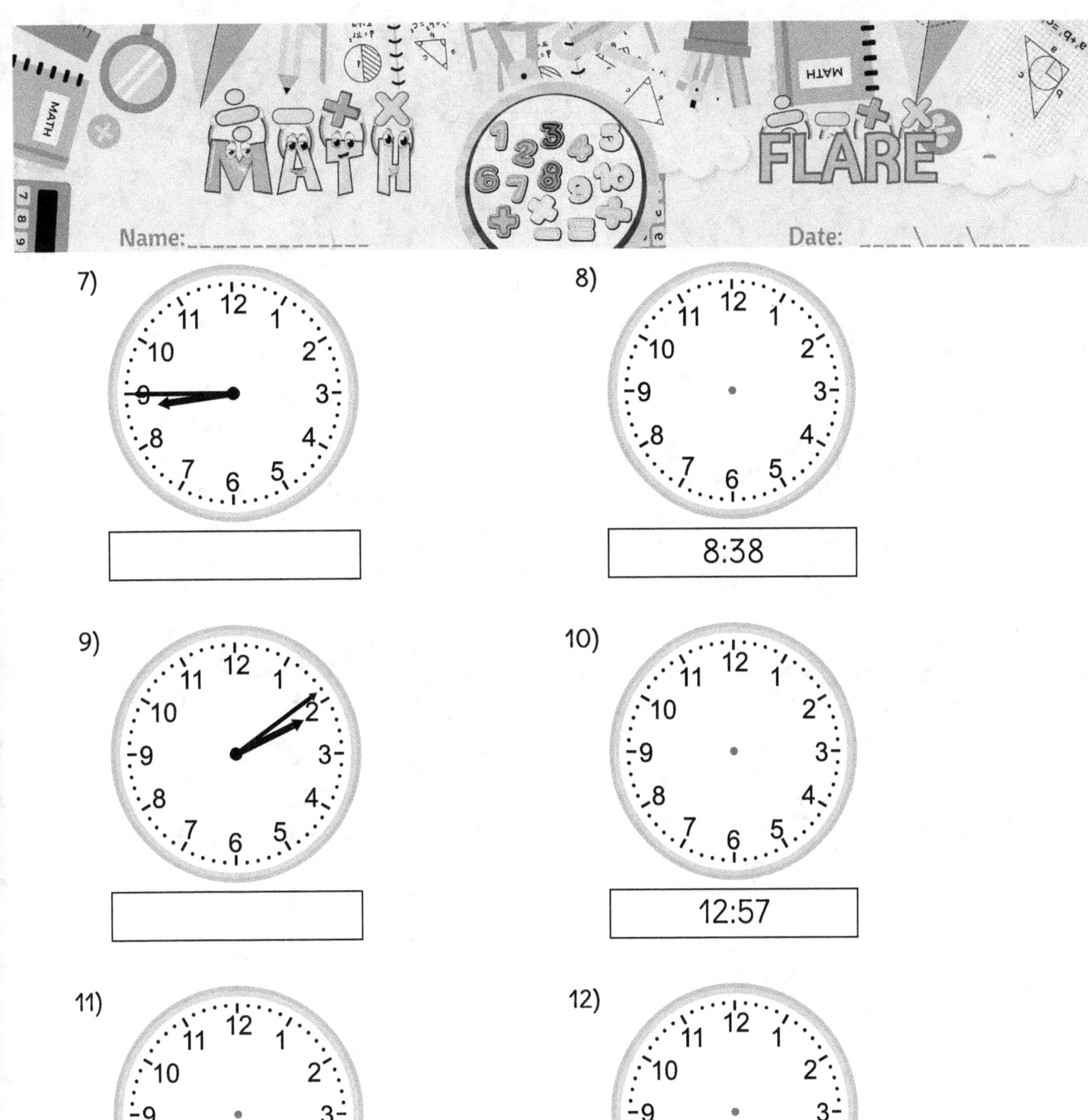

7)

8)

8:38

9)

10)

12:57

11)

3:47

12)

1:48

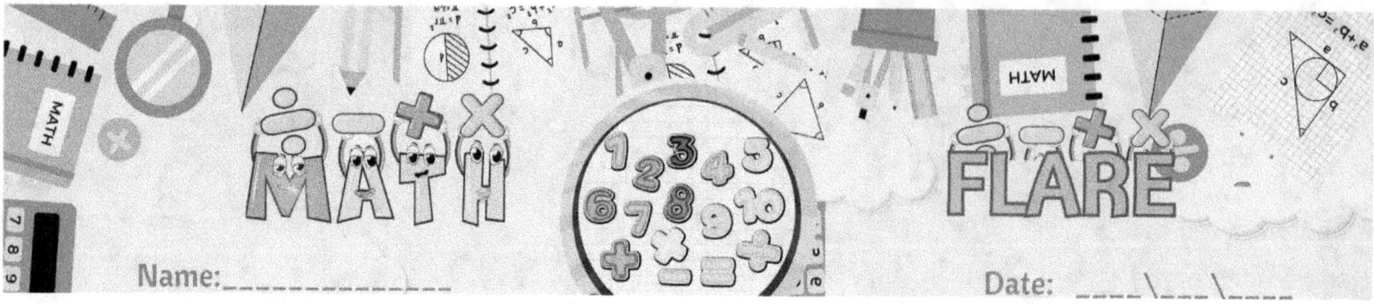

13)

8:34

14)

7:13

15)

1:00

16)

7:44

17) 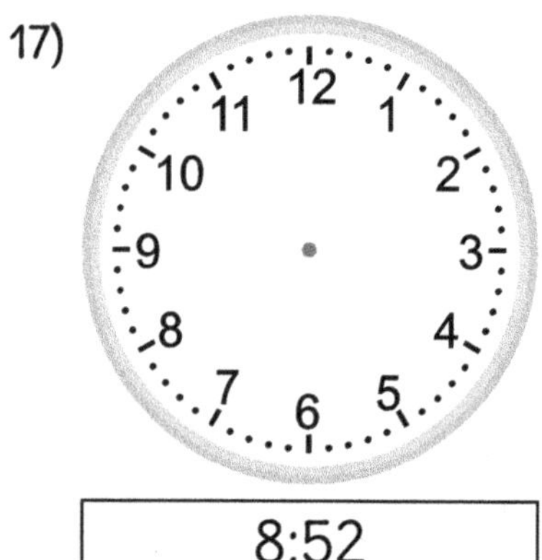

8:52

18) 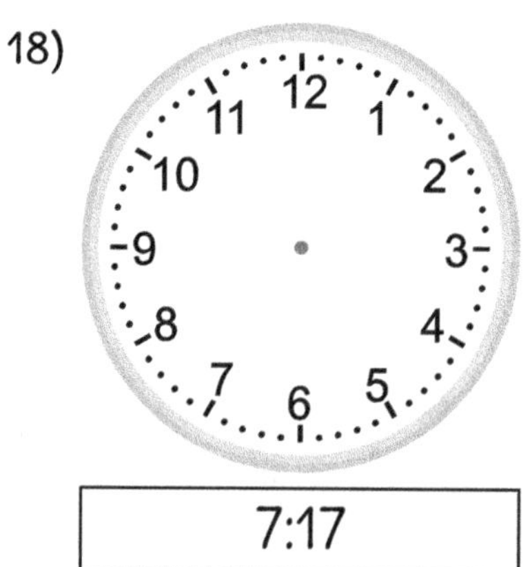

7:17

ANSWERS

Page 1: Counting Up

1.

327	326	325	324	**323**	322	321	320	319	**318**

2.

602	**601**	600	599	598	597	596	595	594	593

3.

821	820	**819**	818	**817**	816	815	814	813	812

4.

275	274	273	272	271	270	269	**268**	267	266

5.

114	113	112	**111**	110	109	**108**	107	106	105

6.

929	928	927	926	925	924	923	922	**921**	920

7.

416	415	**414**	413	412	411	410	409	408	407

8.

856	855	854	853	**852**	851	850	**849**	848	847

9.

379	378	**377**	376	375	374	373	372	371	**370**

10.

422	421	420	419	418	417	416	**415**	414	413

11.

| 786 | 785 | 784 | 783 | 782 | 781 | **780** | 779 | **778** | 777 |

12.

| 879 | 878 | 877 | 876 | 875 | 874 | 873 | **872** | 871 | **870** |

13.

| 364 | **363** | 362 | 361 | 360 | 359 | 358 | 357 | 356 | **355** |

14.

| 360 | **359** | 358 | 357 | **356** | 355 | 354 | 353 | 352 | 351 |

15.

| 852 | 851 | 850 | 849 | 848 | **847** | 846 | **845** | 844 | 843 |

16.

| **377** | 376 | 375 | 374 | 373 | 372 | 371 | 370 | **369** | 368 |

17.

| 136 | 135 | 134 | 133 | 132 | 131 | 130 | **129** | 128 | **127** |

18.

| 500 | **499** | 498 | 497 | 496 | 495 | 494 | **493** | 492 | 491 |

19.

| **357** | 356 | 355 | 354 | 353 | **352** | 351 | 350 | 349 | 348 |

20.

| 781 | 780 | 779 | 778 | 777 | **776** | 775 | 774 | **773** | 772 |

21.

| 853 | 852 | 851 | 850 | **849** | 848 | 847 | 846 | 845 | **844** |

22.

| 322 | 321 | 320 | 319 | **318** | 317 | 316 | 315 | **314** | 313 |

23.

| 91 | 90 | 89 | 88 | 87 | **86** | 85 | **84** | 83 | 82 |

24.

| 831 | 830 | **829** | 828 | 827 | 826 | 825 | **824** | 823 | 822 |

25.

| **162** | 161 | 160 | 159 | 158 | 157 | **156** | 155 | 154 | 153 |

26.

| 209 | 208 | **207** | 206 | 205 | 204 | 203 | 202 | 201 | **200** |

27.

| **382** | 381 | 380 | 379 | 378 | 377 | **376** | 375 | 374 | 373 |

28.

| 815 | 814 | 813 | 812 | **811** | 810 | 809 | **808** | 807 | 806 |

29.

| 684 | **683** | 682 | 681 | 680 | 679 | 678 | 677 | 676 | **675** |

30.

| 707 | 706 | **705** | 704 | 703 | 702 | 701 | **700** | 699 | 698 |

31.

| 307 | 306 | 305 | 304 | **303** | 302 | 301 | 300 | 299 | **298** |

32.

| 424 | 423 | **422** | **421** | 420 | 419 | 418 | 417 | 416 | 415 |

33.

| 429 | **428** | 427 | 426 | 425 | 424 | **423** | 422 | 421 | 420 |

34.

| **354** | 353 | 352 | 351 | 350 | 349 | 348 | 347 | 346 | **345** |

35.

| 25 | 24 | **23** | 22 | **21** | 20 | 19 | 18 | 17 | 16 |

36.

| 862 | 861 | 860 | 859 | 858 | 857 | **856** | **855** | 854 | 853 |

37.

| 921 | **920** | 919 | 918 | 917 | 916 | 915 | 914 | **913** | 912 |

38.

| 78 | 77 | 76 | 75 | **74** | 73 | 72 | 71 | **70** | 69 |

39.

| 857 | 856 | 855 | **854** | 853 | **852** | 851 | 850 | 849 | 848 |

40.

| 460 | 459 | **458** | 457 | 456 | 455 | 454 | 453 | 452 | **451** |

41.

| 171 | 170 | 169 | 168 | 167 | 166 | **165** | 164 | **163** | 162 |

42.

| 120 | 119 | 118 | 117 | **116** | 115 | 114 | **113** | 112 | 111 |

43.

| 797 | **796** | 795 | 794 | 793 | 792 | 791 | 790 | **789** | 788 |

44.

| 430 | 429 | 428 | 427 | 426 | 425 | 424 | 423 | 422 | 421 |

45.

| 885 | 884 | 883 | 882 | 881 | 880 | 879 | 878 | 877 | 876 |

46.

| 196 | 195 | 194 | 193 | 192 | 191 | 190 | 189 | 188 | 187 |

47.

| 553 | 552 | 551 | 550 | 549 | 548 | 547 | 546 | 545 | 544 |

48.

| 432 | 431 | 430 | 429 | 428 | 427 | 426 | 425 | 424 | 423 |

Page 8: Counting Down

1.

| 249 | 248 | 247 | 246 | 245 | 244 | 243 | 242 | 241 | 240 |

2.

| 64 | 63 | 62 | 61 | 60 | 59 | 58 | 57 | 56 | 55 |

3.

| 844 | 843 | 842 | 841 | 840 | 839 | 838 | 837 | 836 | 835 |

4.

| 379 | 378 | 377 | 376 | 375 | 374 | 373 | 372 | 371 | 370 |

5.

| 726 | 725 | 724 | 723 | 722 | 721 | 720 | 719 | 718 | 717 |

6.

| 616 | 615 | 614 | 613 | 612 | 611 | 610 | 609 | 608 | 607 |

7.

| 100 | 99 | 98 | 97 | 96 | 95 | 94 | 93 | 92 | 91 |

8.

| 14 | 13 | 12 | 11 | 10 | 9 | 8 | 7 | 6 | 5 |

9.

| 521 | 520 | 519 | 518 | 517 | 516 | 515 | 514 | 513 | 512 |

10.

| 971 | 970 | 969 | 968 | 967 | 966 | 965 | 964 | 963 | 962 |

11.

| 123 | 122 | 121 | 120 | 119 | 118 | 117 | 116 | 115 | 114 |

12.

| 885 | 884 | 883 | 882 | 881 | 880 | 879 | 878 | 877 | 876 |

13.

| 557 | 556 | 555 | 554 | 553 | 552 | 551 | 550 | 549 | 548 |

14.

| 581 | 580 | 579 | 578 | 577 | 576 | 575 | 574 | 573 | 572 |

15.

| 181 | 180 | 179 | 178 | 177 | 176 | 175 | 174 | 173 | 172 |

16.

| 652 | 651 | 650 | 649 | 648 | 647 | 646 | 645 | 644 | 643 |

17.

| 124 | 123 | 122 | 121 | 120 | 119 | 118 | 117 | 116 | 115 |

18.

| 372 | 371 | 370 | 369 | 368 | 367 | 366 | 365 | 364 | 363 |

19.

| 459 | 458 | 457 | 456 | 455 | 454 | 453 | 452 | 451 | 450 |

20.

| 20 | 19 | 18 | 17 | 16 | 15 | 14 | 13 | 12 | 11 |

21.

| 344 | 343 | 342 | 341 | 340 | 339 | 338 | 337 | 336 | 335 |

22.

| 436 | 435 | 434 | 433 | 432 | 431 | 430 | 429 | 428 | 427 |

23.

| 67 | 66 | 65 | 64 | 63 | 62 | 61 | 60 | 59 | 58 |

24.

| 624 | 623 | 622 | 621 | 620 | 619 | 618 | 617 | 616 | 615 |

25.

| 878 | 877 | 876 | 875 | 874 | 873 | 872 | 871 | 870 | 869 |

26.

| 620 | 619 | 618 | 617 | 616 | 615 | 614 | 613 | 612 | 611 |

27.

| 742 | 741 | 740 | 739 | 738 | 737 | 736 | 735 | 734 | 733 |

28.

| 506 | 505 | 504 | 503 | 502 | 501 | 500 | 499 | 498 | 497 |

29.

| 641 | 640 | 639 | 638 | 637 | **636** | **635** | 634 | 633 | 632 |

30.

| 926 | 925 | **924** | **923** | 922 | 921 | 920 | 919 | 918 | 917 |

31.

| 947 | 946 | 945 | 944 | **943** | **942** | 941 | 940 | 939 | 938 |

32.

| 637 | 636 | 635 | 634 | **633** | **632** | 631 | 630 | 629 | 628 |

33.

| 931 | 930 | **929** | **928** | 927 | 926 | 925 | 924 | 923 | 922 |

34.

| 576 | **575** | **574** | 573 | 572 | 571 | 570 | 569 | 568 | 567 |

35.

| 629 | 628 | 627 | **626** | **625** | 624 | 623 | 622 | 621 | 620 |

36.

| 843 | 842 | 841 | 840 | **839** | **838** | 837 | 836 | 835 | 834 |

37.

| 909 | 908 | 907 | 906 | 905 | 904 | 903 | **902** | **901** | 900 |

38.

| 678 | 677 | **676** | **675** | 674 | 673 | 672 | 671 | 670 | 669 |

39.

| 794 | 793 | 792 | **791** | **790** | 789 | 788 | 787 | 786 | 785 |

40.

| 264 | 263 | 262 | 261 | **260** | **259** | 258 | 257 | 256 | 255 |

41.

| 21 | 20 | 19 | 18 | 17 | 16 | 15 | 14 | 13 | 12 |

42.

| 350 | **349** | **348** | 347 | 346 | 345 | 344 | 343 | 342 | 341 |

43.

| 930 | 929 | 928 | 927 | 926 | 925 | 924 | **923** | **922** | 921 |

44.

| **936** | **935** | 934 | 933 | 932 | 931 | 930 | 929 | 928 | 927 |

45.

| 953 | 952 | 951 | 950 | 949 | 948 | **947** | **946** | 945 | 944 |

46.

| 884 | 883 | 882 | 881 | **880** | **879** | 878 | 877 | 876 | 875 |

47.

| 570 | **569** | **568** | 567 | 566 | 565 | 564 | 563 | 562 | 561 |

48.

| 920 | 919 | 918 | 917 | 916 | 915 | 914 | **913** | **912** | 911 |

Page 15: Counting Patterns

1.

| 312 | 314 | **316** | 318 | 320 | 322 | 324 | 326 | 328 | 330 |

2.

| 722 | 726 | 730 | 734 | 738 | 742 | **746** | 750 | 754 | 758 |

3.

| 90 | 94 | 98 | 102 | **106** | 110 | 114 | 118 | 122 | 126 |

4.

| 611 | 614 | 617 | 620 | 623 | **626** | 629 | 632 | 635 | 638 |

5.

| 741 | 746 | 751 | 756 | 761 | **766** | 771 | 776 | 781 | 786 |

6.

| 986 | 991 | 996 | 1,001 | 1,006 | **1,011** | 1,016 | 1,021 | 1,026 | 1,031 |

7.

| 489 | 492 | 495 | **498** | 501 | 504 | 507 | 510 | 513 | 516 |

8.

| 47 | 52 | 57 | **62** | 67 | 72 | 77 | 82 | 87 | 92 |

9.

| 254 | 256 | 258 | **260** | 262 | 264 | 266 | 268 | 270 | 272 |

10.

| 6 | 10 | 14 | 18 | **22** | 26 | 30 | 34 | 38 | 42 |

11.

| 796 | 800 | 804 | 808 | 812 | **816** | 820 | 824 | 828 | 832 |

12.

| 678 | 680 | 682 | 684 | 686 | 688 | 690 | 692 | **694** | 696 |

13.

| 741 | 745 | 749 | 753 | 757 | 761 | 765 | **769** | 773 | 777 |

14.

| 633 | 636 | 639 | 642 | **645** | 648 | 651 | 654 | 657 | 660 |

15.

| 105 | 108 | **111** | 114 | 117 | 120 | 123 | 126 | 129 | 132 |

16.

| 985 | **989** | 993 | 997 | 1,001 | 1,005 | 1,009 | 1,013 | 1,017 | 1,021 |

17.

| **810** | 812 | 814 | 816 | 818 | 820 | 822 | 824 | 826 | 828 |

18.

| 333 | **336** | 339 | 342 | 345 | 348 | 351 | 354 | 357 | 360 |

19.

| 234 | 237 | 240 | 243 | 246 | 249 | **252** | 255 | 258 | 261 |

20.

| **850** | 852 | 854 | 856 | 858 | 860 | 862 | 864 | 866 | 868 |

21.

| 21 | **24** | 27 | 30 | 33 | 36 | 39 | 42 | 45 | 48 |

22.

| 177 | 179 | 181 | 183 | 185 | 187 | **189** | 191 | 193 | 195 |

23.

| 805 | 810 | 815 | 820 | 825 | 830 | **835** | 840 | 845 | 850 |

24.

| 514 | 519 | 524 | 529 | 534 | 539 | 544 | 549 | **554** | 559 |

25.

| 893 | 896 | 899 | 902 | 905 | **908** | 911 | 914 | 917 | 920 |

26.

| 709 | 714 | 719 | **724** | 729 | 734 | 739 | 744 | 749 | 754 |

27.

| 567 | 570 | 573 | 576 | 579 | **582** | 585 | 588 | 591 | 594 |

28.

| 342 | 345 | 348 | 351 | 354 | 357 | 360 | **363** | 366 | 369 |

29.

| 836 | 838 | 840 | 842 | 844 | 846 | 848 | 850 | 852 | **854** |

30.

| 794 | 796 | 798 | 800 | **802** | 804 | 806 | 808 | 810 | 812 |

31.

| 612 | 617 | 622 | **627** | 632 | 637 | 642 | 647 | 652 | 657 |

32.

| 688 | 690 | 692 | 694 | 696 | 698 | 700 | **702** | 704 | 706 |

33.

| 842 | 844 | 846 | **848** | 850 | 852 | 854 | 856 | 858 | 860 |

34.

| 516 | 521 | 526 | 531 | 536 | 541 | 546 | 551 | 556 | **561** |

35.

| 535 | 537 | 539 | **541** | 543 | 545 | 547 | 549 | 551 | 553 |

36.

| 907 | 911 | 915 | 919 | 923 | 927 | **931** | 935 | 939 | 943 |

37.

| 749 | 751 | 753 | 755 | 757 | **759** | 761 | 763 | 765 | 767 |

38.

| 513 | 517 | 521 | 525 | 529 | 533 | 537 | **541** | 545 | 549 |

39.

| 14 | 18 | 22 | 26 | 30 | 34 | **38** | 42 | 46 | 50 |

40.

| 833 | 838 | **843** | 848 | 853 | 858 | 863 | 868 | 873 | 878 |

41.

| 806 | 811 | 816 | 821 | 826 | 831 | **836** | 841 | 846 | 851 |

42.

| 584 | **586** | 588 | 590 | 592 | 594 | 596 | 598 | 600 | 602 |

43.

| 936 | 939 | 942 | 945 | 948 | **951** | 954 | 957 | 960 | 963 |

44.

| 474 | 478 | 482 | 486 | 490 | **494** | 498 | 502 | 506 | 510 |

45.

| 19 | 22 | 25 | 28 | 31 | 34 | **37** | 40 | 43 | 46 |

46.

| 565 | 567 | 569 | 571 | **573** | 575 | 577 | 579 | 581 | 583 |

<table>
<tr><td>47.</td><td>292</td><td>294</td><td>296</td><td>298</td><td>300</td><td>302</td><td>304</td><td>306</td><td>308</td><td>310</td></tr>
</table>

<table>
<tr><td>48.</td><td>702</td><td>704</td><td>706</td><td>708</td><td>710</td><td>712</td><td>714</td><td>716</td><td>718</td><td>720</td></tr>
</table>

<table>
<tr><td>49.</td><td>360</td><td>365</td><td>370</td><td>375</td><td>380</td><td>385</td><td>390</td><td>395</td><td>400</td><td>405</td></tr>
</table>

Page 25: Compare the Numbers

1. <	2. >	3. <	4. >	5. <	6. <	7. >	8. <	9. <
10. >	11. >	12. >	13. <	14. <	15. <	16. >	17. >	18. <
19. <	20. >	21. >	22. >	23. <	24. <	25. >	26. <	27. >
28. <	29. >	30. <	31. >	32. >	33. >	34. >	35. >	36. <
37. <	38. >	39. <	40. <	41. >	42. >	43. >	44. >	45. >
46. <	47. >	48. <	49. >	50. >	51. >	52. <	53. >	54. >
55. <	56. <	57. <	58. <	59. >	60. >	61. <	62. <	63. >
64. >	65. >	66. <	67. <	68. <	69. <	70. >	71. >	72. <
73. >	74. <	75. >	76. >	77. <	78. >	79. <	80. <	81. >
82. <	83. <	84. >	85. <	86. <	87. <	88. <	89. >	90. <
91. >	92. >	93. >	94. >	95. >	96. <	97. >	98. >	99. <
100. <	101. <	102. >	103. <	104. <	105. <	106. <	107. <	108. <
109. <	110. >	111. <	112. >	113. >	114. <	115. <	116. <	117. <
118. <	119. >	120. <	121. <	122. >	123. >	124. <	125. >	126. <
127. <	128. >	129. <	130. <	131. >	132. >	133. <	134. >	135. >

136. <   137. <   138. >   139. >   140. >   141. >   142. <   143. >   144. >

145. >   146. >   147. >   148. >   149. <   150. >   151. >   152. <   153. >

154. >   155. <   156. >   157. >   158. >   159. >   160. >   161. >   162. <

163. <   164. <   165. >   166. <   167. >   168. >   169. <   170. >   171. >

172. >   173. >   174. <

Page 36: Circle the Numbers

1. (948)   2. 602   3. (111)   4. 918   5. (570)   6. (974)
   (69)   642   (581)   628   222   267
   529   661   538   (989)   (8)   (49)
   523   (363)   242   (23)   282   477
   82   (729)   186   40   126   173

7. (735)   8. 670   9. (41)   10. 514   11. 717   12. (726)
   (125)   (782)   378   935   245   (61)
   560   254   520   597   812   248
   191   246   (828)   (195)   (192)   397
   304   (8)   157   (988)   (857)   107

13. 336   14. (986) 15. 136   16. 193   17. (40)   18. 490
    594   (21)   374   (702)   669   (312)
    (184)   348   743   180   (854)   369
    190   938   (15)   (126)   489   333
    (993)   516   (998)   612   455   (577)

19.
609
535
(856)
(140)
672

20.
447
194
330
(835)
(171)

21.
(494)
588
658
679
(852)

22.
344
502
(797)
(193)
665

23.
(25)
(881)
123
785
68

24.
666
(740)
695
735
(504)

25.
674
651
(15)
362
(906)

26.
600
517
(604)
(343)
551

27.
(998)
372
344
954
(119)

28.
452
(12)
176
(636)
112

29.
(987)
514
(177)
668
552

30.
(728)
413
72
73
(6)

31.
(707)
499
595
(331)
496

32.
(842)
573
297
772
(252)

33.
826
(898)
(455)
641
666

34.
652
537
(168)
(667)
616

35.
(655)
564
(59)
624
516

36.
(160)
475
347
(809)
179

37.
(188)
446
532
337
(844)

38.
499
(777)
(14)
458
276

39.
(878)
715
403
384
(285)

40.
90
60
535
(2)
(899)

41.
(191)
246
404
(457)
350

42.
(143)
440
(971)
815
337

43.
367
227
487
(594)
(65)

44.
380
367
(118)
(797)
168

45.
(875)
524
709
(392)
737

46.
(940)
(162)
674
339
426

47.
(101)
940
345
909
(988)

48.
942
(43)
76
(987)
702

49. (59)
806
198
122
(909)

50. 652
(228)
809
320
(904)

51. 723
(941)
737
833
(25)

52. 666
536
(13)
(719)
410

53. (980)
766
632
389
(236)

54. 427
(881)
578
606
(123)

55. (338)
292
131
(95)
109

56. (70)
327
(587)
482
86

57. (713)
(353)
355
434
703

58. (159)
203
512
(884)
322

59. 406
(31)
356
578
(721)

60. 293
(174)
808
(885)
483

61. (770)
649
203
(198)
567

62. (431)
811
643
725
(955)

63. (340)
(949)
530
634
696

64. 628
411
198
(686)
(77)

65. (224)
370
693
284
(716)

66. (308)
(935)
553
374
816

67. 895
518
701
(999)
(315)

68. (64)
150
158
(867)
272

69. (348)
560
786
929
(982)

70. 457
500
722
(881)
(94)

71. 881
(975)
(123)
809
259

72. 401
(956)
919
481
(259)

73. 496
258
269
(909)
(61)

74. (821)
(248)
530
320
633

75. 478
(254)
331
414
(729)

76. 664
583
(763)
302
(260)

77. 807
(214)
671
280
(934)

78. (919)
(396)
892
741
913

79. (108)   80. (90)   81. (210)   82. 628   83. (817)   84. 282
231   291   (970)   645   (193)   587
677   (877)   403   (708)   617   (988)
608   869   249   (80)   221   974
(776)   162   615   595   452   (141)

85. 425   86. (248)   87. 373   88. (837)   89. 274   90. (914)
(355)   577   706   811   687   613
(788)   (722)   (894)   423   (812)   456
406   638   141   665   147   (157)
526   639   (51)   (307)   (96)   494

91. 503   92. 854   93. (51)   94. (112)   95. 470   96. (738)
(302)   (182)   (923)   298   (164)   542
(902)   (996)   71   477   324   642
728   723   441   170   668   (310)
736   367   222   (614)   (867)   611

97. (635)   98. (72)   99. 655   100. (350)   101. (616)   102. 340
(121)   (803)   (815)   617   136   978
565   167   700   372   286   (235)
144   404   298   924   543   861
136   197   (256)   (984)   (24)   (998)

103. 312   104. (929)   105. 309   106. (655)   107. (121)   108. 499
539   359   132   463   171   (835)
687   926   (74)   (26)   718   (23)
(112)   306   (973)   412   326   120
(732)   (151)   958   517   (994)   796

109. (94) 110. (117) 111. (991) 112. 485   113. 876   114. 141
     569   128   691   (63)   (952)   (820)
     306   (588)   (66)   313   822   361
     406   566   773   (584)   (344)   (117)
     (884)   327   675   369   877   233

115. 95   116. 740 117. 527 118. 430 119. (437) 120. (141)
     337   826   (874)   (105)   523   746
     (806)   667   460   (944)   438   (961)
     510   (90)   (86)   650   751   528
     (58)   (842)   525   510   (919)   743

Page 46: Missing Numbers

1. 297   2. 472   3. 232 234   4. 884 886

5. 717   6. 659   7. 223 225   8. 842

9. 493 495   10. 818   11. 38   12. 710 712

13. 796 798   14. 899   15. 591   16. 994

17. 139   18. 547   19. 404   20. 855

21. 545 547   22. 229 231   23. 851   24. 300 302

25. 911   26. 649   27. 144   28. 707

29. 58   30. 536 538   31. 757   32. 967

33. 943   34. 258   35. 197   36. 599

37. 883   38. 903   39. 648   40. 273

41. 146 148   42. 270   43. 722   44. 640

45. 703 705   46. 592   47. 114 116   48. 582

49. 773   50. 784   51. 502   52. 318

53. 129   54. 179   55. 774   56. 109

57. 388 390   58. 683   59. 531   60. 75

61. 239   62. 379   63. 775 777   64. 836

65. 906   66. 971   67. 700   68. 357

69. 855 857   70. 881   71. 353 355   72. 433

73. 805 807   74. 33   75. 901   76. 982 984

77. 185   78. 452   79. 507   80. 360

81. 314 316   82. 838   83. 811 813   84. 854

85. 936 938   86. 104 106   87. 319   88. 716 718

89. 630   90. 883   91. 154 156   92. 316

93. 718   94. 665   95. 865   96. 480

97. 169   98. 107   99. 804   100. 997

101. 704 706   102. 354   103. 710   104. 269

105. 628 630   106. 556   107. 836 838   108. 241

109. 688   110. 874 876   111. 504   112. 63 65

113. 378   114. 714   115. 932 934   116. 968 970

117. 573   118. 263   119. 698   120. 116

121. 554   122. 471

Page 53: Addition 1 through 20

1. 20   2. 11   3. 20   4. 19   5. 11   6. 15   7. 8

8. 19   9. 29   10. 17   11. 31   12. 19   13. 15   14. 24

15. 10   16. 24   17. 15   18. 20   19. 15   20. 15   21. 22

22. 28   23. 11   24. 28   25. 17   26. 27   27. 26   28. 25

29. 32   30. 23   31. 19   32. 8   33. 21   34. 18   35. 14

36. 19   37. 17   38. 15   39. 15   40. 6   41. 39   42. 33

43. 29   44. 10   45. 25   46. 13   47. 19   48. 22   49. 20

50. 23   51. 11   52. 19   53. 16   54. 20   55. 25   56. 20

57. 34   58. 22   59. 16   60. 18   61. 8   62. 16   63. 9

64. 25   65. 6   66. 27   67. 18   68. 36   69. 17   70. 22

71. 23   72. 22   73. 7   74. 10   75. 26   76. 23   77. 22

78. 21   79. 2   80. 26   81. 36   82. 37   83. 30   84. 38

85. 19   86. 31   87. 12   88. 20   89. 25   90. 24   91. 35

92. 29   93. 14   94. 24   95. 12   96. 20   97. 11   98. 18

99. 18   100. 22

Page 57: Addition 1 through 20

1. 15   2. 18   3. 1   4. 17   5. 11   6. 20   7. 19

8. 15   9. 11   10. 23   11. 17   12. 3   13. 18   14. 19

15. 14   16. 17   17. 9   18. 17   19. 16   20. 31   21. 6

22. 5   23. 5   24. 30   25. 7   26. 4   27. 19   28. 33

29. 17   30. 10   31. 4   32. 12   33. 31   34. 1   35. 16

36. 20   37. 20   38. 17   39. 16   40. 27   41. 7   42. 21

43. 19	44. 10	45. 36	46. 5	47. 23	48. 6	49. 34
50. 4	51. 14	52. 6	53. 8	54. 4	55. 15	56. 9
57. 9	58. 29	59. 25	60. 23	61. 3	62. 6	63. 6
64. 25	65. 26	66. 4	67. 2	68. 26	69. 20	70. 20
71. 18	72. 15	73. 22	74. 14	75. 11	76. 4	77. 30
78. 22	79. 9	80. 15	81. 13	82. 35	83. 13	84. 8
85. 3	86. 16	87. 18	88. 9	89. 15	90. 18	91. 1
92. 2	93. 16	94. 14	95. 8	96. 23	97. 12	98. 10
99. 24	100. 8	101. 11	102. 24	103. 3	104. 11	105. 37
106. 2	107. 18	108. 6	109. 18	110. 18	111. 8	112. 11
113. 5	114. 22	115. 19	116. 4	117. 10	118. 17	119. 9
120. 8	121. 7	122. 20	123. 30	124. 1	125. 20	126. 19
127. 8	128. 10	129. 20	130. 20	131. 7	132. 6	133. 11
134. 11	135. 1	136. 16	137. 17	138. 19		

Page 64: Addition 1 through 50

1. 71	2. 31	3. 67	4. 62	5. 71	6. 89	7. 5
8. 40	9. 26	10. 54	11. 57	12. 44	13. 29	14. 31
15. 80	16. 27	17. 74	18. 43	19. 10	20. 50	21. 56
22. 34	23. 45	24. 62	25. 81	26. 59	27. 45	28. 22
29. 70	30. 59	31. 75	32. 52	33. 61	34. 71	35. 64
36. 32	37. 47	38. 17	39. 54	40. 55	41. 47	42. 28

43. 59   44. 53   45. 31   46. 10   47. 36   48. 62   49. 53

50. 77   51. 19   52. 23   53. 40   54. 47   55. 66   56. 34

57. 27   58. 63   59. 29   60. 48   61. 41   62. 75   63. 55

64. 56   65. 50   66. 31   67. 74   68. 26   69. 38   70. 79

71. 75   72. 52   73. 30   74. 24   75. 32   76. 34   77. 65

78. 30   79. 24   80. 70   81. 83   82. 47   83. 8   84. 24

85. 42   86. 49   87. 84   88. 55   89. 77   90. 92   91. 94

92. 44   93. 58   94. 46   95. 54   96. 53   97. 43   98. 15

99. 71   100. 26   101. 87   102. 60   103. 44   104. 80   105. 65

106. 59   107. 66   108. 31   109. 19   110. 75   111. 64   112. 64

113. 73   114. 46   115. 12   116. 51   117. 53   118. 72   119. 41

120. 32   121. 58   122. 33   123. 72   124. 51   125. 50   126. 90

127. 81   128. 53   129. 35   130. 48   131. 63   132. 39   133. 50

134. 78   135. 32   136. 17   137. 79   138. 51   139. 18   140. 78

141. 31   142. 58   143. 76   144. 64   145. 43   146. 27   147. 68

148. 57   149. 86   150. 33

Page 70: Subtraction 1 through 20

1. 0   2. 7   3. 0   4. 15   5. 1   6. 4   7. 2   8. 6   9. 14

10. 0   11. 7   12. 1   13. 0   14. 0   15. 10   16. 2   17. 17   18. 3

19. 0   20. 2   21. 4   22. 3   23. 3   24. 3   25. 11   26. 13   27. 14

28. 5   29. 2   30. 3   31. 2   32. 2   33. 2   34. 6   35. 15   36. 5

37. 0   38. 5   39. 8   40. 0   41. 3   42. 0   43. 7   44. 4   45. 7

46. 4   47. 3   48. 1   49. 13   50. 12   51. 9   52. 4   53. 3   54. 1

55. 9   56. 1   57. 1   58. 2   59. 9   60. 9   61. 6   62. 8   63. 1

64. 14   65. 8   66. 2   67. 3   68. 11   69. 7   70. 5   71. 2   72. 4

73. 4   74. 7   75. 12   76. 2   77. 9   78. 0   79. 1   80. 1   81. 2

82. 3   83. 3   84. 11   85. 0   86. 17   87. 2   88. 1   89. 10   90. 4

91. 5   92. 10   93. 16   94. 0   95. 2

Page 74: Subtraction 1 through 20

1. 13   2. 5   3. 1   4. 13   5. 7   6. 6   7. 5   8. 1

9. 5   10. 1   11. 15   12. 3   13. 1   14. 8   15. 5   16. 6

17. 2   18. 1   19. 10   20. 4   21. 11   22. 3   23. 8   24. 11

25. 5   26. 1   27. 2   28. 7   29. 7   30. 11   31. 3   32. 13

33. 7   34. 3   35. 7   36. 16   37. 0   38. 11   39. 3   40. 11

41. 5   42. 4   43. 1   44. 18   45. 6   46. 10   47. 1   48. 2

49. 8   50. 16   51. 2   52. 3   53. 7   54. 13   55. 14   56. 9

57. 5   58. 3   59. 16   60. 3   61. 13   62. 6   63. 6   64. 2

65. 3   66. 0   67. 9   68. 6   69. 4   70. 4   71. 20   72. 12

73. 2   74. 18   75. 2   76. 1   77. 13   78. 11   79. 4   80. 14

81. 8   82. 4   83. 9   84. 19   85. 9   86. 2   87. 8   88. 14

89. 4   90. 8   91. 1   92. 11   93. 2   94. 9   95. 1   96. 1

97. 6   98. 8   99. 4   100. 18   101. 18   102. 18   103. 11   104. 7

105. 11   106. 10

Page 80:   Subtraction 1 through 50

1. 1   2. 1   3. 7   4. 2   5. 3   6. 7   7. 0   8. 1   9. 10

10. 1   11. 6   12. 14   13. 5   14. 3   15. 8   16. 4   17. 0   18. 7

19. 6   20. 6   21. 3   22. 4   23. 11   24. 0   25. 0   26. 1   27. 9

28. 3   29. 9   30. 11   31. 4   32. 1   33. 3   34. 5   35. 4   36. 10

37. 1   38. 3   39. 8   40. 6   41. 3   42. 4   43. 6   44. 4   45. 15

46. 7   47. 17   48. 1   49. 11   50. 7   51. 3   52. 2   53. 4   54. 5

55. 1   56. 2   57. 4   58. 5   59. 1   60. 1   61. 3   62. 11   63. 9

64. 11   65. 0   66. 10   67. 5   68. 6   69. 1   70. 0   71. 4   72. 5

73. 3   74. 3   75. 10   76. 4   77. 12   78. 17   79. 2   80. 6   81. 2

82. 2   83. 4   84. 1   85. 5   86. 7   87. 2   88. 9   89. 13   90. 11

91. 4   92. 8   93. 1   94. 5   95. 6

Page 84:   Commutative Property of Addition

1. 16   2. 4   3. 12   4. 12   5. 7   6. 14   7. 4   8. 16

9. 7   10. 11   11. 7   12. 14   13. 18   14. 12   15. 9   16. 4

17. 12   18. 3   19. 1   20. 19   21. 17   22. 17   23. 2   24. 12

25. 8   26. 7   27. 8   28. 15   29. 2   30. 15   31. 1   32. 5

33. 14   34. 14   35. 7   36. 8   37. 7   38. 7   39. 18   40. 13

41. 14   42. 5   43. 14   44. 17   45. 5   46. 12   47. 10   48. 9

49. 2   50. 6   51. 16   52. 4   53. 4   54. 17   55. 15   56. 18

57. 13   58. 19   59. 10   60. 8   61. 8   62. 2   63. 6   64. 9

65. 5   66. 11   67. 3   68. 3   69. 3   70. 15   71. 9   72. 15

73. 11   74. 8   75. 14   76. 18   77. 18   78. 18   79. 19   80. 8

81. 5   82. 7   83. 10   84. 14   85. 1   86. 12   87. 6   88. 9

89. 20   90. 8   91. 16   92. 12   93. 3   94. 8   95. 5   96. 7

97. 17   98. 20   99. 18   100. 6   101. 7   102. 2   103. 7   104. 11

105. 1   106. 13

Page 90: Make 50

1. 34   2. 27   3. 10   4. 36   5. 13   6. 41   7. 11   8. 43

9. 24   10. 31   11. 48   12. 28   13. 14   14. 35   15. 46   16. 23

17. 40   18. 19   19. 21   20. 12   21. 32   22. 26   23. 18   24. 38

25. 17   26. 37   27. 45   28. 49   29. 25   30. 22   31. 47   32. 29

33. 39   34. 30

Page 92: Matching the answers.

1. a.A b.F c.C d.G e.D f.H g.J h.I i.B j.E

2. a.E b.G c.D d.A e.I f.C g.H h.J i.B j.F

3. a.G b.B c.D d.E e.C f.A g.H h.I i.F j.J

4. a.I b.C c.J d.A e.G f.F g.D h.B i.H j.E

5. a.I b.J c.D d.E e.G f.H g.A h.B i.C j.F

Page 97: Addition Word Problems

1. 6   2. 10   3. 8   4. 15   5. 4   6. 12   7. 15   8. 9

9. 14   10. 18   11. 13   12. 11   13. 9   14. 16   15. 13   16. 14

17. 10   18. 11   19. 12   20. 15   21. 6   22. 14   23. 4   24. 17

25. 16   26. 3   27. 10   28. 14   29. 9   30. 19   31. 8   32. 15

33. 8   34. 9   35. 13   36. 11   37. 11   38. 19   39. 6   40. 10

Page 107: Subtraction Word Problems

1. 8   2. 6   3. 5   4. 2   5. 6   6. 2   7. 0   8. 0   9. 5   10. 2

11. 0   12. 5   13. 1   14. 3   15. 0   16. 1   17. 7   18. 2   19. 2   20. 2

21. 6   22. 1   23. 6   24. 0   25. 0   26. 3   27. 1   28. 1   29. 5   30. 3

31. 0   32. 2   33. 4   34. 2   35. 2   36. 2   37. 6   38. 1   39. 0   40. 1

Page 117: Place Value

1. 1 hundred

2. 8 ones

3. 8 tens

4. 7 hundreds

5. 0 ones

6. 1 hundred

7. 6 ones

8. 2 hundreds

9. 6 tens

10. 8 ones

11. 8 tens

12. 5 hundreds

13. 8 hundreds

14. 2 tens

15. 8 tens

16. 5 ones

17. 7 tens

18. 2 hundreds

19. 9 tens

20. 3 ones

21. 3 ones

22. 9 tens

23. 7 tens

24. 1 hundred

25. 4 ones

26. 8 ones

27. 2 hundreds

28. 5 tens

29. 9 hundreds

30. 8 tens

31. 1 one

32. 0 tens

33. 7 ones

34. 3 hundreds

35. 2 tens

36. 8 hundreds

37. 0 ones

38. 2 ones

39. 6 tens

40. 2 ones

41. 8 ones

42. 4 ones

43. 3 hundreds

44. 3 ones

45. 6 tens

46. 8 hundreds

47. 8 hundreds

48. 9 ones

49. 5 ones

50. 8 ones

51. 7 ones

52. 0 ones

53. 2 hundreds

54. 3 tens

55. 1 hundred

56. 3 tens

57. 7 ones

58. 2 tens

59. 4 hundreds

60. 5 tens

61. 9 hundreds

62. 2 hundreds

63. 7 ones

64. 6 hundreds

65. 6 hundreds

66. 3 hundreds

67. 7 tens

68. 7 hundreds

69. 1 hundred

70. 8 hundreds

71. 6 hundreds

72. 5 hundreds

73. 8 tens

74. 0 ones

75. 7 hundreds

76. 7 hundreds

77. 5 ones

78. 4 hundreds

79. 3 ones

80. 2 tens

81. 4 ones

82. 2 tens

83. 1 one

84. 3 tens

85. 5 tens

86. 5 ones

87. 2 hundreds

88. 2 hundreds

89. 7 ones

90. 5 hundreds

91. 0 tens

92. 4 hundreds

93. 3 ones

94. 6 hundreds

95. 4 ones

96. 5 ones

97. 0 ones

98. 3 hundreds

99. 2 tens

100. 2 hundreds

101. 2 ones

102. 7 ones

103. 5 ones

104. 8 tens

105. 4 ones

106. 6 ones

Page 123: Place Value: Expanded Notation

1. 260	2. 490	3. 443	4. 94	5. 290	6. 674	7. 808
8. 438	9. 756	10. 600	11. 252	12. 543	13. 462	14. 152
15. 319	16. 165	17. 821	18. 796	19. 782	20. 577	21. 366
22. 952	23. 332	24. 853	25. 755	26. 398	27. 739	28. 572
29. 675	30. 330	31. 927	32. 562	33. 670	34. 682	35. 888
36. 938	37. 744	38. 517	39. 270	40. 475	41. 148	42. 547
43. 305	44. 550	45. 24	46. 56	47. 569	48. 815	49. 950
50. 679	51. 46	52. 16	53. 894	54. 538	55. 112	56. 942
57. 919	58. 411	59. 699	60. 185	61. 925	62. 921	63. 58
64. 615	65. 900	66. 482	67. 637	68. 277	69. 883	70. 53
71. 266	72. 308	73. 892	74. 805	75. 785	76. 847	77. 304
78. 732	79. 343	80. 171	81. 757	82. 725	83. 651	84. 498
85. 913	86. 668	87. 133	88. 571	89. 946	90. 501	91. 825
92. 107	93. 223	94. 626	95. 248	96. 935		

Page 130: Place Value: Expanded Notation

1. 1 hundred + 2 tens + 4 ones

2. 5 hundreds + 7 tens + 4 ones

3. 9 hundreds + 3 tens + 2 ones

4. 5 hundreds + 3 tens + 9 ones

5. 6 tens + 8 ones

6. 6 hundreds + 2 tens + 8 ones

7. 7 hundreds + 8 tens

8. 7 hundreds + 7 ones

9. 3 ones

10. 7 hundreds + 3 tens + 4 ones

11. 3 hundreds + 2 tens + 8 ones

12. 9 tens + 6 ones

13. 1 hundred + 3 tens + 4 ones

14. 1 hundred + 8 tens + 8 ones

15. 6 tens + 9 ones

16. 5 hundreds + 2 tens + 9 ones

17. 4 hundreds + 2 tens + 8 ones

18. 2 hundreds + 1 one

19. 2 hundreds + 7 tens + 1 one

20. 5 hundreds + 6 tens

21. 7 hundreds + 3 ones

22. 2 hundreds + 3 tens + 2 ones

23. 3 hundreds + 5 tens

24. 6 tens + 7 ones

25. 3 hundreds + 3 tens + 1 one

26. 3 hundreds + 8 tens + 3 ones

27. 2 hundreds + 2 tens + 8 ones

28. 1 hundred + 6 tens

29. 7 hundreds + 3 tens + 8 ones

30. 6 hundreds + 2 ones

31. 5 hundreds + 8 tens + 3 ones

32. 6 hundreds

33. 3 hundreds + 7 tens

34. 6 hundreds + 9 ones

35. 7 hundreds + 6 tens + 9 ones

36. 2 hundreds + 3 tens + 9 ones

37. 2 hundreds + 1 ten + 9 ones

38. 6 hundreds + 5 tens + 8 ones

39. 2 tens + 4 ones

40. 7 hundreds + 1 ten + 8 ones

41. 2 hundreds + 6 ones

42. 6 hundreds + 6 tens + 6 ones

43. 3 hundreds + 9 tens + 9 ones

44. 2 hundreds + 4 tens + 4 ones

45. 8 hundreds + 5 tens + 1 one

46. 3 hundreds + 6 tens + 8 ones

47. 6 hundreds + 3 tens + 8 ones

48. 4 tens

49. 4 tens + 3 ones

50. 8 hundreds + 6 tens + 2 ones

51. 2 tens + 3 ones

52. 3 hundreds + 5 tens + 5 ones

53. 6 hundreds + 8 tens + 8 ones

54. 2 hundreds + 3 tens + 3 ones

55. 8 hundreds + 9 tens + 1 one

56. 2 hundreds + 2 tens + 5 ones

57. 8 hundreds + 6 tens + 6 ones

58. 2 hundreds + 9 ones

59. 6 hundreds + 8 tens + 5 ones

60. 4 hundreds + 1 one

61. 6 hundreds + 2 tens + 1 one

62. 9 hundreds + 7 tens

63. 1 hundred + 5 tens + 2 ones

64. 1 hundred + 6 tens + 9 ones

65. 4 hundreds + 9 tens + 6 ones

66. 7 hundreds + 6 tens + 5 ones

67. 5 hundreds + 7 tens + 9 ones

68. 3 hundreds

69. 2 hundreds + 9 tens + 1 one

70. 2 hundreds + 1 ten

71. 5 hundreds + 4 tens + 3 ones

72. 2 hundreds + 4 tens + 8 ones

73. 8 hundreds + 4 tens + 2 ones

74. 4 hundreds + 9 tens + 7 ones

75. 5 hundreds + 6 tens + 6 ones

76. 9 hundreds + 5 tens + 1 one

77. 8 hundreds + 2 tens + 3 ones

78. 4 hundreds + 8 tens

79. 1 ten + 6 ones

80. 5 hundreds + 9 tens

81. 1 hundred + 2 tens + 1 one

82. 6 hundreds + 9 tens + 6 ones

83. 7 hundreds + 4 tens

84. 5 hundreds + 6 tens + 1 one

85. 8 hundreds + 4 ones

86. 9 hundreds + 1 ten + 3 ones

87. 1 hundred + 3 tens + 7 ones

88. 5 hundreds + 4 tens + 4 ones

89. 3 hundreds + 7 tens + 3 ones

90. 1 ten + 1 one

91. 9 hundreds + 7 tens + 4 ones

92. 6 hundreds + 2 tens + 3 ones

93. 9 tens + 8 ones

94. 2 hundreds + 3 tens + 6 ones

95. 2 hundreds + 6 tens + 7 ones

96. 2 hundreds + 4 tens + 7 ones

Page 137: Understanding Time

1. 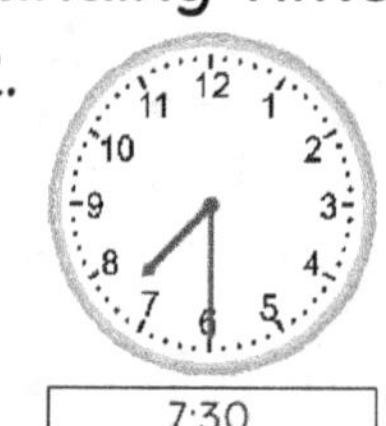
4:00

2.
7:30

3.
3:30

4.
3:20

5. 
11:55

6. 
6:35

7. 
12:50

8.
12:45

9. 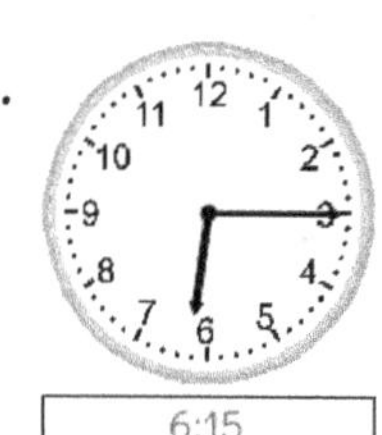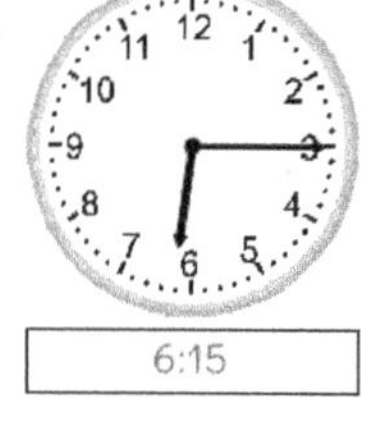
7:45

10. 
2:00

11.
6:15

12.
5:55

13. 
1:40

14. 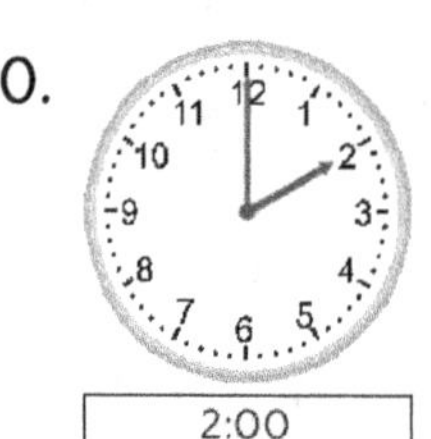
12:40

15. 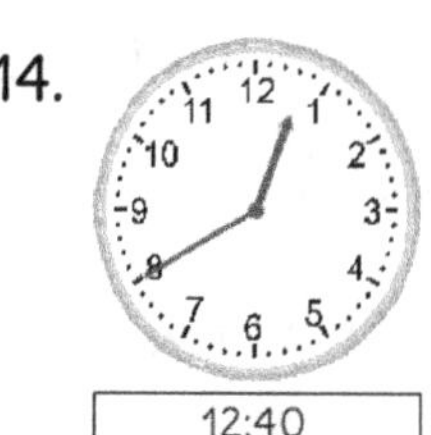
10:50

16. 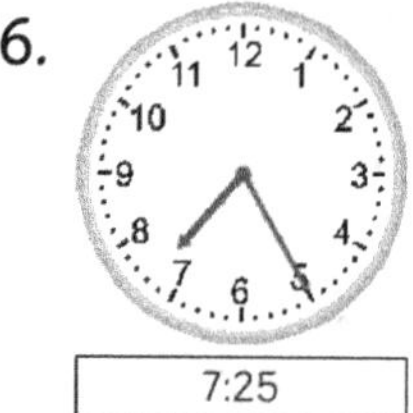
7:25

17. 

10:30

18. 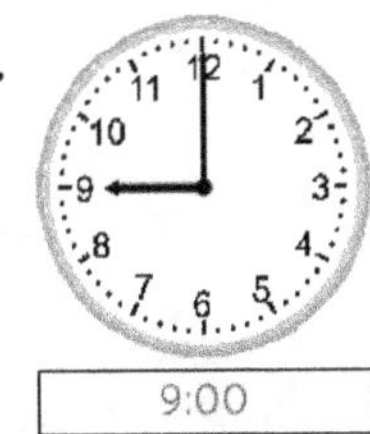

9:00

Page 140: Understanding Time

1. 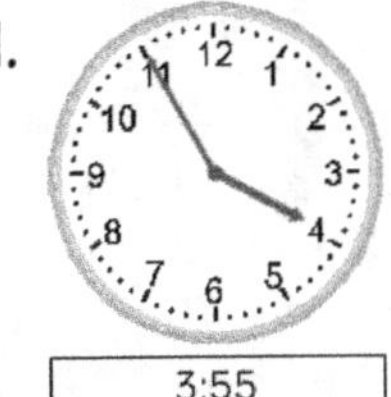

3:55

2. 

12:46

3. 

5:28

4. 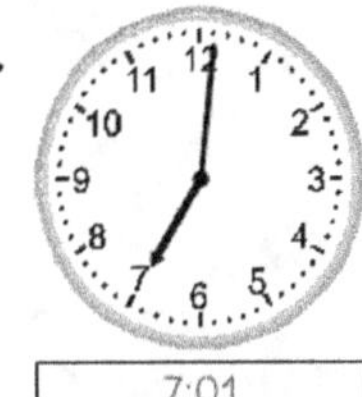

7:01

5. 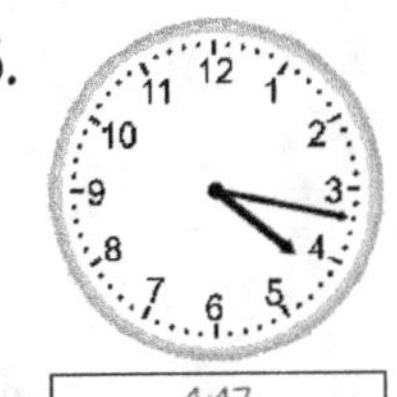

4:17

6. 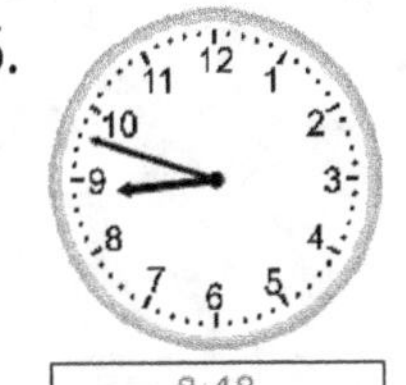

8:48

7. 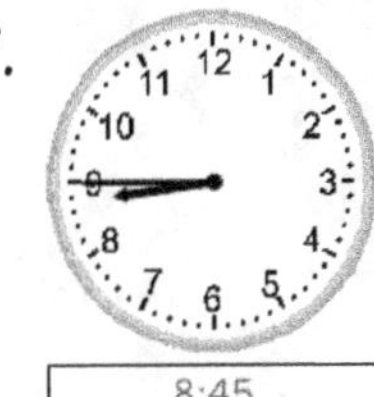

8:45

8. 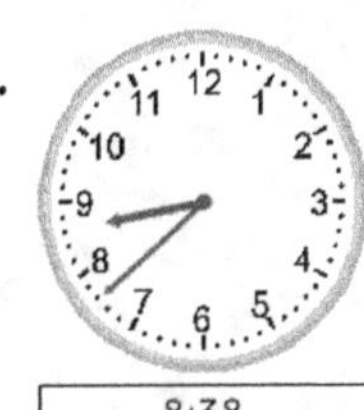

8:38

9. 

2:09

10. 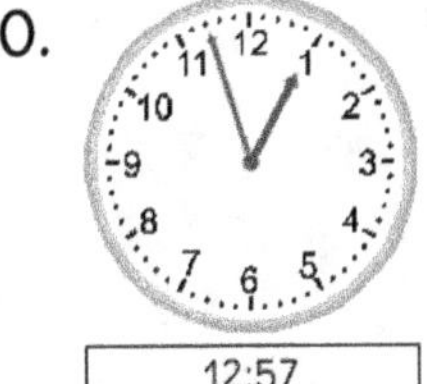

12:57

11. 

3:47

12. 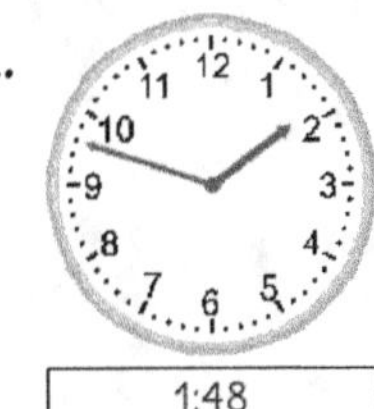

1:48

13. 

8:34

14. 

7:13

15. 

1:00

16. 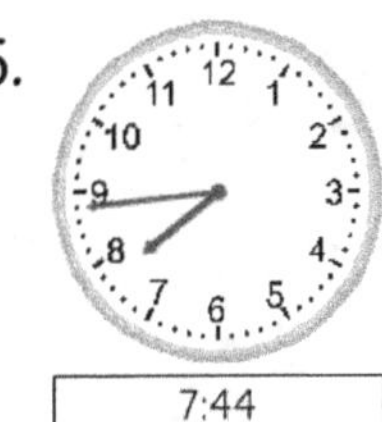

7:44

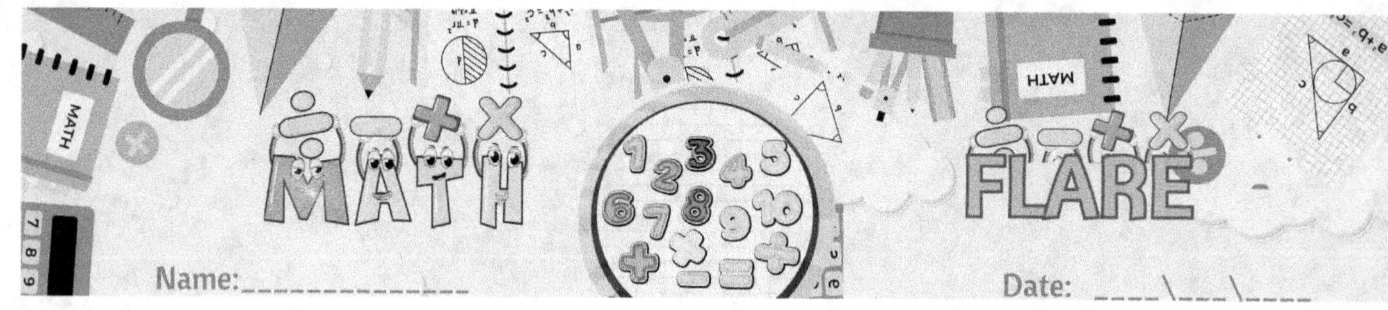

17. 

8:52

18. 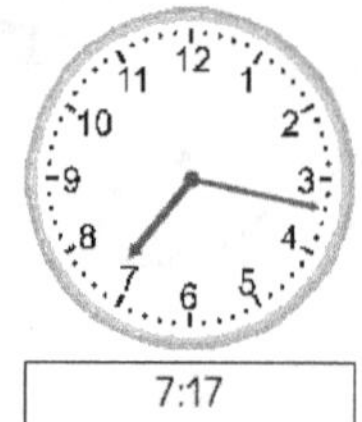

7:17